Dynamics of Higher Education

DYNAMICS OF HIGHER EDUCATION

Local, National and Global Perspectives

Edited by

Joram Begi

Commonwealth

Dynamics of Higher Education

First Published : 2008

ISBN 978-81-311-0190-2

Published by :

COMMONWEALTH PUBLISHERS
4831/24, Prahlad Street,
Ansari Road, Darya Ganj,
New Delhi - 110002
Ph. : 23272541, 23257835
Fax : 91- 011- 23257835
e-mail : campusbooks@hotmail.com

Typesetting by :
Arjun Computers
Delhi - 110051

Printed at :
Roshan Offset Printers
Delhi

Foreword

Education is one of the key indices for judging the status of a Nation. As a matter of fact, it is an important component in determining the Development Index of a country as practices by U.N.D.P. in its annual Human Development Report. And it is apparent for us in India that one of the major factors that is responsible for pushing India to a place quite low, only above the Sub-Saharan African Countries, is because of the tardy progress we have made in the area of education. Similarly Higher Education is at cross roads today. Even though we have seen a phenomenal increase in the field of higher education over the last sixty years since we attained independence, with an impressive increase in the number of Universities from 30 to 300, Colleges from 750 to about 18,000 and students from 0.2 to over 17 million, the rate of enrolment is rather poor with only 7–8 percent of the total population in the age group of 17-23 going to colleges. In sharp contrast to this, the rate is as high as 51 percent in many of the Developed nations. In view of this, Kothari Commission in its report in 1968 expressed its dismay over the declining standards in higher education in the country and pointed out that rapid expansion has, in fact, resulted in lowering the quality.

The Higher Education scene in the case of Arunachal Pradesh does not present a rosy picture. But it is to be acknowledged that the Directorate of Higher and Technical Education has been playing a proactive role in furthering the cause of higher education as is evident in the fact that there has been a two fold increase in the number of institutions and students over the last decade. I am happy that the proceedings of the Seventh Conference of Higher and Technical Education are being brought in the form of a book. This is indeed the best way of commemorating the Decennial Year of the establishment of the Directorate. The book consists of articles that cover a wide ranging of topics relating to Higher Education. While most of them are specifically related to the state of Arunachal Pradesh, there are quite a few articles that explore general issues relating to Higher Education in India. Dr. Joram Begi has given a comprehensive account of the status of the Institutes of Higher Education in the state. This is well documented with all relevant data at the end of the book. Incidentally, he has recently authored a book on Education in Arunachal Pradesh which, in my view, is a monumental work.

It is appropriate to take a look at the backwardness of the state in order to remind ourselves of the challenges that lie ahead of us. According to the *The National Human Development Report: 2001* published by the Planning Commission in 2002, Arunachal Pradesh ranks last in Human Development Index and the second in Human Poverty Index among the North Eastern states. And sadly, the state has the lowest literacy rate as well as the highest urban-rural gap and the highest gender gap in literacy. In rural areas, the gender gap in literacy is sharper than in urban areas. The access to higher education is abysmally low in the stat at the ration of 6.37% in comparison with the national ration of 8.97%. Even in the North East, its ratio is only marginally higher than the states of Sikkim, Tripura and Nagaland. And when it comes to enrolment of Scheduled Tribe girl students in higher education, the share of the girls is only 38.32%. It compares favourably with the national figure of 35.02%. However, in the North East it is ahead of only Tripura that occupies the last place with 34.58%. But the other states are relatively doing well with Sikkim and Meghalaya leading with 53.48% and 50.09% respectively.

Dr. Manmohan Singh announced that every district in the country should have a college and every state must have a Central University in the meeting of the State Education Ministers held last April. In this connection, the Ministry of Human Resource Development has already initiated steps to establish sixteen new Central universities all over the country. This, along with the setting up of fifteen Institutions of Excellence by the Central Government, should give a real boost to higher education in India. This is where the Government of Arunachal Pradesh must take necessary steps to expand higher education in the state. It is sad to note that eight districts in the state do not have a college. And it was only last year that a college was started in Yachuli after a long gap of ten years. One is aware of the financial constraints faced by the state. But this is the time when the Directorate should push its case strongly and strive for the establishment of eight new colleges in the next five years. This would be an important step in the right direction, for higher education in Arunachal Pradesh is crying for immediate attention and expansion.

K.C. Belliappa

Acknowledgements

Any academic activity is a shared experience. It may be planned by an individual and the end result may be ascribed to an individual, but there are contributions of many in one way or other in the process of the academic pursuit. The end product of an academic venture comes after a long preparation and perseverance. This is evident in the case of present volume which is a bye-product of the idea conceived in 2006 in connection with VII Conference of Higher and Technical Education held on 22nd and 23rd February, 2007. The idea was to interact with education practitioners especially of institutes of higher and technical education in order to understand the challenges faced by higher education in Arunachal Pradesh in the context of globalisation. The process of interaction happened in the form of presentation of papers on various aspects of higher education. Undoubtedly, the present volume owes its beginning to the paper presenters in the conference. So I gratefully acknowledge the scholarships of the contributors of the papers in the conference. The conference was organized by the Directorate of Higher and Technical Education involving all the officers and officials in the department of higher education. Obliviously, I am grateful for the help rendered by them in making the conference a success. Drawing on the inspiration from the deliberations I decided to bring out a volume incorporating the papers presented there. So I invited revised papers from the contributors. The revised papers received have been included in the present volume. I would like to put on record my highest sense of gratitude to the paper contributors who obliged my request.

While preparing this volume Dr. M.C. Behera, Dr. Deepak Pandey, Dr. M.Q. Khan, Dr. A.K. Jha and Dr. V.N. Sharma helped me in many ways. I am grateful to all of them. I am specially grateful to Dr. Deepak Pandey for designing the cover page. I am also grateful to Prof. K.C. Belliappa, Vice-Chancellor, Rajiv Gandhi University for writing the foreword of the book. I also express my sincere gratitude to Shri Tatar Kipa, Hon'ble Minister for Education, Arunachal Pradesh and Shri Hage Khoda, IAS, Secretary (Education), Government of Arunachal Pradesh for their encouragement to any academic pursuit which I want to undertake. I am also grateful to my colleagues in the Directorate who helped me in different ways in the process of editing this work. I am specially thankful to Mr. Praveen G, who typed out the MSS with a smiling face. Lastly, I am grateful to Mr. Ajay Verma, Commonwealth Publishers, New Delhi for publishing this volume in time.

Dr. Joram Begi

Introduction

—Joram Begi

Education was a State subject till 1976 when it was included in the Concurrent list. That is why education manifests unitary spirit at least at ideological and structural levels through various regulating bodies and national goals of education. There are national education policies and reports of various committees and commissions which provide an ideological base and functional frame for implementation of national goals of education. We have NCERT, UGC, NCT and AICT which provide guidelines for the structure of syllabi and curriculum design and regulate the standard of education. SCERT in states follow the guidelines of NCERT not only in the matter of course structure but also in designing general curriculum. There are CBSE, Kendriya Vidyalaya Sangathan, JNV and other regional and national boards of education which also influence the educational system at school level mostly in private sector.

UGC, NCT, AICT, etc. also prescribe guidelines according to which they approve a course and an educational institution of higher learning. The academic recognition of UGC to colleges and universities under 12(f) is necessary for recognition of degree of one university by the other. The B.Ed degree of an educational institution does not have any value unless approved by NCTE. There is NAAC to assess the programmes and functioning of institutes of higher education as a measure of quality assurance.

The unitary character of education at the level of higher and technical education has been more strengthened and even expanded beyond national boundary in the era of globalization. One of the characteristics of globalization is movement of human resource across the countries. The human resource of the developing countries migrates to developed countries in the field of science and technology, AICTE, business management etc. This has two implications. The human resource of developing countries must meet the set-standard of quality of developed countries. This requires the standard of education in developing countries to rise to a level of producing human resource to meet the demand and expectations of the employing industries in developed countries.

Secondly, to meet the level of quality and prescribed standard of human resource as demanded by developed countries, the standard of education in developing countries has to be raised accordingly. Obviously, systems of education in developing countries are required to be standardized keeping in the line of the set-standard of developed countries. In other words, the systems of education in developing countries have been assuming uniform characteristics in terms of standard and course content as far as they are designed in the line of meeting the global demand.

The context has again a deeper implication. In an obvious line of reasoning, it appears that national goals of education have been converging into a global phenomenon responding to the quality demand of developed countries. In a way it is so. That is why globalization is condemned in different quarters for its homogenizing tendency. At the same time globalization recognizes diversities and releases forces for the maintenance and promotion of such diversities. Local and regional co-operations, recognition to the importance of local knowledge, community involvement in development process, decentralized development, rising voice of *'dalits'* and other weaker sections, etc. are reckoners to the importance that the diversities are assuming in the era of globalization.

The UNESCO, UNDP and other international agencies have been promoting ideas which also have homogenizing tendency in one way or the other. In human development reports, education has been recognized as an important component of enlarging choices and thus human development. All nations now emphasize education unlike earlier priority given to economic factors for national development. It is not mere literacy but the level of education that matters and so accessing of higher education to large percentage of eligible population group of the nation has been in the priority list of educational planners. An example to the point is the growing popularity of distance mode in almost all countries of the world.

The example cited has two implications. The first one relates to the acceptance of the principle that higher percentage of access to higher education is positively related to higher level of development. This principle has global acceptance and all the countries are looking towards achieving this objective through various means of which distance mode is an important one. The system of education has assumed a uniform look as far as distance mode of delivery is concerned. Herein manifests the second implication—the use of ICT in delivery mechanism.

In the era of globalization the example of distance education gives us some idea about how education system assumes global character. It responds to the ideological commitment concerning the humanity and acts in a line that resembles the lines followed by different nations.

The above discussions lend us in apparent contradictions. In the era of globalization there is a tendency towards homogenization. At the same time we talk of locality and local space. In fact we encounter importance of diversities and promotion of local strength in different ways. One example can be the attempt to link local craft of tribal areas to the global market.

The reality is not then the contradictions; it is the manifestation of continuity through different levels—from local to global.

The system of higher education in India is not an exception. In spite of being a state subject it responds to national demand and thus assumes national character. At the same time it does not ignore its role to cater to the needs of the state; it very well attends to the aspirations of local (people of state and its various regions as contrast to national) people. When there is a changing societal need for education in a global perspective, the system also responds to it both in spirit and form.

The context of higher education is clear. It displays local (regional), national and global perspectives. The three perspectives are not competing; they are rather a continuum of complementary realities. This is the essence of the present volume *Dynamics of Higher Education : Local, National and Global Perspectives.*

Continuum of Complimentary Realities

There was a time when nations lived in isolation. Even the communities and regions within a nation had very limited interaction. In course of time some countries interacted with other countries in terms of trade and commerce. India's trade with different countries is an example to the point. This trade and commerce later became a pretext to colonise technology-poor but natural resource rich countries. This phase of history is marked by colonial expansion and dominance; some countries became dependent on others. There grew resentment and discontent among 'dependent' countries which led to their independence.

The countries tried to develop independently, depending on other countries in agreeable terms and conditions.

This was, however, a situation of isolation but with a little improvement. Independent countries interacted with other countries as far as their respective interests were safeguarded. In the process international inequalities appeared showing gnawing teeth. The efforts to share resources resulted into the phase of interdependence, a visible and important characteristic of globalization.

Evidently, globalization has the base in national co-operations and collaborations. It promotes interest of nations through a networking of sharing. In this sense globalization is a continuum of national endeavours to realize national goals objectively and meaningfully.

National goals, on the other hand, are not mere abstractions; these are reflections of demands and aspirations of citizens who live in different regions, belong to different cultures and possess different levels of resource and skill endowment. No doubt, national goals are continuum of diverse local and regional goals.

In other words, the global forces operate with a foot on local needs through national aspirations. Local and national needs have been linked to global solution. The strength of global solution to national and local needs/problems also depends on local and national resources. The vertical arrangement of forces from local to global are not hierarchically isolated, they are complementary, interwoven and inter-dependent.

So is the case with the system of education. The national system doesn't ignore the local and regional context of education. A nation is not the manifestation of an abstraction; it is rather an actualization of local and regional realities. The national curriculum is the reflection of a strategy to fulfil diverse local and regional needs. In the same line of reasoning, it also incorporates factors with a view to prepare its human resources to face the global challenges and to meet the global standard of employability. Necessarily, local, national and global perspectives of education, precisely of higher and technical education, are different phases on the same scale, depending on and striving for one another.

Thematic Dimensions of Perspectives

The perspectives of higher and technical education are contextual, but display a continuum from local to global. This is the focus of the papers included in this volume. The perspectives are not exclusive; a local perspective, say quality assurance measures adopted in Arunachal Pradesh, has a context of globalization. This is because quality consciousness relates to global standard of human resource development. At the same time, the paper on the education system of Arunachal Pradesh is not independent of national perspective; the education system of the state is a sub-set of national education policy and programmes.

Keeping the overlapping perspectives in view the papers however, have been grouped under five thematic divisions. The first division *i.e. Dynamics of Higher Education in Arunachal Pradesh* includes three papers focusing on the issues of growth of higher and technical education after independence. The second division entitled *Context of Globalization* includes seven papers on various issues relating to globalization. There are six papers in the third section which reflect rule of conduct in ensuring quality of education and thus is entitled *Normative Dimensions*. Three papers included in the fourth section entitled *Positive Concerns* deal with strategy formulation and scientific approaches to issues relating to quality assurance measures. The fifth one has included two papers on co-curricular activities and thus is entitled *Other Frontiers*.

I. Dynamics of Higher Education in Arunachal Pradesh

Education has its significance because it conforms to the contemporary societal needs. As we know, no society is static and hence the societal needs change over time. Needless to say, the role of education also changes consequent upon the changes in societal needs. In other words, education is a dynamic process concomitant to the dynamic nature of the society.

Unsurprisingly then, the system of higher education in Arunachal Pradesh has displayed its dynamics after 1964 when the first degree college of the state was established at Pasighat in erstwhile Siang district. The dynamics displayed in the system of higher education is not unidirectional. This has been the focus of the three papers included under the present thematic scheme.

The first paper entitled *"Higher and Technical Education in Arunachal Pradesh Since 1964"* has outlined the evolution of higher education in the state from 1964 to 2005. Its author Joram Begi has discussed the growth and evolution of higher education in terms of increase in enrolments, number of colleges in both private and government sectors, diverse courses and different streams such as Arts, Science and Commerce introduced and also in terms of vertical growth with the establishment of Rajiv Gandhi University (formerly Arunachal University) in the state. Thus, the institutes of higher education, as Begi believes, have grown horizontally and vertically.

Not only there has been a growth in general education, but there has been a growth in technical and medical education in the state, even though the number of institutes in the above two areas are less. Establishment of institutes of technical education is indicative of changing societal needs and expanding horizon of the system of education.

Begi has also discussed the budget allocation under higher education. To Begi, teacher training institutes have also added to the growing dimensions of higher education though administratively these are under the control of Director of School Education, Government of Arunachal Pradesh. As is evident, the courses introduced in colleges and in the university are of conventional types. Moreover, there are few technical and medical institutes in the state. Therefore, the state government subsidises higher and technical education pursued by Arunachalee students outside the state. This practice has been a factor of expending higher education in the state in terms of accessing Arunachalee students to institutes outside.

The growth of higher education, however, faces challenges from within. This is another dimension of dynamics about higher education in the state. The emerging challenges themselves are dynamic in nature for they are bye-products of the process of growth in higher education. Moreover, efforts to address the challenges incorporate dynamism to the process by modifying or introducing something new into it. In this line of reasoning, Deepak Pandey's paper entitled *Higher Education in Arunachal Pradesh—Growth and Challenges* identifies some issues which plague the quality of higher education in spite of its quantitative expansion. He has enlisted absence of selective admission, emphasis on money and monetary incentives in place of human touch in formal system of education, centralized nature of educational policies and aimless admission as major challenges before the higher education. In Arunachal Pradesh, Pandey writes, "higher education is becoming a substitute for a job" for students "seek admission in colleges" to avail stipends (emphasis added) because *there is nothing else to do*!

Similarly, A.K. Thakur links the challenges of higher education in Arunachal Pradesh to the challenges it has generally faced in course of its growth and expansion. He identified them in terms of the means adopted in teaching learning process and negligence of accountability in the system of higher education. As a result, higher education has been divorced from the larger society and producing unemployable persons. He has also mentioned of its questionable orientation, poor functioning and continued exclusion of poor and disadvantaged section of our society as challenges in the present system of higher education. Then he prescribes for an inclusive type of the system of higher education. He argues that education system in order to be dynamic enough needs to address the issue outside class-room teaching. The present social needs require the education system to inculcate the spirit of democracy and the feeling for living together in pluralistic society. The system of education need not have a narrow vision of employability but a wider vision of linking it to collective community wisdom outside the text book knowledge. So he mentions A.P.J. Abdul Kalam's view on linking herbal farm and conservation of bio-diversity resources to educational curriculum. Here the emphasis is laid on conservation aspect that college education is required to take care.

II. Context of Globalisation

Globalisation has added a new dimension to the societal role of education in terms of content and context. As a result, the system of higher education faces new challenges. There are again different dimensions to these challenges, because education system needs to respond to the challenges that emerge at local, national and global levels. At one level there is the concern for qualitative education while at the other the emphasis is on its empowering role. Still at the other, the system of higher education is required to play a positive role in human development in contrast to earlier emphasis on economic development.

There are seven papers under the thematic section of *Context of Globalisation* which broadly focus on the above issues outlined. These are but few popular issues which globalisation has placed as challenges before the system of higher education. The challenges are general and specific; they have bearing on local and national issues also.

At national level the challenges are many; at one hand there are local concerns and aspirations and at the other there is global demand. Moreover, there are national perspectives which need to be safeguarded. A nation faces the challenges of technology divide and impact of technology in the attempts to preserve culture from being blown away. The challenges before higher education come from the drawbacks in elementary and secondary system. Arup K. Das, in his paper entitled *"Education Scenario of our Country—Challenges Ahead"*, has focused on the above issues which our country confronts in the context of globalisation. He has identified the challenges before the system of education in general and the higher education in particular. He holds that unlimited accessing to higher and technical education in itself is a challenge as far as employability is linked to higher education. Unrestricted opportunity of accessing to higher and technical education exerts pressure on limited national resources and keeps many educated youths jobless as is evident from our country's situation. For Das, the issue of greater accessing to higher and technical education is not a challenge in India, but the issue of their employment is a challenge and hence he emphasizes better quality of education at the present rate of accessing. The remedial measures to be required to meet the challenges are themselves also challenges in our country for the country has many priorities of which education is one.

As has been mentioned, one of the challenges before a nation in the context of higher education is the production of qualitative and competitive human resources in the line of the demand in global market. Understanding this challenge in the global perspective M.A. Salam in his paper entitled *"Higher Education in India in the Liberalised Economic Era : Addressing to Threats of Higher Educational Potentials"* highlights the challenges before our country in view of addressing the challenges of higher education in the global context. He looks into the challenges in terms of employment generation role of higher education. The most important drawback in this regard is non-standardisation of higher education system as the standard and quality do vary from state to state.

In a similar veiw P.C. Swain in his paper entitled *"Globalisation and Higher Education in India : Issues and Concerns"* threats the new meaning and role attached to education in the context of globalisation as challenges before the system of education of our country. It needs a change in the national perception, globalisation treats education as a commodity and as non-merit goods. Further, globalisation has unlashed the operational forces of *laisez faire*, de-professionalisation in teaching process and has commercialized the system of education. Besides these issues, the rush for technical education, as Swain observes, has created a sense of negligence towards conventional type of disciplines. Implicitly, the challenge before the nation is to shift the conventional set up to fit into the emerging technical and technology oriented operational frame consequent upon globalisation. The process of integration of the system of higher education into the process of globalisation in fact is a challenge which is clearly spelt out in Swain's paper.

Globalisation has recognized the importance of quality education not in any unequivocal terms which every nation strives for achieving. The first step in this regard is identification of challenges encountered in the process of quality assurance and then to suggest measures to address the challenges and ensure quality in higher education. These steps are quite discernible in the paper of A.R. Parhi which is entitled as the *"Quality Package and Higher Education"*. Parhi finds the concern for quality in higher education as a bundle of contradictions in terms of unequal standard, enthusiasm to accessing to higher education but without scrutiny to institution, infrastructural and professional back-up and in terms of profiteering attitude in the process of assuring quality education. He finds people's attitude, bureaucratization, issue of language, political interference, standard of text books and delivery mechanism as factors affecting the quality of education. He finds addressing to all these problems together is necessary in ensuring quality in higher education to which he calls 'quality package', a catch word in the era of globalisation.

R.K. Mandal in his paper entitled *"Quality Assurance in Higher Education in Arunachal Pradesh : Issues and Challenges"* has also voiced the similar concern with regard to challenges encountered in quality assurance in the context globalisation. He identifies problems in recruitment system, reservation policy and in examination system and suggests measures to tackle these problems for quality assurance in higher education.

U. Talukdar also highlights the challenges before the higher education consequent upon its privatization in response to globalisation in his paper entitled *"Privatization and Quality Assurance in Higher Education"*. He has based his discussion on the initiatives taken by privately managed St. Claret College, Ziro, as case study. In his paper he has outlined seven criteria the college has adopted following NAAC parameters of quality assurance. Following measures initiated by the college, Talukdar suggests the establishment of Internal Quality Assurance Cell (IQAC) and preparation of a vision document for a seven year period along with annual action plan for quality assurance in higher education. Like Mandal he also suggests internal reform revamping the measures like teaching-learning process and the evaluation system in order to assure quality in higher education.

As has been mentioned, the globalisation has shifted the development discourse from the emphasis on economic development to comprehensive and holistic understanding in terms of human development. Human development, on the other hand, is inclusive in that it seeks the involvement of all sections of the society in the process of development. In other words, human development is participatory in nature and participation on equal terms requires empowerment of the weaker section. Herein lies the challenge to higher education in the era of globalisation.

Alternatively, globalisation emphasises the empowering role of education. D. Neogi's paper entitled *"Education as a Key to Women Empowerment in Arunachal Pradesh : A Perspective"* focuses on the issue of women empowerment in the process of participatory and equitable human development. Neogi points out the importance of empowerment of women in general and that of Arunachalee women in particular. So he emphasises the empowering role of education in case of women in order to bring about human development as is understood in the context of globalisation.

III. Normative Dimensions

A system of education has its signification as long as it takes care of social needs and fulfils individual aspirations. Social needs do not exist in compartmentalized sections, though more often they look so apparently. The economic need of the society cannot be perceived differently from its political or moral needs. Social needs are integrated in nature though one need may assume significance for time being in a given situation. But the significance of a need does not mean its absolute separation from other needs.

Similarly, individual aspirations are not independent of social aspirations. Even at family level, the individual's need is related to the needs of other members of the family. An individual cannot satisfy his hunger keeping other members of the family in starvation.

What follows from the above outline of discussion on the nature of social and individual needs is the integrated characteristic of these needs. In other words, any attempt to deal with these needs must take this characteristic into account; the attempt needs to be comprehensive and holistic in perspective.

Education having a social purpose needs to be comprehensive enough to accommodate both subjective and objective aspects of social needs. Herein lines the significance of normative character of education and educational planning. More often people think of what the education should be, what its role should be given a social purpose, what its constituents should perform and so on. Then follows intellectual dissection why it should be so. When the why comes in conformity with a what then there begins the exercise for how it should be. The usual course of contemplation and action gives priority to normative discourse in planning the system of education with a social purpose. The value loaded debates often reflect individual biases but unequivocally these show the social concern of the time. This is evident in the paper of R.B. Tripathy which is entitled *"Compulsions to Commitment : The Value Dynamics of Higher Education"*. Though the phrase 'Compulsions to Commitment' does not provide any conceptual clarity, it apparently prescribes 'compulsions' in ensuring loyalty to 'commitment' in the field of examination system and science education. He finds deteriorating conditions in both the areas, more in different constituents of examination system. He wishes change towards betterment in both examination system and science education through the efforts of 'higher education managers'. This is what Tripathy concludes as his 'commitment' prescription with a 'compulsion' of 'introspection' for value dynamics of higher education.

Anil Choudhary in his paper entitled "Professional, *Technical and Value Education for Socio-Economic Development"* recognizes the significance of professional and technical education in ensuring socio-economic development. But he feels that the socio-economic development will not be humanized development without value addition to professional and technical education. By "value' he does not mean economic value; he emphasises cultural values and prescribes for value based formal education by linking values (cultural values) with knowledge of contemporary society.

Hage Hassang objectively studies the normative factor in his paper entitled *"The Attitude of Parents towards Higher Education for Girls : A Case Study of Deomali Town of Arunachal Pradesh"*. He finds that the attitude of parents towards daughters' education is positive but varies inversely with the socio-economic condition in the family. Parents with lower income and formal education do not favour post graduate education for girls for traditional reasons. They fear that such girls may 'reject family traditions and social customs and neglect religious duties'.

Similar attitudinal factor is noticed in the paper of Madhuparna Bhattacherjee entitled *"Students' Perception of Quality in Higher Education : A Case Study"*. She has objectively studied the perception of students on the quality of higher education in Arunachal Pradesh along five axes, namely process and mode of entry into the courses, quality of teaching, nature of curriculum, evaluation process and infrastructure availability. Her findings are startling and points to parental approach in education system, for the students are not satisfied with what is given to them. They are afraid of dilution of their study interest because of entry of disinterested students into the course consequent upon wrong selection process. Students have poor opinion on course structure, 'chalk and talk' method of teaching and on evaluation procedure which lack transparency and objectivity. Then follows what should be the improvement drive in higher education. Bhattacharjee has identified the problems of higher education in the state from students' perspective. The paper has both theoretical grounding and empirical strength, nevertheless its normative character reflects in the long list of suggestions.

When the society is changing, the system of education changes in order to be compatible to the concomitant change in social needs. This is evident in the paper of Milorai Modi which is entitled *"Role of Education in the Development of Nation."* He has perceived the development of nation in terms of knowledge-based economy within the frame of knowledge society. His perception of the 'development of nation' has a local space in that he has based his argument drawing on experience from Arunachal Pradesh. Modi has identified the area of weakness in the system of higher education and has suggested for strengthening those areas so that the role of education in the development of nation becomes meaningful.

The role of education in order to be meaningful assumes quality of components which make up the system of education. The important components, as mentioned by Ajay Kr. Mishra in his paper entitled *"Role of Teacher as a Catalyst of Change"*, are content and technique of education, teachers, student and infrastructure. However, Mishra emphasises the role of the teacher because it is the quality of teacher that ensures quality in the content and technique of education and in students. It is teacher who motivates and shapes the personality of students.

IV. Positive Concerns : Planning the Action

Not contemplation but action is considered to be the key to success. But action without contemplation has no base and mere contemplation is like day dream that one never realizes. What is important is contemplation or dream-based action. The contemplation shows the way for action through strategy formulation, approach design, etc. The three papers included in this thematic division are not normative in nature but they suggest scientific approaches for objective realisation in one of the other aspect relating to the system of education in general and higher education in particular.

M.C. Behera's paper entitled *"Reaching Out the Unreached : Higher Education in Arunachal Pradesh through Distance Mode at Perspective"* outlines a strategy for accessing higher education to the large section of eligible and aspiring population group of the tribal state of Arunachal Pradesh through distance mode. The basis of his strategy draws on the logic of greater opportunity for greater accessing to higher education to meet the growing market demand for quality human resource in the era of globalisation. His strategy gives distance mode a complementary role rather than the role of a competitive alternative and hence is synergistic in nature.

Unless teaching takes the learners needs, capability and interest into consideration, it becomes a futile exercise. The objective of teaching-learning is least realised in terms of learners' achievements. Hence what is important is to understand the learners. T. Madhusudan in his paper *Understanding the Learners* analyses the characteristic strengths and preferences of two domains of brain, left and right. He then maintains that the world is moving toward conceptual age on greater emotional and creative levels. To meet this emerging challenge, he suggests for an understanding of the learners' level and style of learning so that a good instruction design can be framed to the benefit of learners.

Debabrata Maji in a similar line of reasoning suggests a system approach for quality training. He provides a conceptual frame of system approach and applies it in designing models of quality training in both open and closed loops in his paper entitled *System Approach to Quality Training*. He argues that the approach not only defines the process clearly but also contains methods which are self evaluating in nature to the performance. It is flexible enough to accommodate modifications of training process on the basis of results. He has used the concept of training in a wider sense to mean teaching learning process in both general and technical education and as such his system approach is comprehensive and widely applicable in nature.

V. Other Frontiers

Education is an integrated concept; it integrates both body and mind; it believes in the adage that a healthy mind dwells in a healthy body. A healthy body and a healthy mind grow out of punctuality, disciplined life, regular exercise and the feeling for the community, whether it is clan, caste, tribe or country. Feeling for the community requires learning together and believing in a common cause. That is why games and sports, NCC, NSS, scouts and guides have been integrated with educational curriculum.

The above line of thinking happens to be the essence of two papers, namely *"Role of NCC in Arunachal Pradesh"* by A.K. Gupta and *"Role of NSS in Higher Education"* by V.N. Sharma included under the thematic heading *Other Frontiers.*

NCC, NSS, etc. have their core area outside educational curriculum. NCC, for example, is not the compulsory part of the general education system and hence an added merit from its frontier. Nevertheless, the role of NCC in harnessing the potential of youths for the betterment of the nation in general and the society in particular has greater significanc. NCC plays a constructive role in creating awareness about the evils like AIDS, terrorism, about consumer and human rights and in controlling drug abuse in youths. In brief, the role of NCC is to bring about the overall development of personality of an individual through inculcating the courage and confidence, the values of community feeling and optimism with the aim of engaging him/her in the process of Nation Building. This is the thrust area of discussion in the paper of A.K. Gupta.

The paper of V.N. Sharma resounds in the same tone the role of NSS as 'extension education' that tries to develop the social behaviour of the people. Though implicit, Sharma's paper emphasizes the additional knowledge youths receive through NSS which develops their personality through physical labour, service, character and renouncement. Youth learn the dignity of labour and the feeling of 'Not Me, But You', *i.e.* the feeling for the community.

To sum-up, the papers included in this volume deal with the challenges of higher education from local, national and global perspectives given the new societal role of education in the context of globalisation.

Contents

SECTION—III
Normative Dimensions

Section—IV
Positive Concerns : Planning the Action

Section—V
Other Frontiers

List of Contributors

1. **Ajay Kr. Mishra** — Ph.D., Reader, Deptt. of Political Science, Tirap Govt. Degree College, Deomali, Tirap District, Arunachal Pradesh.
   Phone No. 03786–255219
   Mobile No. 09436046148
2. **Amarendra Kr. Thakur** — Ph.D., Reader, Deptt. of History, North Eastern Hill University, Shillong, Meghalaya.
   Phone No. 0364-272301
   Mobile No. 09436333397
3. **Anil Choudhury** — M.Sc., MCA, Head, Deptt. of Electronics and Electrical Engg., Rajiv Gandhi Govt. Polytechnic, Itanagar, Papum Pare District, Arunachal Pradesh.
   Phone No. 0360-2218742
4. **Akhilesh Kr. Gupta** — Ph.D., Lecturer and ANO, NCC, North Eastern Regional Institute of Science and Technology, Nirjuli, Papum Pare District, Arunachal Pradesh.
   Phone No. 0360-2257401
   Mobile No. 09436058269
5. **Arup K. Das** — Ph.D., Dean, Faculty of Life Science, Rajiv Gandhi University, Rono Hills, Itanagar, Papum Pare District, Arunachal Pradesh.
   Phone No. 0360-2277252.

6. **Asim Ranjan Parhi** — Ph.D., Lecturer (S.G), Deptt. of English, Indira Gandhi Govt. College, Tezu, Lohit District, Arunachal Pradesh.
Phone No. 03804–222668
Mobile No. 09436049212

7. **Debashis Neogi** — Ph.D., Lecturer (S.G.), Deptt. of Economics, Indira Gandhi Govt. College, Tezu, Lohit District, Arunachal Pradesh.
Phone No. 03804–222300
Mobile No. 09436254366

8. **Debabrata Maji** — M.Tech, Lecturer, Deptt. of Mechanical Engineering, North Eastern Regional Institute of Science and Technology, Nirjuli, Papum Pare District, Arunachal Pradesh
Phone No. 0360–2257401

9. **Deepak Pandey** — Ph.D., Principal, Govt. College, Yachuli, Lower Subansiri District, Arunachal Pradesh.
Phone No. 03788–277311
Mobile No. 09436043434

10. **Hage Hassang** — Ph.D., Lecturer, Deptt. of Economics, Tirap Govt. College, Deomali, Tirap District, Arunachal Pradesh
Phone No. 03786–255219

11. **Joram Begi** — Ph.D., Director of Higher and Technical Education, Govt. of Arunachal Pradesh, Itanagar,
Phone No. 0360–2214416
Mobile No. 09436040316

12. **Madhuparna Bhattacharjee** — M.Phil., Lecturer (S.G.), Deptt. of Geography, Dera Natung Govt. College, Itanagar, Papum Pare District, Arunachal Pradesh.
Phone No. 0360–2212516
Mobile No. 09862036084

13. **M.C. Behera** — Ph.D., Director, Distance Education, Rajiv Gandhi University, Rono Hills, Itanagar, Papum Pare District, Arunachal Pradesh.
Phone No. 0360–2278087
Mobile No. 09436252229

14. **Milorai Modi** — Ph.D., Reader, Deptt. of Political Science, Dera Natung Govt. College, Itanagar, Papum Pare District, Arunachal Pradesh.
Phone No. 0360–2212516
Mobile No. 09862173115

15. **M.A. Salam** — Ph.D., Reader, Deptt. of Economics, Govt. College, Bomdila, West Kameng District, Arunachal Pradesh.
Phone No. 03782–222120
Mobile No. 09436057826

16. **P.C. Swain** — Ph.D., Reader, Deptt. of Political Science, Indira Gandhi Govt. College, Tezu, Lohit District, Arunachal Pradesh.
Phone No. 03804–222667
Mobile No. 09436049506

17. **R.B. Tripathi** — Ph.D., Reader, Deptt. of Political Science, Dera Natung Govt. College, Itanagar, Papum Pare District, Arunachal Pradesh.
Phone No. 0360–2212516
Mobile No. 09436050037

18. **R.K. Mandal** — Ph.D., Lecturer (S.G), Dera Natung Govt. College, Itanagar, Papum Pare District, Arunachal Pradesh.
Phone No. 0360-2212516

19. **T. Madhusudan** M.E., M.Tech, Principal,
Rajiv Gandhi Govt. Polytechnic,
Itanagar, Papum Pare District,
Arunachal Pradesh
Phone No. 0360–2218781
Mobile No. 09436068605

20. **Utpal Talukdar** Ph.D., Lecturer, Deptt. of
Geography, St. Claret College, Ziro,
Lower Subansiri District,
Arunachal Pradesh.
Phone No. 03788–201052

21. **V.N. Sharma** Ph.D., State Liaison Officer, NSS,
Directorate of Higher & Technical
Education, Govt. of Arunachal
Pradesh, Itanagar.
Phone No. 0360–2291432
Mobile No. 09436221555

SECTION—I
Dynamics of Higher Education in Arunachal Pradesh

1

Higher and Technical Education in Arunachal Pradesh Since 1964

—*Joram Begi*

Map of Arunachal Pradesh showing Locations of Higher Educational Institutions in Arunachal Pradesh as in 2007

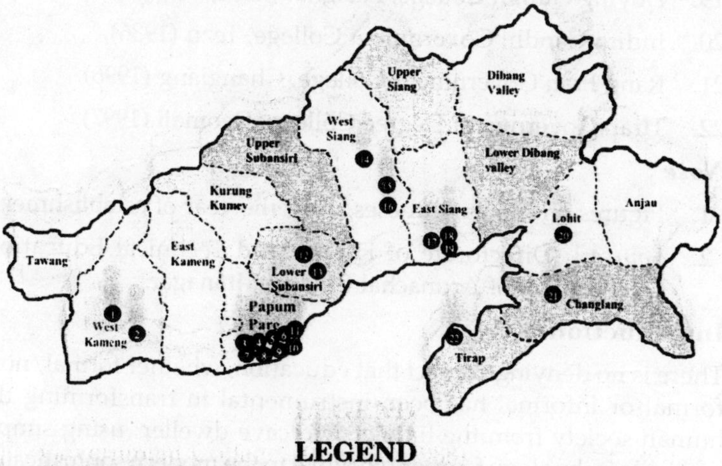

LEGEND

1. Government College, Bomdila (1988).
2. Central Institute of Himalayan Culture Studies (2004).
3. Rajiv Gandhi Government Polytechnic, Itanagar (2002).

4. Dera Natung Government College, Itanagar (1979).
5. North East Homoeopathy Medical College and Hospital, Itanagar (2001).
6. Donbosco College, Jully (2002).
7. Hills College of Teacher Education, Naharlagun (2006).
8. St. Thomas Institute of Legal Studies (2007).
9. IGNOU, Regional Centre (2000).
10. North Eastern Regional Institute of Science & Technology, Nirjuli (1984).
11. Rajiv Gandhi University, Rono Hills (1984).
12. St. Claret College, Ziro (2003).
13. Government College, Yachuli (2007).
14. Donyi Polo Government College, Kamki (1996).
15. St. Francis College, Aalo (2007).
16. Tomi Polytechnic, Basar (2006).
17. Jawaharlal Nehru College, Pasighat (1964).
18. College of Horticulture and Forestry, Pasighat (2002).
19. Doying Gumin College, Pasighat (2004).
20. Indira Gandhi Government College, Tezu (1986).
21. Rang Frah Government College, Changlang (1996).
22. Tirap Government Degree College, Deomali (1997).

Note :

1. Figures within parentheses show the year of establishment.
2. *Source* : Directorate of Higher and Technical Education, Government of Arunachal Pradesh, Itanagar.

Introduction

There is no denying the fact that education, whether formal/non-formal or informal has been instrumental in transforming the human society from the time of the cave-dweller using simple available technology for mere survival to the modern sophisticated one making and using complex technology for a meaningful living with command and control. In this process of transformation, the higher education has been playing the role of a catalyst not only by speeding up the process through improvement of skills and technology but also by activating and enriching the creative imagination of humankind.

Naturally, it comes to the need for an understanding of what higher education is all about. At the ideological level, it can be understood as a system that adds to skills, expands the horizon of creative imagination and develops a sense of appreciation and understanding for the expansion of individual self to social and global self both in perception and action[1]. But the working definition of higher education has apparently a graded connotation and as such refers to a level in the formal system of education. It is clear from the definition devised and accepted in 1962 by 44 nations participating in a UNESCO conference on higher education in Africa.

As per the definition, higher education refers to all types of education (academic, professional, technological, or teacher education) provided in institutions, such as, universities, liberal arts college for which : *(a)* the basic entrance requirement is completion of secondary education, *(b)* the usual entrance age is about 18 years, and *(c)* the courses lead to the giving of a named award (degree, diploma, or certificate) of higher studies[2]. In short, higher education is a post secondary education resulting in the award of a degree, diploma or certificate. The institutes of higher education include colleges, universities and schools of professional and technological studies including teacher-training schools and junior colleges[3].

The importance of higher education has been well perceived by planners and academics in India. The Approach paper of the steering group, Planning Commission, for the 9th Plan, states in its opening sentence :[4]

> "The crucial role of higher education, in the process of development and modernisation, was well recognised from the beginning of Indian planning 1950-51. This recognition is abundantly evident in the observation of its first Prime Minister, Jawaharlal Nehru that, if all is well with the Universities, it will be well with the Nation".

Kulandaiswamy states that a university is the nursery for the creative talent to sprout; it is the farm that provides fertile soil and favourable climate for one's talent to find the fullest manifestation; it is the environment where leadership develops; it is the place where expeditions into the unknown are initiated and encouraged; it is also the place where inventions and innovations germinate and blossom[5]. Though the statement has been made in a different context, it however, speaks of the significance of higher education in the process of development of a nation and building up human resource.

Conceptualising Higher Education in Arunachal Pradesh

Coming to Arunachal Pradesh, it can be stated that the system of higher education is a late entrant following the formal system of education introduced in 1947. In terms of teachers' training, following the definition of higher education, it can be mentioned that higher education is as old as school education in the state. But in the state of Arunachal Pradesh, teachers' training institutes like DIETs, SIE, Changlang come under the management of school education from administrative point of view. However, B.Ed. course offered by Rajiv Gandhi University and Hills College of Teacher Educaition, Naharlagun comes under higher education. For the purpose of our analysis and discussion, higher education refers to the education imparted in institutes as shown in Table 1. Precisely, it includes degrees, diploma and certificate courses offered by the University, Colleges and technical and professional institutes.

It is to be mentioned in this context that before the establishment of Secondary Education Board of Assam (SEBA), syllabi were prepared and examinations conducted for class IX and class X by Gauhati University. Naturally, the certificate for matriculation examination was awarded by the University[6]. However, education upto matriculation was not considered higher education even though certificate was awarded then by the University. Commonly, education of +3 stage onwards under 10+2+3 pattern has been considered higher education. But, for diploma or certificate courses, it may not always be a post-secondary level of education. Obviously, for general education in arts, science and commerce; higher education stands for the post-higher secondary level of education. While in technical and professional courses, it is the course, which provides diploma degree or certificate, is important.

Table 1
Institutions of Higher Education in the State

Sl. No.	*Name of the Institute/Centre*	*Year of Establishment*	*Nature/ Mode of Course Offered*	*Location*
1	2	3	4	5
1.	Jawaharlal Nehru College	1964	Regular mode, General Course	Pasighat (East Siang)
2.	Dera Natung Government College	1979	-do-	Itanagar (Papum Pare)
3.	Indira Gandhi Government College	1986	-do-	Tezu (Lohit)
4.	Government College Bomdila	1988	-do-	Bomdila (West Kameng)
5.	Donyi-Polo Government College	1996	-do-	Kamki (West Siang)
6.	Rang-Frah Government College	1996	-do-	Kengkhu (Changlang)
7.	Tirap Degree College	1997	-do-	Deomali (Tirap)
8.	Government College	2007	-do-	Yachuli (Lower Subansiri District)
9.	Don Bosco College	2002	-do-	Jully, Itanagar (Papum Pare)
10.	St. Claret College	2003	-do-	Ziro (Lower Subansiri)
11.	Doying Gumin College	2004	-do-	Pasighat (East Siang)
12.	St. Fransico De Sales College	2007	-do-	Aalo (West Siang)
13.	North-East Homeopathy Medical College	2001	Regular mode, professional course	Itanagar (Papum Pare)

Contd. . . .

Table 1 (Cond. . . .)

1	2	3	4	5
14.	St. Thomas Institute of Legal Studies	2007	Regular mode, professional course	Itanagar (Papum Pare)
15.	Rajiv Gandhi Polytechnic	2002	Regular Mode, Technical and Professional course	Itanagar (Papum Pare)
16.	Tomi Polytechnic College	2006	-do-	Basar (West Siang)
17.	College of Horticulture and Forestry	2001	-do-	Pasighat (East Siang)
18.	NERIST	1984	-do-	Nirjuli, Itanagar (Papum Pare)
19.	IGNOU Regional Centre	2000	Distance mode, General and Tech. courses	Naharlagun (Papum Pare)
20.	Rajiv Gandhi University	1984	Regular course, General, Technical and Professional	Rono Hills (Papum Pare
21.	Hills College of Teacher Education	NA	Regular course, Technical course	Naharlagun (Papum Pare)
22.	Central Institute of Himalayan Culture Studies.	2003	-do-	Dihung (West Kemeng)

Source : Annual Report (of various Years) of Rajiv Gandhi University and field study.

The technical institutes like NERIST, Rajiv Gandhi Polytechnic and Tomi Polytechnic College offer courses after completion of class-X. Though the courses are not post-secondary level of education they nevertheless come under higher education.

Institutional Categories and Mode of Course Offered

In Table 1, 20 institutes/centres have been enumerated which provide higher education in the state. All the colleges mentioned in serial number 1 to 8 in the table of reference are government colleges and they impart general courses under both regular and private mode. However, from this session onwards University is abolishing private – mode in phase – wise manner. Table 2 shows that, of these eight colleges only two colleges, namely, J.N. College, Pasighat and D.N. Government College, Itanagar have Science Stream. Commerce stream runs in four colleges, namely, J.N. College, D.N. College, I.G. Government College, Tezu and D. P. G. College, Kamki.

The science stream at D.N. Government College was introduced in 2001-02, while at J.N. College it commenced in 1973-74. Similarly, the commerce stream was introduced at D. P. G. College in 2007-2008, at I.G. Government College in 2004-05, at D.N. Government College in 1995-96 and at J.N. College in 1983-84. Obviously, J.N. College, being the pioneering institute of higher education, had the privilege of starting new streams first among all.

Table 2
Year of Introducing Different Streams in the Colleges of the State

Stream	*Name of Colleges*	*Year of Opening*
Humanities	J.N. College, Pasighat;	1964–65
	D.N. G. College, Itanagar;	1979–80
	I.G.G. College, Tezu;	1986–87
	Govt. College, Bomdila;	1988–89
	D.P.G. College, Kamki;	1996–97
	R.F.G. College, Changlang;	1996–97
	T.D. College, Deomali;	1997–98

	D.B. College, Jully;	2002–2003
	St. Claret College, Ziro;	2003–2004
	D.G. College, Pasighat;	2004–2005
	Govt. College, Yachuli	2007–2008
	St. Francis College, Aaalo	2007–2008
Science	J.N. College, Pasighat	1973–74
	D.N.G. College, Itanagar	2000-01
Commerce	J.N. College, Pasighat	1983–84
	D.N.G. College, Itanagar	1995–96
	I.G.G. College, Tezu	2004–05
	Donyi Polo Govt. College, Kamki	2007-08

Source : Directorate of Higher and Technical Education.

The colleges mentioned in serial number 9 to 12 in Table 1 are general colleges under non-government sectors (details in following sections) and all of them offer regular mode of education. At present the Doying Gumin College is the only evening college in the state. Though the present D.N. Government College, Itanagar was started as evening college in 1979, the evening shift was abolished subsequently making it exclusively a day college in the year (academic) 1987–88.

The North-East Homoeopathy Medical College and Hospital (NEHMCH) is also being run by a non-governmental organisation and is the only institution in the state that provides degree course in alternative medical education. Rajiv Gandhi Polytechnic began as a project in 2002 under Technician Education III of MHRD, and the institution has been taken over by the state government since 1st July,' 2007 after the completion of project period on 30th June 2007. It provides diploma in technical and professional courses.

Another Polytechnic called Tomi Polytechnic College at Basar has been established in 2006 under Private sector. The other two institutes namely NERIST and College of Horticulture and Forestry (CHF) are in central government sector, which provide technical and professional courses under regular mode only.

The St. Thomas Institute of Legal Studies, a Law College, has been established in the year 2007 at Itanagar under Private Sector. The Institute offers 5 years' integrated Bachelor Degree Course in Law.

Formal and conventional institutes of education provide education through regular and private modes. Courses having laboratory subjects, of course, do not have private mode. Over the years there are innovations in the system and in recent years distance mode is gaining popularity. Essentially, distance mode is neither a supplement, nor an alternative to the conventional system providing regular and private modes. It is a new stage in the evolution of education and it recognizes the fact that in many situations, it is easier to transport knowledge to people than transport people to the places of knowledge.[7] Distance education has its own significance and different universities go for distance mode through multimedia communication, off campus centres or through centres providing services along with its conventional mode. However, there are many universities like IGNOU, Netaji Subhash Open University, Dr. B.R. Ambedkar Open University which provide education exclusively through distance mode. IGNOU has its regional Centre in the state at Itanagar (Naharlagun). Rajiv Gandhi University has also introduced distance mode by opening the Centre for Distance Education (CDE) in 2004–05. Regional Centre of IGNOU offers wide range of courses of general, technical and professional nature through its 10 study centres located in different parts of the state. The centres are located at Itanagar (1987), Bomdila (1988), Jawaharlal Nehru College, Pasighat (1988), Khonsa (2003), Tezu (2004), Ziro (2005), Changlang (2005), DIET, Pasighat (2005), Block Resource Centre, Doimukh (2005) and DIET (seppa) 2006.The CDE of the RGU has begun with general courses at undergraduate level. During 2005-06, 64 students have been enrolled in four centres at I.G. Government College, Tezu; Tirap Government College, Deomali; Bomdila Government College, Bomdila and at the University centre itself.

Hills College of Teacher Education, established under private sector at Naharlagun is running B.Ed. programme from 2006–07 academic session. The Central Institute of Himalayan Culture Studies at Dahung offers Shastri Degree in Buddhist Studies, particularly pertaining to Buddhism of Tibetan origin. The Institute has been affiliated to Sampurnanand Sanskrit University, Varanasi and is being run with grants-in-aid from Ministry of Culture, Government of India.

Private Colleges

Don Bosco College, Jully (2002), St. Claret College, Ziro (2004), Doying Gumin College, Pasighat (2004) and St. Francis De Sales College, Aalo (2007) are the general colleges under private sector offering Bachelor degree courses mostly in Arts and Humanities. North East Homeopathy Medical College and Hospital, Itanagar (2002), Hills College of Teacher Education, Naharlagun (2006) and St. Thomas Institute of Legal Studies, Itanagar (2007) are professional private colleges offering Bachelor Degree in Homeopathy, Education and Law respectively. Doying Gumin College, Pasighat also started B.Ed. Programme from the Academic Year 2007–2008.

Course Structure at Degree Level

In general education in colleges, one has to appear in twelve papers of 100 marks each under pass course. In 1st year, one has to offer one paper each in three elective subjects and another one in compulsory English. In the second year, there are two papers of compulsory English and one paper each in two elective subjects, which one has to opt for out of the three elective subjects offered during 1st year. In the 3rd year one has to study two papers in each of the two elective subjects offered during 2nd year. For honours one has to appear in 17 papers of 100 marks each. The course structure for honours differs from that of the pass course from 2nd year onwards. Of the two elective subjects one opts for honours in either subject and studies 2 papers more in the subject than a pass student does. In the third year one is to study 3 papers more in the honours subject. The 500 more marks for honours course is due to 5 more papers (*i.e.* 2 in 2nd year and 3 in 3rd year) in honours subject only.

Similarly, for commerce pass course, there are 15 papers of 100 marks each, while there are 19 papers of 100 marks each for honours course in commerce.

In Science stream, *i.e* B.Sc. (Pass course) has 1400, while (Honours course) has 2000 marks.

Quality Assurance Measures

For assuring quality in higher education, the Directorate of Higher and Technical Education has been conducting Conference since 1998. Delegates from Colleges, University, UGC, IGNOU, NERIST etc. deliberate upon the problems both general and institution specific and prepare action plan for incoming academic session. This also gives a chance for feed back to the government for planning and formulating education policies in a right perspective.

Moreover, a Quality Assurance Cell (QAC) with the financial assistance from National Assessment and Accreditation Council (NAAC), Bangalore has been established in 2003 under the Directorate of Higher and Technical Education. The State Level Quality Assurance Coordination Committee headed by Education Minister has also been constituted in 2003. Since then, the Cell and the Committee have been consistently monitoring the quality improvement, particularly, in collegiate education. The cell also conducts workshop to sensitise NAAC Assessment and Accreditation of the colleges and University from time to time.

Besides, the University and Colleges of the state are being assessed by NAAC peer team to know where they objectively stand in the matter of academics and governance. D.N. Government College, Itanagar was assessed in October 2005 and was placed in B+ grade. J.N. College, Pasighat was assessed in March 2006 and was placed in B++ grade. Indira Gandhi Government College, Tezu after being assessed in February, 2006 was given B+ grade. Government College, Bomdila and Donyi Polo Government College, Kamki were assessed during August - September 2006 and were placed in B grade. The lone University of the state after assessment in 2002 was awarded B grade. Rang Frah Government College, Changlang is under preparation for assessment.

Situation of Higher Education Before 1964

Students of the State, after completing their matriculation, if wanted to pursue higher education, had to migrate to Guwahati, Shillong and other towns of the region where colleges were available. Cotton College, Guwahati (established in 1901) and St. Edmund College, Shillong (established in 1924) were the usual destination[8]. Arunachalees who had the opportunity to receive formal education first and proceeded for higher education during 1950s and 1960s studied mostly in these colleges. To name a few among the pioneer students of the state receiving higher education: Daying Ering, who matriculated from the High School at Sadiya in 1948, studied in the Cotton College; Shri Matin Dai who matriculated in 1952 from High School, Sadiya did his graduation in 1956 from St. Edmand College, Shillong; Oshong Ering, the first matriculate from Pasighat High School in 1954 took admission in St. Edmund College in 1955; Toi Dai, the first science graduate amongst the Arunachalees, took his B.Sc. degree (Agri) from Jorhat Agriculture College (now Assam Agriculture University), C. T. Manpong, the first engineering graduate (1969) of the state, studied in Assam Engineering College, Guwahati while Odang Lego, the first doctor took his MBBS degree from the Guwahati Medical College, Guwahati in 1969.

Collegiate Education—A Historical Overview

Jawaharlal Nehru College, Pasighat

Due to slow but steady increase of educational activities in the then NEFA since 1947, at the school level, the desire for higher education amongst the students gradually increased. The economic condition of most of the students did not permit them to go outside the state for the purpose. Government of India, especially after the Chinese aggression of 1962, realised this and as such the first ever college of the state was established at Pasighat on 4th July 1964. The college initially named as Pasighat Government College was renamed, Jawaharlal Nehru College, after the name of the first Prime Minister of India who died in office in the month of May that very year. In the year of its establishment, the college (a government institution), started with forty two students only, in pre-university (Arts course). It is important to note that all the students were *bona fide* Arunachal Pradesh Scheduled Tribe (APST) students. Of the five Frontier Divisions of the state they were mostly from the then Siang and Lohit Frontier Divisions, a few from the Tirap and the Kameng Frontier Divisions, none from the Subansiri Frontier Division. There was not a single female student[9]. At the time of starting the college, there were 3 lecturers. The post of the principal was temporarily held by the Director of Education. Later on, a regular principal, Dr. J. B. Ganguly[10], was appointed. Five more lecturers joined later in the same year. The initial departments were English, Assamese, Hindi, History, Political Science, Economics and Education. Geography was added later. In the following year *i.e.* during academic year 1965-66, 30 students were admitted in the first year of the three year degree course (Arts). Science faculty in the college was started from the academic session 1973-74 and commerce from 1983-84.

The college site was selected at the outskirt of the Pasighat town, 3 kms away from the town. The site consists of a hill top, called upper campus, and down below, some level areas, called lower campus. It started functioning in Ordinary Basa Type (OBT) buildings at lower campus. Later on, semi-permanent buildings were constructed in upper campus. One has to reach the upper campus from the lower campus either by climbing 277 cement - concrete steps or 3 kms. by road. All class rooms, office, library, laboratories etc. are housed in the upper campus, while Hostels (10 nos), play ground and auditorium are in the lower campus. However, the college in course of time has become the nerve centre of higher education in the state. Till early 1980s almost 90% of students from the state going for higher studies, used to enrol themselves in this college. Besides degree courses in Arts, Science and Commerce, post-graduate courses in Political Science and History under the Punjab University and later under Arunachal University, were conducted here during the period from 1980 to 1988, *i.e* till the beginning of academic courses by Arunachal university at Rono Hills. Post-graduate courses in Botany and Zoology under Arunachal University (now Rajiv Gandhi University) were also started in this college. At present, the college has 1786 students and 62 faculty members. More than 50% of civil servants, intellectuals and political elites of the state are alumni of the college. Thus, the college has made significant contribution to the socio-economic development of the state.

Dera Natung Government College, Itanagar

The 2nd college of the state, another government institution, was established on 6th September, 1979 at Itanagar (then New Itanagar). The necessity of establishing a college in the newly established state capital was felt by the then government headed by Shri P.K. Thungon as the Chief Minister of the Union Territory. Many employees of the Secretariat and the Directorates were reluctant to leave Shillong due to children's education. Two schools, a Kendriya Vidyalaya (K.V–1) at Naharlagun, the temporary capital, on 25th April, 1974, and another a state government Higher Secondary School at Itanagar (permanent capital) were established on 2nd Oct. 1978. The college was established to meet the demand of the employees for their children's higher education. The college, started functioning with the nomenclature of Government College,

Itanagar, has been renamed as Dera Natung Government College in 2001 after the sudden demise of illustrious Education Minister of the state, Late Dera Natung in a helicopter crash while on touring duty.

The college was started as an evening college with three lecturers and 13 students, who were all office-goers, in the lower campus buildings of the present government higher secondary school, Itanagar. Initially the college started with Arts faculty with English, Hindi, History and Economics as subjects. Subsequently, more subjects like Political Science, Education and Geography were introduced. Faculties of Commerce in 1995-96 and Science in 2000-01 were also started.

The college has been allotted 82 acres of land in the heart of the capital town. The college was shifted to its permanent campus in the month of July 1986. Along with evening classes, day classes were also started on 16th August 1986; but evening classes were finally abolished during 1987-88 and the college now has become a premier institution with Arts, Science and Commerce faculties. There is a heavy rush of students for admission in the college from all over the state in spite of demarcation of catchment areas for each college in the state. The college at present has more than 2634 students, 61 teachers and 40 non-teaching staff.

Here it is worth while and relevant to mention that the college has been successfully running a *Career Counselling Cell* sponsored and financed by the Directorate of Higher and Technical Education, Govt. of Arunachal Pradesh since 2003. The importance of this counselling cell further enhances as it is the only centre of its kind in the state which imparts effective coaching to prepare aspirants for various competitive examinations focussing mainly on examinations conducted by UPSC and APPSC. Apart from this the cell also gives guidance to the needy in order to decide their future prospects and career according to their interests and specialisation.

Indira Gandhi Government College, Tezu

The 3rd college was established at Tezu in 1986, after 7 years from the year of establishment of the 2nd college. This is also a Government College named as Indira Gandhi Government College, Tezu. Initially there was no proper planning to start the college. Hence, existing teaching and non-teaching staff from J.N.

College, Pasighat and D.N. Government College Itanagar were transferred to start the college. The college temporarily functioned in the buildings of the Department of Industry. It was shifted to its permanent campus of 200 acres of land just in the outskirt of Tezu township in 1990. The college is the 3rd largest college in the state with enrolment of 1150 students and 28 teachers and 22 Non-teaching staff during academic session 2007-08.

Initially, the college was an Arts college with subjects—English, Hindi, History, Political Science, Economics and Geography. Commerce faculty has been introduced in the academic session 2004-05. Education subject has also been introduced with effect from the Academic year 2007-2008.

Government College, Bomdila

The 4th college was established in 1988 at Bomdila with the simple nomenclature as Government College, Bomdila. It is also an Arts college with subjects—English, Hindi, History, Political Science, Economics and Geography. The college has 589 students and 18 teachers during academic year 2007-08. Although the college started functioning in the Bomdila Government Higher Secondary School premises, its permanent site was allotted at a place called 'Wangkho', 5 kms. away from Bomdila township where the foundation stone of the college was laid on 17th October 1988 by Shri Gegong Apang, the then Chief Minister of the State. Due to lack of proper approach road and scarcity of water at the site, infrastructure like buildings could not be constructed there. Another attempt was made to shift the college to a place called 'Dahung', 25 kms away from Bomdila but with no concrete step. Thus, due to lack of a concrete decision on its permanent site, the college suffered a lot in its growth. However, in 2001 the state government constituted a committee headed by Shri Roding Pertin, the then Minister of State for Education, to decide the issue once for all. The committee decided to locate the college at its present location, sharing a part of Higher Secondary School campus with certain adjustment.

The college has exchanged a newly constructed three storeyed building with the existing two-storeyed building meant for Middle section of the school in 2005. Efforts are also on to get the Special Service Bureau (SSB) vacated land at new Bomdila allotted for hostels and residences for staff.

Rang Frah Government College, Changlang

The 5th college called Rang Frah Government College was started on 17th July 1996 at Changlang. The college started functioning for a few years at the Buniyadi Siksha Bhawan (BSB) building in Changlang town. The college was shifted on 13th February 1997 to a place called Longbusung, 15 kms away from Changlang township.

The college was originally planned to meet the demand of higher education in the undivided district of Tirap. However, due to bifurcation of the district into Tirap and Changlang districts and as Mr. Somcham Ngemu, was the then Dy. Minister of Education, the college was located in Changlang. The college offers degree programme in Arts. The subjects taught are—English, Hindi, History, Pol. Science, Economics and Geography. The College has 239 students as per enrolment of academic session 2007–08 and 13 teachers.

The biggest problem of the two colleges–Donyi Polo Government College, Kamki and Rang Frah Government College, Changlang is the locational disadvantage. No ancillary facilities like—Market, Hospital, School, Post Office, police station, and public transport exist in those places. All students are to be accommodated in hostels and all staff are to be provided with residential accommodation in the college campus itself. Due to resource constrains, the state government has not been able to fulfil all these requirements. As a result many teachers do not want to be posted in these colleges.

Donyi Polo Government College, Kamki

The 6th college of the state was opened on 22nd July 1996 at Kamki with 190 students and 5 lecturers. Mr. Lijum Ronia, the then Minister of Education was instrumental for establishment of the college. The college is named as Donyi Polo Government College and is located at a distance of 25 kms. away from Aalo township, the district Head-quarters of West Siang District. The college was established without any prior planning mainly for the reason to avoid frequent clashes between the Galo and the Minyong students at J.N. College, Pasighat especially during the time of the students' union elections resulting in communal problem between the two communities.

The college is running degree programmes in Arts with subjects—English, Hindi, Economics, Education, History, Political Science, and Geography. Commerce faculty has also been added to the college from the academic session 2007-2008. As per enrolment record of the current Academic year, the college has 839 students and 22 teachers.

Tirap Government Degree College, Deomali

The 7th college was established in 1997 at Charju (Khela) 8 kms. away from Khonsa, the district headquarters of Tirap District. The College was named as the Tirap Government Degree College. The college has 377 students and 11 teachers during the academic session 2007-08.

Like Rang Frah Government College, Changlang and Donyi Polo Government College, Kamki, the Tirap Government Degree College at Charju too, had locational difficulties apart from lacking in basic infrastructure. Hence, in 2001 when late Dera Natung and Late Sanghe Lhaden were the Minister and the Secretary respectively of Education department, they made a sincere attempt to merge both Tirap Government College, Charju and Rang Frah Government College, Changlang into one college and to relocate it at Deomali, a convenient place for both the districts. The justification in this regard was that :

(1) both the colleges in their existing locations had the locational disadvantages lacking in ancillary facilities,

(2) both the places were infested with insurgency problem, and

(3) the number of students enrolled in both the colleges was low and thus a wastage of resources.

Accordingly, Tirap Government Degree College was shifted in 2001 to Deomali and started functioning temporarily in a building meant for T.B. Hospital. However, the Rang Frah Government College, Changlang could not be shifted due to opposition from the people of Changlang District. Tirap Government Degree College has continued to function at Deomali without its own land and building. An attempt was made by administration to get a plot of land in the Coffee Board area of Deomali. But the elected representatives of Tirap district in a meeting held on 27th August 2003 decided to shift back the college to the original site at Charju with a rider that the college has to continue functioning at Deomali till the creation of infrastructure at Charju[11].

Government College, Yachuli

The college has been established at Yachuli, 25 kms. before reaching Ziro; the district headquarters of Lower Subansiri. The college is temporarily functioning at the DIET building and a plot of land measuring 150 acres approximately has been donated by the local people free of cost for the establishment of the college. The college started functioning w.e.f. 19th July' 2007 with 57 nos of students and 5 nos of teachers in the subjects—English, Hindi, Economics, History and Political Science.

Private Colleges

The State Government, especially after it has become a full-fledged state, has no adequate resources to establish more Government Colleges in the state, nor it has been able to provide basic infrastructure to the existing colleges. Keeping this view, it has decided to encourage Non-Governmental Organisations (NGOs) and other voluntary organisations to establish private colleges in the state.

The state government issues No Objection Certificate (NOC) to establish colleges subject to the following conditions :

1. The college is to be affiliated to Arunachal University (now Rajiv Gandhi University).
2. The college is to be established as per the terms and conditions laid down by the provisions of the relevant ordinance of the university.
3. Prior approval is to be obtained from the concerned statutory body (if the proposed college is a professional and technical institution).
4. The college shall abide by the rules and regulations framed from time to time by the state government for maintaining standard of education in the state.
5. It shall include a state government nominee in the Governing Board of the institution.

Accordingly, 7 private colleges, 4 general and 3 professional and 1 Polytechnic, have been established in the state since 2001.

Don Bosco College was established in 2002 at Jully, 5 km. away from Itanagar by the Catholic Mission. The college offers Bachelor Degree programme in Arts in subjects—English, History, Political Science, Economics and Sociology. *St. Claret College* was established in 2003 at Salaya near Old Ziro by Cleration Formation Society, Shillong. The College offers Bachelor degree in Arts in the subjects English, History, Political Science Economics and Anthropology. *Doying Gumin College* was established in 2004 at Pasighat by the Murang Education Society, Pasighat. The college also offers B.A programme in the subjects English, History, Political Science and Economics and B.Ed. *St. Francis De Sales College,* Aalo has been established w.e.f. the Academic Session 2007-2008. The college offers Degree programme in Arts and Humanities.

The *North East Homoeopathy Medical College and Hospital* (NEHMCH), the only medical professional college, was established in 2001 at Itanagar by Abotani Charitable Society, Itanagar. The college offers BHMS degree. The *Hills College of Teacher Education, Naharlagun* has been established from the academic session 2006-2007. The college offers B. Ed. Programme. The *St. Thomas Institute of Legal Studies, Itanagar,* the first Law College has been established in 2007 under private sector.

Tomi Polytechnic, College, Basar has been established in the year 2006. It is the first Technical Institutions under private sector. The college offers Diploma course in Civil Engineering, Computer Science and Engineering, Electrical and Electronics Engineering and Electronics and Telecommunication Engineering.

In the context of college education it is to be noted that each of 16 districts does not have a college Table 1; only eight districts are covered with all the institutes of higher education. Colleges and other institutes of higher education are mostly located in capital complex and in Pasighat, the oldest town in the state. Except Donyi Polo Government College, Rang-Frah Government College and Tirap Government Degree College, other colleges are located in district headquarters or in Capital complex.

Another striking point about college education is that the courses are conventional Arts, Science and Commerce. Except in J.N. College, Science and Commerce streams are very recent in DNGC and so is Commerce in I.G.G. College Table 2. Further, it is to be noted with reference to the Table 3 below, that honours courses were offered in colleges much late as compared to their respective years of establishment. Again honours courses in certain subjects were offered still later, say Hindi in 1989-90 in J. N. College though the subject has been introduced in the year of its establishment. Even in D.N. Government College, despite it being located in the heart of the capital of the state, there is no honours in Mathematics and Physics. In D.P. Government College, Kamki there is no honours in Education. *Rang Frah Government College* offers honours in three subjects out of six subjects taught. Similarly Tirap Government Degree College has honours only in two out of six subjects introduced. Some of the private colleges, do not have honours courses in all subjects.

Table 3
Number of Students and Teachers in the Year of Establishment of the Colleges and Their Corresponding Number during 2007-08

College	*Year of Establish-ment*	*No. of Students during Year of Estt.*	*No. of Teachers during Year of Estt.*	*2007-08 Students*	*2007-08 Teachers*
J.N. College, Pasighat	1964	42	8	1789	62
D.N.G. College, Itanagar	1979	13	5	2634	61
I.G.G. College, Tezu	1986	42	8	1150	28
Govt. College, Bomdila	1988	90	4	589	18
D.P.G. College, Kamki	1996	190	5	839	22
R.F.G. College, Changlang	1996	124	2	239	11
T.D. College, Deomali	1997	87	5	377	11
D.B. College, July	2002	NA	NA	418	15
St. Claret College, Ziro	2003	NA	NA	206	13
D.G. College, Pasighat	2004	16	NA	239	06
Govt. College, Yachuli	2007	57	05	57	05
St. Francis De Sales College, Aalo	2007	53	NA	53	NA

Source : Same as Table – 2.

In J.N. College, there are 13 subjects with 62 teachers Table - 3, the average ratio of subjects and teachers is 4.77. In DNGC it is 4.69, in IGGC 3.5, in Government College, Bomdila 3.00, in DPGC

3.14, in RFGC 2.2 and in TDC 2.2. Though this average is not a proper measure in terms of dividing individuals, it is indicative of proportionate share of distribution of teachers. Two things emerge. First, locationally advantaged colleges have more teachers and students and second, all the subjects in a college do not have proportionate representation of teachers. In general it may be pointed out that there is an over all shortage of teachers in different subjects. It further indicates that subjects have been introduced in different colleges without creation of corresponding posts.

Technical and Professional Education

North Eastern Regional Institute of Science and Technology (NERIST)

The North Eastern Regional Institute of Science and Technology (NERIST) is the first technical institute in the state, established in 1984 at Nirjuli, 19 kms from Itanagar, the State Capital of Arunachal Pradesh.

In 1979, the Arunachal Pradesh government submitted a proposal for setting up an Institute of Science and Technology, with multiple inputs and terminal facility. This proposal was accepted in principle by the North-Eastern Council in 1981. At the behest of North Eastern Council, the Indian Institute of Management, Ahmedabad submitted an initial project report in 1982.

The same year, Planning Commission approved the proposal. However, the Education Ministry called for detailed report and action plan for evaluation. For this purpose, a working group was constituted by North Eastern Council in 1982. The Working Group Report along with Action Plan was placed before Education Ministry in September, 1983.

In May, 1984, the Planning Commission suggested scaling down of the project in view of the Arunachal University (now Rajiv Gandhi University) located in the same place.

In June 1984, an inter-ministerial meeting was held to consider scaling down or retention of the proposed project including provision of degree courses. The consensus was for retention of the project including degree programme. For awarding its own degree, it was agreed that NERIST would be conferred university status by an Act of Parliament.

The institute started its academic programme with the admission of students through an Entrance Examination in August, 1986.

North Eastern Regional Institute of Science and Technology (NERIST) has been endeavouring since its existence, to be a leading institute of learning in the field of applied science and engineering not only in the north eastern region but in whole of India. In its short existence of 22 years it is pursuing the policy of educating a whole human being. At the institute both technical and social science subjects are emphasized in order to prepare students to perform equally well as educationists, scientists, leaders in industry, trained engineers and technicians.

The academic programme in Engineering and Technology at NERIST consists of three successive modules of two years each after matriculation. The three modules are called Certificate, Diploma and Degree. In applied science, a 2 year base module and a 4 year degree module are offered. Each module provides facility for corresponding to an occupational level, and at the same time provides entry to the next higher module, finally leading to a Degree in Engineering or Technology about 6 years after matriculation. It, thus, provides vertical and lateral linkages between different occupational levels. The system also allows lateral entry from outside with necessary pre-requisites at the base of each level.

The Institute is a new experiment in the field of Scientific and Technical Education.

The Institute was affiliated to North Eastern Hill University (NEHU), Shillong. However, it attained the Deemed to be University status in 2005.

Rajiv Gandhi Polytechnic, Itanagar

Arunachal Pradesh Polytechnic, now Rajiv Gandhi Polytechnic, is the first of its kind in the state. It was established in 2002 with financial assistance from the World Bank under Technician Education III Project of the Ministry of Human Resource Development, Government of India. The institute was functioning initially in a rented building. In January 2005 it was shifted to its permanent campus near Dera Natung Government College, Itanagar.

The Institute offers Diploma courses in seven streams namely, Travel and Tourism (TT), Hotel Management & Catering Technology (HMCT), Computer Science & Engineering (CSE), Herbal Technology (HT), Garment & Fashion Technology (GFT), Automobile Engineering (AUE) and Electrical and Electronics

Engineering (EEE). The duration of each course is three years. The entry qualification for HMCT is class XII passed and for the rest it is Class X passed. The admission is given through a Joint Entrance Examination conducted by the Directorate of Higher and Technical Education, Government of Arunachal Pradesh, Itanagar.

The Rajiv Gandhi Polytechnic has earned the credit of being the first institution in the state to achieve ISO 9001: 2000 certification in June' 2006.

Tomi Polytechnic College, Basar

The second Polytechnic called Tomi Polytechnic College, Basar has been established in 2006 under private sector. The institute has started Diploma Course in four streams namely, Civil Engineering, Electrical Engineering, Electronics & Telecommunication Engineering and Computer Science Engineering.

The College of Horticulture and Forestry, Pasighat

The College of Horticulture and Forestry (CHF) was established at Pasighat, East Siang District of Arunachal Pradesh on 7th March, 2001 under the aegis of the Central Agriculture University, Imphal, Manipur. The mandate of the college is to impart quality education in various disciplines of Horticulture and Forestry primarily for the benefit of the students of North East Hilly region; to perform need based resource and extension education relevant to NEH region and to establish linkages with Indian Council of Agricultural Research (ICAR) institutions and other related institutions located in NEH region.

The college offers undergraduate programme in the field of Horticulture with a total intake capacity of 32 students in first year. The allocations of seats for admission to B.Sc. (Horticulture) degree Programme for 7 states are : Manipur-5, Arunachal Pradesh-5, Tripura-5, Mizoram-4, Meghalaya-4, Sikkim-4, and Nagaland-2, while ICAR has a quota of 3 seats. Post-graduate Programme in Horticulture and undergraduate Programme in Forestry are proposed to be started soon.

North East Homoeopathy Medical College and Hospital, Itanagar

The North East Homoeopathy Medical College and Hospital was established in 2002 by Abotani Charitable Society, Itanagar to meet the demand of homoeopathy medical education of the students of NE region in general and of Arunachal Pradesh in particular. The college offers Bachelor degree in Homoeopathy

Medicine and Surgery (BHMS). The college is affiliated to Rajiv Gandhi University and is recognised by the Central Council of Homeopathic (CCH), New Delhi.

Selection of students to pursue various Technical and Professional Courses outside the State

Since Arunachal Pradesh does not have sufficient technical and professional institutions of its own, it is allotted 150 degree engineering, 160 diploma engineering and about 60 medical and allied degree seats from Government of India every year in different states of the country. These seats are allocated through Joint Entrance Examination. Seats are allotted as per the state government reservation policy under the following 4 categories :

Category I — 80% seats to Arunachal Pradesh Schedule Tribe candidates.

Category II — 12% seats to the children of State Government employees.

Category III — 4% seats to the children of Central Government employees who are presently posted in Arunachal Pradesh.

Category IV — 4% seats to the Children of *Bona fide* residents in Arunachal Pradesh minimum for a period of 3 years and who do not fall within the above three categories State quota of seats is also available in National Institute of Technology (NIT), Silchar and NERIST.

Table 4

Number of Diploma and Degree (Engineering and Medical etc.) Seats Nominated by the State Government during 2003-04 to 2005-06 against GOI, NEC and State Quota to outside the State.

Sl.No	*Course*	*2003-04*	*2004-05*	*2005-06*	*Total*
1	2	3	4	5	6
1.	BE/B.Tech. etc	134	153	150	437
2.	MBBS/BVS etc	95	83	92	270
3.	Diploma	121	160	151	432
	Total	350	396	393	1139

Source : Directorate of Higher & Technical, Education.

University Education

The University education in the state made a beginning with the establishment of Arunachal University (Now Rajiv Gandhi University) in 1984. However, the college-education of the state is at least two decades older than this with the establishment of J.N. College at Pasighat in 1964. The J.N. College and the present Dera Natung Government College at Itanagar, established in 1979, were affiliated to Guwahati University in Assam. In 1973, a Central University, namely North-Eastern Hill University was established to meet the demand for higher education in the hill regions of North-East India. The NEHU Act, 1973 provides under section 6(1) of North Eastern Hill University, Act 1973 (Jurisdiction) that the privilege of advantage of the University shall be extended to all the Hill States/Union territories (*i.e.* Meghalaya, Nagaland, Arunachal Pradesh and Mizoram) of North Eastern region. The Headquarters of the University was to be located at Shillong and the University Campuses to be established in all hill states of the region, *i.e.* Arunachal Pradesh, Nagaland and Mizoram[12]. Accordingly the Kohima and Aizwal campuses of the University were established as per the Act and all the existing colleges of the state of Meghalaya, Mizoram and Nagaland were de affiliated from the Gauhati University and affiliated to the new University. The then government of Arunachal Pradesh did not take any initiative neither to establish the University campus in Arunachal Pradesh nor the J. N. College, the lone College of the state was affiliated to NEHU rather preferred to continue under Gauwahati University. During this period, (i.e. 1970s) mainly owing to language issue in Assam and the policies adopted by Gauhati University to introduce Assamese as medium of instruction in affiliated colleges. Consequently there was a student demand from Arunachal Pradesh for affiliation of colleges to NEHU. But the government of the Union Territory did not favour such a demand because there was a strong apprehension that the Arunachalee-students at NEHU would be exposed to Christianity. As Arunachalee communities are tradition-bound, the exposure to Christianity was apprehended to be a potential threat to their rich-cultural heritage. On 1st March 1976, while addressing the students community at Pasighat, K.A.A. Raja, the then Lt. Governor of the state, clearly voiced this concern of the government. He even assured them to have a separate university in the state if there be problem of affiliation, but strongly denounced the idea of affiliation to NEHU. This was perhaps the first casual thought of the government for having a university in the state.

In the meantime, the situation in Assam, (*i.e.* the Assam agitation since late-70s), created irregularities in academic administration and management; examinations could not be conducted in time and declaration of results became most uncertain. As a result, the ground to withdraw affiliation from Gauwahati University became strong and imperative. At the same time, the state government had its own reason for not affiliating its colleges to NEHU. As an alternative, the colleges of Arunachal Pradesh were affiliated to Punjab University, Chandigarh in 1980. During initial years, examination were conducted on the basis of the syllabi of Gauwahati University till the syllabi of Punjab University were adopted and introduced in colleges. But the new situation created various problems because of the distance from Arunachal Pradesh to Chandigarh.

The problem further ignited the urge of the Arunachalees for a University. This urge got a leadership in Shri Gegong Apang, the then Chief Minister of the state, who took up the matter tenaciously with the Central Government. Consequent upon his initiatives and consistent persuasion, the foundation stone of Arunachal University (now Rajiv Gandhi University) was laid by Mrs. Indira Gandhi, the then Prime Minister, on 4th February, 1984 in its present campus. However, the university started functioning initially at the present Arunachal Pradesh Public Service Commission office building from 1985-86 conducting examinations initially under Punjab University. The University shifted to its Rono Hills campus in 1988-89 with three departments, namely Education, History and Political Science.

In this connection, it is to be mentioned that the students passing out from colleges of Arunachal Pradesh faced difficulties to pursue post-graduate courses level of education. The colleges, being affiliated to Punjab University, Chandigarh, there was problem of distance along with financial problems of those who wanted to go for post-graduate studies. Availability of seats was also another problem. So P.G. departments in History and Political Science were opened in J.N. College, Pasighat in 1981-82 session under the Punjab University. These two departments were taken over by Arunachal University (now Rajiv Gandhi University) during 1985-86 session[13] and shifted to its present site in 1988. Thus the Department of Education, was the first department established in 1988 at the Arunachal University (now Rajiv Gandhi University) permanent Campus, Rono Hills.

The object of the university is to disseminate and advance knowledge by providing instructional and research facilities in such branches of learning as it may deem fit, and endeavour through research, education, training and extension to play a positive role in the socio-economic and cultural development of Arunachal Pradesh based on the rich heritage of its people[14]. Towards this it shall undertake :

(i) to strengthen and diversify certificate and diploma courses related to the needs of employment, and building the economy of the region on the basis of its natural resources;

(ii) to introduce relevant undergraduate courses for enhancing knowledge and skills;

(iii) to provide education and training in the various arts, crafts and skills of the region, raising their quality, and improving their availability to the people;

(iv) to provide or arrange training of teachers required for such activities or institutions;

(v) to provide training and other facilities to equip persons for different categories of jobs;

(vi) to provide suitable postgraduate courses of study;

(vii) to undertake and organize research to develop the creative potential of its people for optimal use of the resources of the territory particularly that which is related to regional development; and

(viii) to provide for counselling and guidance and facilities for helping in placement of students.

The growth of the University in terms of departments, enrolment etc. is presented in Table – 5. It is to be mentioned that the Department of Botany and Zoology were opened in 1997 in J.N College Pasighat and later shifted in 1999 to the University campus. The Job-oriented courses introduced and those underway during 2007-08 are shown in Table – 6. Besides the above courses,

Table 5
Growth of University Departments

Name of Department Courses	Year of Establishment in the Campus	Teaching Faculties: Year of Est.	Teaching Faculties: 2007-08	Enrolment: Year of Est.	Enrolment: 2007-08	Year from which Ph.D. Programme started
1	2	3	4	5	6	7
Botany	1997	4	7	12	30	2000
Commerce	1995	3	7	30	51	1997
Economics	1991	4	5	18	54	1995
Education	1988	7	9	15	124	1999
English	1990	4	4	18	52	1994
Geography	1992	5	7	15	61	1994
Hindi	1999	3	5	20	80	2000
History	1988	4	6	30	92	1995
Pol. Science	1988	5	5	30	95	1996
Arunachal Institute of Tribal Studies (AITS)	1995	3	6	3	13	1996

Contd. . . .

Table – 5 (Contd. . . .)

1	2	3	4	5	6	7
Zoology	1997	3	6	12	30	2000
Anthropology*	2001			15	35	
Mathematics	2005		2	15	25	
Computer Science and Engineering	2004		1	25	64	
Mass Communication	2004		1	25	23	
Management	2006		1		65	
Total			72		894	

Sources : RGU, Various Annual Report and Registrar, RGU.

* Anthropology is not a separate department. It is a P.G. Course conducted by the Department of Tribal Studies. The faculties appointed are under Tribal Studies.

** Department of Tribal Studies is upgraded and designated as Arunachal Institute of Tribal Studies during 2005-06.

a Pre-Test Coaching Centre is attached to the University which conducts coaching programmes for students appearing in NET/SLET and Central Civil Service Examinations. The Department of Education along with Post-graduate degree also provides B. Ed. course. The Department of Tribal Studies (Arunachal Institute of Tribal Studies) provides language package course in tribal languages along with Post-graduate course in Anthropology. This is the only non-conventional department that provides M. Phil. degree of inter-disciplinary studies. Among other achievements, mention may be made of the establishment of Physical Education Branch in 1999 to look after sports activities in the University.

Table 6
Growth of the University
(Job oriented and other degree/diploma/certificate courses)

Name of the Course	*Year of Establish-ment*	*Students Enrolment (2006-2007)*	*Faculties*
1	2	3	4
PG Diploma in Journalism and Mass Communication	2004	25	1
Certificate course in Teaching of Mathematics	2005	18	Run by the faculty of Mathematics
Bachelor of Computer Application (B.C.A)	2005	25	1
Certificate course in Computer Applications	2004	25	Run by the faculty of Computer center
Diploma courses in Computer System Maintenance	2005	10	-do-
P.G Diploma courses in Hospitality Management and Tourism	2005	04	Run by the faculty of Commerce
B.A. in Distance Education.	2005	64	No regular faculty

1	2	3	4
Certificate Course in IT in Accounting	2006	17	Run by the faculty of Commerce
Certificate course in Geographic information System	2005	04	Run by the faculty of Geography
Certificate course in Disaster Management	2005	15	Run by the faculty of Geography .

Source : Rajiv Gandhi University, Rono Hills, Itanagar.

The academic growth of the University has been manifested in the assessment of the University by the National Assessment and Accreditation Council during 14th-18th April 2002. The NAAC assessed the University in terms of its academic performance, research performance and governance and assigned B grade as a whole. Since 2001, the University has been recognized as a Centre with a potential for Excellence on Biodiversity by UGC amongst the select group of 12 Universities out of 90 competing Universities in the country. Besides, the departments of History and Education have been granted Special Assistance Programme (SAP) during 2003-04 for advance researches.

Though academic growth of the university has become visible, it still has not been able to keep pace with the diverse needs of higher education due to fund and infrastructure constraints. The University got academic recognition in 1985 under section 2(f) but got financial recognition on 25th March 1994 under section 12(B) of the UGC Act, 1956. Without any UGC grants, it started functioning with an adhoc grant of Rs. 1.69 crores from the state government in 1989 which increased to Rs. 8.59 crore in 2005-06.[15] As has been said, only from 1994-95, UGC started giving development grants—Rs. 75 lakhs during the last three years of the 8th Plan, Rs. 2.20 crores during the 9th Plan and Rs. 4.00 crores during the 10th Plan. During 2003-04, the UGC has additionally sanctioned Rs. 96 lakhs under the scheme of special assistance for a young university.

Table 7 presents a discouraging picture as to the share of higher education in general and of colleges (DHE) and university in

Table 7
Budget Grant of Education Department (Rs. in Crore)

Finance Year	*Higher and Technical Education*				*School Education*	*Total Allocation to Education Department*
	DHE	*R.G. University*	*R.G. Polytechnic*	*Total*		
2001-02	9.66 (39.57)	3.75 (13.81)	11.00 (45.06)	24.41 (12.10)	177.51	201.92
2002-03	9.21 (38.04)	4.00 (16.52)	11.00 (45.44)	24.21 (13.70)	152.63	176.84
2003-04	14.08 (59.71)	4.00 (16.96)	5.50 (23.32)	23.58 (11.43)	182.80	206.38
2004-05	10.72 (35.37)	8.59 (28.34)	11.00 (36.29)	30.31 (22.60)	103.77	134.08
2005-06	12.64 (28.13)	8.59 (19.12)	23.70 (52.75)	44.93 (18.59)	196.81	241.74

Source : Directorates of Higher and Technical Education and School Education.

Note : *(i)* The total grant includes both plan and non-plan grants.

(ii) Figures in the parentheses show % to total of each category.

particular so far total financial outlay under education is concerned. The share is around 20% for 2004-05 and 2005-06 though for other three years from 2001-02 it was less than 15%. The share of university education has been increasing over the years right from 12.10 in 2001-02 to 22.60 in 2004-05, though during 2005-06 it is still more than the share in 2003-04. The share in college education is fluctuating. The fluctuation is due to inter head adjustments. For example, during 2004-05, low share under DHE can be attributed to increasing share of university and technical education. Table– 8 presents the gloomy picture in terms of budget allotment under education head in general which was declining for four years and is around 10%. Obviously, education in general and higher education in particular suffer from financial constraints.

Table 8

State Budget of Government of Arunachal Pradesh from 2001–02 to 2005–06

(Rs. in Crore)

Financial Year	*Plan*	*Non-Plan*	*Total*	*% Under Education*
2001-02	885.36	677.92	1563.28	12.92
2002-03	935.93	713.25	1649.18	10.72
2003-04	1045.86	1141.48	2187.34	9.44
2004-05	1014.22	1094.63	2108.85	6.36
2005-06	1248.61	1146.49	2395.10	10.09

Source : Directorate of Planning, Government of Arunachal Pradesh and Table 6.

The impact of University education can be seen from the number of NET/SLET qualified candidates from Arunachal University (now Rajiv Gandhi University) along with the development other human resource. There are a large number of Arunachalee-teachers working in Colleges, University, DIETs, SIE and in Higher Secondary Schools. The departments as shown in Table - 9 have been organized under different faculties as follows:-

1. *Faculty of Social Sciences*

   Department of Economics

   Department of History

Department of Political Science

Department of Tribal Studies

2. *Faculty of Language*

Department of English

Department of Hindi

3. *Faculty of Commerce*

Department of Commerce

4. *Faculty of Education*

Department of Education

5. *Faculty of Environmental Science*

Department of Geography

6. *Faculty of Life Sciences*

Department of Botany

Department of Zoology

Table 9

Seats Available in each Department

Name of Deptt./ Course	*Seats allotted*			
	Opening		*Subsequent Enhancement of seats*	
	Year	*No.*	*Year*	*No.*
1	2	3	4	5
Botany	1997	12	2003	15
Commerce	1995	30		
Economics	1991	30	1999	35
Education*(a)*				
(a) B.Ed.	1988	20	1995	40
(b) M.A	1992	20	1995	30
English	1990	25	1999	30
Geography	1992	20	2003	30
Hindi	1999	30	2003	40

Contd. . . .

1	2	3	4	5
History	1988	30	1994	40
Political Science	1988	30	1994	40
Tribal Studies	1995	05	1997	07
(Anthropology)	2000	15	2002	20
Zoology	1997	12	2003	15
Mathematics	2005	15	—	
Computer Science	2005	40	—	
Mass Communication	2006	25	—	
Management	2006	25	—	

Source : Rajiv Gandhi University, Rono Hills, Itanagar.

The University introduced semester system from the session 1999 – 2000. This is a measure of learning by part in other words; when a lesson is divided into more parts learning becomes more intensive; involvement in curricular activities by both teachers and taughts become more intense.

The University education has been more diversified in terms of technical and professional courses introduced Table 6 and Table 9. Though there is no adequate number of regular faculties in many courses, the existing resource has been utilised to the optimum. Since it is the beginning, its impact can be judged after some years. Among the old departments, all are of conventional type with more enrolment in subjects like Political Science, History, Economics, English, Education, etc. Table 9. By introducing more professional and job-oriented courses Table 6, the University has come forward to solve the growing unemployment problems of the state and the region.

Arunachal University (now Rajiv Gandhi University), even after its existence for last more than 20 (Twenty) years has not been able to create basic infrastructure. This is due to the fact that the State Govt. has not been able to fund the University adequately. Keeping this in view the people of the state especially the Students Community, Teaching Community and the State Govt. made a rigorous persuasion to the Central Govt. for conversion of the existing state University to a Central University. As a result the

University has been converted into a Central University w.e.f. 9th April' 2007 by the Act of Parliament. The conversion has definitely helped the University to enhance its quantum of funding but there are other teething problems as for example the number of faculty members has been reduced to 72 (Seventy Two) against the total sanctioned post of 124 (One Hundred and Twenty Four). University has not been able to hold the selection committee meeting due to non availability of the visitors nominee which is a must as per the Central University Act.

Conclusion

The state of Arunachal Pradesh needs to do a lot in the field of Higher and Technical Education. As per U. G. C. report[16] of Academic year 2006–2007, the National Gross Enrolment Ratio (GER) is 10% within the age group of 18–24 years, whereas the Gross Enrolment ratio of Arunachal Pradesh is only 6.37% which is one of the lowest in the country. From the Table 10 it appears that even in the North Eastern Region, most of the states like Manipur, Meghalaya, Mizoram, Assam have much higher Gross Enrolment Ratio (GER) than Arunachal Pradesh in Higher Education.

Table 10
Distribution of Higher Education Institution in North East Region (NER) and the Gross Enrolment Ratio (GER) (2006–2007)

State	*No. of University*	*No. of Arts Science & Commerce Colleges*	*Engineering Colleges*	*GER%*
Arunachal Pradesh	01	10	01	6.37
Assam	05	317	03	8.67
Manipur	02	58	01	13.19
Meghalaya	01	48	0	10.94
Mizoram	01	26	0	9.51
Nagaland	01	36	0	4.33
Sikkim	01	02	01	6.29
India	217	9427	1068	10

It is also to be noted that out of 16 (Sixteen) districts of the state, 15 (Fifteen) districts are recorded as educationally backward districts as per census report of 2001.

Moreover, all the institutions of higher education are located in 8 (Eight) districts and the remaining 8 (Eight) districts are not having any.

Perhaps, this fact has been realised by the State and the Central Government and expected to reduce this gap during the 11th plan period as education in general and higher education in particular has been given priority by the planning commission in its outlay.

REFERENCES

1. "Education is the basic tool for the development of consciousness and reconstitution of society". Mahatma Gandhi; The New Education Policy states that education refines sensitivities and perceptions that contribute to national cohesion, a scientific temper and independence of mind and spirit thus furthering the goals of socialism, secularism and democracy enshrined in our Constitution (GOI, MHRD, Department of Education, National Policy on Education 1986, with modification taken in 1992, p. 45).
2. The New Encyclopedia Britanica Micropodia, 1985, vol.v.p.917.
3. *Ibid.*, Vol. XVIII, p. 1.
4. GOI, Planning Commission, 1996, p. 1.
5. V.C.K. Kulandaiswamy, 1999, 'Higher Education leads towards Leadership', *University News*, September 27.
6. Barthakur, Anada Prasad, *Chan Poharat Arunachal* (in Assamese), 2004, pp. 38-39.
7. Kulandaiswamy, V.C., 'Open University' in *Higher Education Reform in India*, Suma Chatnis and Phillip G. Altbach (ed), Sage, 1993, p. 366.
8. Ering, Oshong, *The Lingering Memories* Published by Siang Literary Society , 2005, p. 8-9, 16.
9. From Admission Register of 1964-65, Jawaharlal Nehru College, Pasighat, p. 1-5.
10. Phukan B.N., *Higher Education in Arunachal Pradesh: A Retrospect,* Silver Jubilee Souvenir 1979–2004 : Dera Natung Government College, Itanagar, p. 16.
11. Minutes of the meeting held under the Chairmanship of the Minister (Education) on 27.08.2003 at 1030 hrs. to discuss the problem regarding selection of permanent site of Tirap Government College,

p. 120-121 of File no. Ed/HE-146/2000, Directorate of Higher and Technical Education, Government of Arunachal Pradesh, Itanagar.

12. It is worth mentioning that the NEHU Campuses in Nagaland and Mizoram have become full fledged Central Universities namely, the Nagaland University and the Mizoram University. Had NEHU Campus been started in Arunachal at the same time, Arunachal should have also got a Central University by now.
13. Though the University was established in 1984, it got academic recognition under section 2 (f) from the UGC on 28th March, 1985 and started functioning since 1st April, 1985.
14. Under Section 4 and First Schedule of Arunachal University Act. 1984, as amended upto 1993.
15. Arunachal government has increased the grants to Rs. 8.59 crores as statutory grants in 2004-05.
16. *University Education in India : Challenges Ahead* by K. Sudha Rao published in the University News, Volume 45, No. 02, January 8 to 14, 2007.

APPENDIX - I

Vice Chancellors of Rajiv Gandhi University

Prof. C. L. Anand	01.09.87 to 19.01.92
Shri Madan Jha, IAS (Acting)	11.02.92 to 22.01.93
Shri S. Reghunathan, IAS (Acting)	25.01.93 to 05.12.93
Prof. A. C. Bhagbati	06.12.93 to 05.13.98
Dr. K. K. Dwivedi	11.01.99 to 15.11.2002
Prof. Tamo Mibang (Acting)	16.11.2002 to 19.08.2003
Prof. Atul Sarma	19.08.2003 to 30.06.2006
Prof. Tamo Mibang (Acting)	01.07.2006 to 19.11.2006
Prof. S. C. Saha	20.11.2006 to 09.04.2007
Prof. K. C. Belliappa	09.04.2007 to till date

Registrars of Rajiv Gandhi University

Shri A. P. Srivastava	01.07.85 to 05.05.88
Dr. J. Nath	06.05.88 to 04.05.91
Dr. T. Nyori (Acting)	05.05.91 to 21.11.91
Shri Joram Begi	29.11.91 to 28.11.96
Dr. T. Nyori (Acting)	29.11.96 to 09.02.97
Shri Joram Begi	10.02.97 to 31.01.02
Dr. T. Nyori (Acting)	31.01.02 to 30.12.03
Dr. T. Nyori	30.12.03 to 31.12.06
Shri Stephen Hongray (Acting)	01.01.07 to 05.11.07
Prof. A. Mitra (Acting)	06.11.07 to till date

Directors of Higher and Technical Education, Govt. of Arunachal Pradesh

Shri P. Potom	13.02.1996 to 12.02.1999
Mrs. K. Namchoom	13.02.1997 to 18.05.2001
Shri P. Potom	19.05.2001 to 31.01.2002
Dr. Joram Begi	01.02.2002 to till date

2

Higher Education in Arunachal Pradesh—Growth and Challenges

—*Deepak Pandey*

The inability to introduce a system of selective admissions, inordinate rush for higher education and higher education becoming a substitute for jobs rather than a preparation for jobs are some of the challenges faced by the higher education.

It goes without saying that in today's global environment, an accessible and high quality higher education system is imperative for a state's as well as country's economic progress; no developmental work can be undertaken unless the populace is properly educated. Higher education and research are instrumental in the pursuit, advancement and transfer of knowledge and constitute an exceptionally rich cultural and scientific asset. This is more true in the case of Arunachal Pradesh because, owing to historical circumstances, the state was a late entrant in the field of higher education compared to other parts of the country. Geographically, linguistically and culturally, the area of the then NEFA was so fragmented that even primary and secondary education legged behind. The Chinese aggression in the early sixties (1962) proved to be a blessing in disguise for the cause of higher education and the Government of India focused its attention towards the introduction and expansion of higher education. The opening of the Jawaharlal Nehru College at Pasighat in July 1964 can be said to be the beginning of higher education in the state.

I

In the early 60s, Arunachal Pradesh, the then NEFA was gradually emerging from centuries old darkness and isolation and the system of higher education that was initially introduced here followed the all-India pattern. To briefly summarize the education system of India in the 60s, the system introduced by T. B. Macaulay in 1854 that aimed at creating a class of educated Indians which would remain loyal and grateful to them and would also provide cheap manpower (clerks) was carried out without no or very little alteration. And this was more or less the trend with which the system of higher education in Arunachal Pradesh started. The system worked well for many years to come and catered to the needs of the society in more than one ways. It not only provided bureaucrats, technocrats, leaders and journalists to the state but also expanded the horizons of the people. Higher education became the gateway of government jobs in the state; for many years to come every graduate was absorbed in job if he so desired. It may, however, be pointed out here that for many years to follow, there was practically no emphasis on technical or 'job-oriented' education and it remained confined to the teaching of traditional subjects like History, Political Science, Education, etc. in humanities.

With higher education becoming the means for acquiring better social and economic status, the demand for it also increased and in 1979 another degree college was opened at Itanagar. The 80s and 90s saw rapid expansion of higher education in the state and new colleges as well as a state university were established during this period. Post-graduation studies were started in 1981 at J. N. College, Pasighat. To make higher education assessable to the students in the remote areas as well as to the employed, Centers of Indira Gandhi National Open University were opened. Today, after more than four and a half decades, Arunachal has one University, eight government colleges and two private colleges besides IGNOU Centers. The number of students seeking higher education in the colleges of the state that was 42 in 1964 has increased to more than six thousand. And this is no mean achievement keeping in view the geographical, historical and financial limitations of the area. Besides, emphasis was also given to technical education and NERIST became functional in the state. One College of Horticulture and Forestry has also been opened.

It would not be wrong to suggest, therefore, that the last 25 years (1981–2006) form the most crowed era in the history of higher education in Arunachal Pradesh. It was during this period that higher education spread its wings to each and every corner of the state and hitherto neglected areas were also provided venues for acquiring the same. It has been subjected to much critical thought and many bold initiatives and innovations during this period. The scales of pay of the university and college teachers have been substantially improved. A limited programme of exchange of university teachers has been introduced and a fairly large programme of Orientation and Refresher Courses has been implemented for upgrading the knowledge of the teachers. The year 2006 has been of considerable significance for higher education in Arunachal. During this year the Rajiv Gandhi University and five colleges have been accredited by the National Assessment and Accreditation Council (NAAC) thus opening the doors for further expansion and improvement of higher education on national standards. The achievements of higher education, both in absolute and relative terms, are by no means inconsiderable.

II

The growth and expansion of higher education in Arunachal Pradesh, however, is not without its drawbacks. What has largely offset the above mentioned achievements, and made higher education a point of critical discussion is its practically uncontrolled expansion. Today, as mentioned earlier, there are more than six thousand students enrolled in the university and colleges of the state. The reasons for this are manifold. The first is the inability to introduce a system of selective admission to higher education so that it is always possible for any student who completed secondary school and who desires to study further to find admission in college in *some* course. The weakness of the secondary education system, for lack of diversification, is the main reason for this. An inordinate rush for higher education is, thus, built into system itself. Also, the social demand for higher education has considerably increased because it is still the *only gateway* to any worthwhile job, and it is increasingly becoming the minimum qualification even for those jobs which can be made open to secondary school leavers. Moreover, with the passage of time, higher education is becoming a substitute for a job rather than a preparation for it. Recalling from personal experience, in the early 80s, most of the students acquired graduation degree to become Circle Officers; in the early 90s this changed to School Teachers; in the late 90s to Clerks; today students seek admission in the colleges because there is *nothing else to do!*

Like other parts of the country, in Arunachal too, the old formal system of education has not been transformed and has merely been expanded with some minor changes here and there. It is also to be noted that higher education in the state has succeeded better where schemes of expansion are concerned. This is because of the over-emphasis on monetary inputs and the relative neglect of the human inputs of ideas and efforts. Expansion has been easy to achieve in higher education because of the pressing social demand. All that is needed is the provision of buildings and teachers, the things that money can easily provide if one does not insist on quality. Quality in higher education, on the other hand is entirely different matter. It does not need much money, but what it needs most is a tremendous input of thought and human effort. By and large, we have not been willing to put in the human effort which needs idealism, commitment, and sustained hard work. Instead we have chosen to depend exclusively on money and monetary incentives to achieve our ends.

Here, it may be pointed out that there are certain weaknesses in the educational planning at the Centre that have put constrains on the state policies towards higher education. Although in theory higher education is a state responsibility, in actual practice planning is mostly done at the Centre and is concentrated there. We must follow an all India pattern laid down by the University Grants Commission. The state authorities, the teachers and the students are not adequately involved in educational planning and development.

A time has come when we should question the model of higher education that we have adopted and think seriously of some alternative measures. Broadly speaking, the major issues before higher education in Arunachal Pradesh can be put under three heads : *(i)* ensuring equity in higher education; *(ii)* the financial crunch, and *(iii)* the move to privatize higher education as a remedial measure. As the time passes we realise that the formal system of higher education of the type we have adopted, serves only a limited purpose. The system is very costly and wasteful. We can no longer to bank upon this type of higher education exclusively because the time is running out and the financial resources available for higher education are becoming scantier as the time passes. It is high time the higher education in Arunachal resorted to long-term resource planning instead of taking the state support for granted. We will now have to identify avenues of resource generation, both, internal as well as external. The Punnayya Committee set up by the UGC and the Swaminathan Panel of the AICTE have made some broad recommendations in this regard. The internal measures, amongst other things, may include proper utilisation of funds, general economy in expenditures, pooling and sharing of departmental and institutional resources and most importantly, rationalisation of fee structure. As far the external resources, the important avenues include donations from alumni, philanthropists and others, consultancy, etc.

We must, therefore focus our attention to evolving different strategies of the advance of higher education in Arunachal Pradesh which suit our conditions better and which can be implemented with the limited financial resources we can provide. No doubt, we cannot isolate ourselves from the rest of the country and we must take into consideration the national experience; yet, keeping in view our peculiar historical, socio-economical and geographical position, what we must evolve should be a unique solution of our own, a system of higher education suited to our needs and aspirations.

3

Higher Education in Arunachal Pradesh : Within and Beyond its Colleges

–Amarendra Kr. Thakur

The planners, politicians, educationalists and capitalists are all together, seriously looking for ways and means to reach out a workable solution for improvement of education in India.

> "If you're not pragmatic, not responsive to changing realities, then you don't succeed."
>
> —*Robert Dallek, The Times of India, October 31, 2006.*

The publication of the above mentioned thought and a report, the same day and the same newspaper as, "Arunachal college facilities in a mess" may be a co-incidence, is certainly a signal and a pointer towards the need of a massive and serious programme of rethinking and restructuring higher education in Arunachal Pradesh. The report is not unfounded fully and uncalled for. In most of the government colleges especially in bigger classes many students are literally on their toes attending lectures from outside their classrooms because of lack of space. The classroom-student ratio is not satisfactory. And in most cases the teacher-student ratio is also unable to cater to the need and aspiration of the students. Certainly, it is not the only case of Arunachal Pradesh. Almost everywhere in India the scenario of higher education is more or less the same. The planners, politicians, educationists and capitalists too, are seriously looking for ways and means to reach out a workable solution for educational improvements in India. This seriousness is more focused in recent past.

It is so because, an educational mortality rate whereby of 100 children enrolled in class I, not more than 26 reach class X, barely 13 qualify for higher secondary education and only six qualify for college education, raises serious concerns with regard to the means adopted in the teaching-learning process and of accountability which is rarely addressed. At a conservative estimate, the total public expenditure on primary education since independence has exceeded $150 billion. If even after spending that amount we are still a largely illiterate country with such a high education mortality rate, surely some seriously rethinking is needed without any further delay. This is not the end, we have been lamenting the crisis of our education system—its divorce from the larger society, its production of unemployable persons, its questionable orientation, its poor functioning, and the continued exclusion of the poor and the disadvantaged. Much of the narratives of the crises have become commonsensical although thorough research on each of the themes is awaited. But, we now need to re-imagine what direction and orientation our education system must take, for we are at a juncture where alongside great and widespread expectation about mass elementary education there is near complete despondency and demoralization about the state of higher education.

I

The pass percentage of students in the colleges of Arunachal Pradesh is certainly very impressive and a good number of students of Arunachal Pradesh are able to qualify the NET; the real contribution of graduates and post-graduates towards impact at all India level is not very visible. Since they are unable to grab the positions and posts in good number at All India level (in central or other state services); thus pressure on government job of Arunachal Pradesh is increasing day by day. There may be several reasons for this handicap. The rising unemployment and several other related socio-economic and political problems cropping up are to be taken care of at this stage itself. It is not possible to prescribe a pragmatic programme as the remedy to the problems in an article with no such expertise. Nonetheless, I have tried to address earlier towards the same through the annual college magazine of Tirap Government College, Deomali, *Rang 'O' vol. II*, 2002-03, p.3 as a novice. Even today I personally feel that our academic endeavour is somewhere lacking in its spirit. The education in some other parts of India or the world has added to its fold the third dimension, unlike the state of affairs in the colleges of Arunachal Pradesh. The first of the basic aspects of it is undoubtedly not compromised but such is not the case of the second dimension *i.e.* research. We are somewhere lacking in starting and continuing our researches. And pathetic is the condition of the third dimension of educational process, i. e. extension or sharing of knowledge. In research as well as in teaching, increasingly, there must be a sense of togetherness and partnership. Indeed, we literally need to work as partners with other scholars, within our own academies and in foreign institutions. Hence, serious and continuous teaching and researches and more importantly extension of the same would certainly make our endeavour really more meaningful. It should not only be extended to the academic fraternity at large but also to the society for its larger benefit. Our administrators need to encourage this and to change the rules that inhibit our doing so.

The remedies of social problems and the role of higher education towards solving the same as expressed by President A. P. J. Abul Kalam for Manipur or Assam or for the whole of the North-Eastern India have also clear and sound bearing upon the state of Arunachal Pradesh. President A. P. J. Abul Kalam, while delivering the 10th Convocation Address of Manipur University recently said, "A university is judged by the level and extent of research work it accomplishes. This sets in a regenerative cycle of excellence. Experience of research leads to quality teaching and quality teaching imparted to the young in turn enriches research." He also emphasized, the university should marshal its resources to develop a data base of bio-diversity resources available in the state and should suggest how best to use it economically without causing environmental degradation. The need towards research and extension of research for society was further called upon. The President said research on development of herbal medicinal products needs greater focus. He added, "I visualize Manipur having herbal farms and also transforming herbs into drugs. Manipur should aim to have a pharma company. This will help in providing employment opportunities to our youths and give fillip to industrialization in the state." Not only through the Address, but also during the entire tour he emphasised towards all round progress of the region and role of higher education in this regard. The President told the media, "All the problems in the North-East will come to an end once there is economic development". He advocated "one village, one product" and was impressed with the achievement of a village on the outskirts of Guwahati, which has taken up duck rearing on a large scale through self help groups, and the centre of Assam's silk production at Sualkuchi village. During his interaction with the students and faculty members of Assam University, President Kalam said progress and peace should go hand in hand. If one of these two aspects is absent, a nation or a region is bound to become cripple, he added. He said this is more true in respect of the North-East. The President suggested that all the universities in the country should involve themselves in the development of the respective areas where the varsities are located. This should be done in collaboration with the government and other agencies and through utilization of its own resources, he said. If higher education (including university) of Arunachal Pradesh gives a serious thought towards the suggestions of President Kalam and acts upon sincerely and timely, through promoting serious researches and extension of researches for the society, there is certainly a bright future ahead. The media covered the visit appropriately and the same can be seen in the newspapers of the region 17th and 18th October, 2006, (*The Times of India* and others).

II

Coming to other aspects of planned growth of higher education in Arunachal Pradesh, the discussion at a wider level around 3A's has its relevance here too; thus needs a little elaboration. It is rightly expressed, if Indian higher education is to fulfil its mission, it must be *'Accessible', 'Affordable', and 'A' class'* (emphasis added by me). These are the three crucial problems that the government, educationists and the public must grapple with. It is important to emphasize the role of all three. The deficiencies of higher education are not simply the fault of governments (though it must be admitted, they have a lot to answer for); the responsibility equally resides with educationists and the public. As India's population grows and the number of young people swells, the gap between the number of college and university seats that are required and what the system provides is increasing.

Sociologically, the demand for higher education has spread further. Social strata that traditionally did not countenance sending their young people to colleges and universities are today far more conscious of the need for higher education. Some portion of these sections now also has the money to pay for higher education. There is little or nothing that can be done about the demographic push for higher education. The rate of population growth is slow but will not stop until mid-century. The structure of India's population is young : compared to Japan, China, and the West, for instance, we will have a huge bulk of young people for another 30–40 years. An increasing proportion of these young people will want access to higher education to better their life chances.

Politically too, there are not too many degrees of freedom available to us. In an open, pluralistic, and democratic society, we cannot contemplate denying young people access to higher education except on academic grounds. To do so would be unfair and dangerous. In any case, the demand for higher education is a positive value. If we want to keep our democracy alive and deepen the attachment of the public to democratic institutions and practices, we must invest in higher education. A better-educated citizenry can only strengthen democracy. Furthermore, in a globalized and highly competitive world, human capital is a vital resource. If young people in India are to live satisfying and productive lives, they must have the intellectual skills to compete with counterparts all over the world.

What can we do about the issue of accessibility? The answer is clear enough : we need more seats in colleges and universities. That means two things in turn : existing institutions must be encouraged to expand, and public and private resources must be funneled towards creating new institutions. None of these factors can be augmented quickly, especially not faculty. In the longer term though, existing institutions can expand. In order to gird up for expansion, they need a clear indication that the central government and state governments will help them as much as possible. Governments have learned to be friendlier to industry; they must now learn to be friendlier to education.

If Indian higher education is to fulfil its mission, it must not only be made more accessible, it must also be more affordable. For it to be available to larger numbers and a wider public, families must be able to pay for colleges and universities. The problem here is not usually the tuition fees. Tuition fees, generally, are ridiculously low and are by no means economically rational in their pricing. That said, paying for a college education is a burden for many families because, in addition to tuition fees, there are the costs of books and materials, hostel fees, rentals (if you don't get hostel accommodation), transportation, and so on.

In addition to the accessibility and affordability of higher education, we must pay attention to the claims of excellence. A college or university education in India should be "A" class. As for the rest, our colleges and universities are in a shambles (again with a few exceptions). An 'A' class education in colleges and universities depends on a teaching and research culture that is conspicuously lacking in India. As anyone who has done both knows, the two inform each other, as they must. It is in the course of teaching that one gets the best research ideas, and it is by doing good research that one enriches one's teaching. This is one of the oldest nutmegs of academic life but nonetheless true for all that and deserves to be repeated till it hurts! The point has also been highlighted by non other than the President of India, Dr. A.P.J. Abdul Kalam as discussed in the first section.

Indian education system has the serious problem of infrastructure. Standards are being ruthlessly ignored and compromises being made with quality of education. Presently education sector scenario faces a challenging environment, similar to that of manufacturing sectors. Competition for Excellence is rapidly going down. No doubt, existing formal accreditation/ affiliations systems being operated through various boards and councils does provide a basis for implementing quantity system but do not address quality system needs. Compounding the problems is the lack of appropriate reading materials. It is not that these materials always do not exist; but they are not assigned mostly. The other problem is the cost of articles and books for students who might be asked to purchase the key materials. This brings us to the general question of the physical facilities in colleges and universities. The situation here is horrendously depressing.

Enter an institution of higher education and prepare to weep : crowded classrooms and corridors, lack of common rooms for boys and girls and reading space in library, cracked walls, floors, and roofs; leakage and seepage everywhere; toilets that are filthy; antiquated equipment; furniture that is an ergonomic disaster and usually broken and unwieldy; canteens that are dingy, dirty and unhygienic; crowded hostel accommodation that deadens the spirit with no attention to design; everywhere student posters and graffiti that have defaced walls, windows and pillars. Sometimes the problem of power supply and water supply even for experiments and researches make the task education (giving and taking) really difficult. Sometimes, for the first generation of people in higher education the affordability is difficult. The rural income is not always supportive of higher education. The challenge, therefore, before us is how to provide satisfactory solutions to such issues.

Initially after independence there was emphasis over capital in agricultural, subsequently it became investment in industrial sector, now a time has come even in Arunachal Pradesh to invest in the human sector. This is so because the young population and the growth of population are in favour of Arunachal Pradesh. It is important to mention that human capital has to be harnessed with new techniques and tools of education and investment of capital. It is important, however, to keep in view the regional imbalances. To cope up the problem, the self help Grameen Bank in Bangladesh is the eye opener. The same can be started in rural areas of Arunachal Pradesh too. Here it is important to mention that the new age is caught in the webs of GOLIT where globalization, open market economy, liberalization and information technology are directing the future course of the world.

Change is extremely rapid. One cannot, in an academic system, educate students in all the details of such a rapidly changing system. One can only provide an environment in which the abilities to reason and to analyze are developed in an individual. When real life problems are encountered, the individual would have the capability to deal with them, and to access the knowledge necessary to do so; earlier when, knowledge was acquired through local discussions, then through books and libraries, and now through Internet and the World Wide Web. Teachers have to see not only their minds or the books but also the vast repertoire stored in thousands of services the world over. Another striking feature of emerging society shall be shift in emphasis from directed learning to self initiated learning. Hence, in addition to planning keeping in view the coming at least 20–30 years, immediately efforts should be made towards growth of e-learning in colleges for both the teachers as well as students. For the same the population trend of Arunachal Pradesh, the impact of the Sarva Siksha Abhiyan and other means of distance education, capital needed and can be provided for, scope of the Public-Private partnership etc. should be taken into account and with the help of some professional and experienced planners a blue-print of the education policy of higher education in Arunachal Pradesh can be prepared. At least for the 21st century it can be "Well begun is half done".

Serious efforts are needed to enable the students and the teachers of higher education of Arunachal Pradesh to excel. It is also important, however, to keep in mind and action that the traditional university systems are still largely public and poorly financed. They have tended to be complacent and resistant to change. They are also unable to meet the increasing demands of members in higher education and of needed quality. Hence, in many of these sectors, commercialized education is rapidly developing. This is turning out to be process for generation of technical experts. The thrust is towards acquisition of power and wealth; knowledge is being regarded as a means towards this rather than as a product of scholarship in its own right. Education is being reduced to becoming as much of a product as anything else in the market place. In an earlier age, education was regarded as sacred; its purpose was to bring out the finest qualities and capabilities intrinsic to a human being. The word of Abraham Lincoln is also important enough to be reminded :

> "The past is the cause of the present, and the present will be the cause of the future. All these are links in the endless chain stretching from the finite to the infinite."

III

In the midst of these extraordinary developments, we must remember that fundamental truths, that will ultimately define a good human society, remain unchanged. The opinion of our first Prime Minister, Jawaharlal Nehru, seems still valid. In his Convocation Address to the Allahabad University in 1947, in the year India became independent, he summed up the basic objectives of a university and its role in national life. He had then remarked that a university stands for humanism, for tolerance, for reason, for adventure of ideas, and for the search for truth. It stands for the adventure of ideas, and for the search of truth. It stands for the onward march of the human race towards even higher objectives. If the universities discharge their duties adequately, then all is well with the nation and the people.

NOTE

It is not occasioned here to provide an exhaustive bibliography related to recent debate and publications on various aspects of higher education in India and the world. I have listed some of them which I have found important in the preparation of this article and even otherwise. For details, see various articles in the issues of *Seminar*, December 1995, "Learning to Change"; April 1998, "Right to Education"; September 2000, "Redesigning Curricula; October 2000, "Unviable Universities"; April 2004, "Are We Learning?"; February 2005 "Reclaiming Childhood"; July 2006, "Education and Livelihood"; September 2006 "The Elusive Triangle – Access, Equity and Excellence in Indian Education" (especially the articles by A. R. Vasavi, Kanti Bajpai and Guilherme Vaz). Some other important publications may be of interest and importance : G. G. Kingdon, "A Political Economy of Education in India: The Case of UP", *Economic and Political Weekly*, 36 (32), 2001; Pratham, *Annual Status of Education Report* (ASER), New Delhi, 2005; P. Shah, "Equity in Education", *Business Standard*, New Delhi, 13 July 2005; R. Govinda, "Building and Sustaining a Quality Education System", Annexure 3, in Ministry of Human Resource Development, New Delhi, NIEPA, 2005; J. B. G. Tilak, *Determinants of Household Expenditure on Education in Rural India*, New Delhi, 2000; S. Despande and Y. Yadav, "Redesigning Affirmative Action : Castes and Benefits of Higher Education", *Economic and Political Weekly*, LXI (4), 2006; *India Education Report*, (NIEPA); A. Kumar and S. Kumar, (eds.), *Dalit Studies in Higher Education : Vision and Challenges*, Delhi, 2005; Gursharan Singh Kainth, "Quality Education", *Yojana*, November, 2006, pp. 57–58; Yogendra Yadav and Satish Deshpande, "Meeting the Challenge of Mandal II", *The Hindu*, 22 May 2006 and M. G. K. Menon, *XVI Convocation Address*, North-Eastern Hill University, 14 November, 2006.

SECTION—II
Context of Globalisation

4

Education Scenario of Our Country—Challenges Ahead

—*Arup K. Das*

Education at secondary level plays a very significant role for the growth of a healthy society and in shaping the destiny of a nation.

The last quarter of twentieth century was marked by tremendous spurt of development in the field of information technology and communication network. For the first time the world has turned into a global village. The spectacular development in the field of satellite communication has brought every nook and corner of the world at the finger tip of a key board. People in one corner of the world with one cultural background have come into close contact with other cultures. The mass media have helped, the smaller ethnic group or communities hitherto secluded in oblivion, to showcase their culture to larger audience albeit the overpowering influence of cultures of dominant nature enjoying more accessibility. There are other reasons like economic and geographic for the isolation and apparent backwardness of regions and pockets in the third world countries of the world. In-spite of abundance of natural resources such regions have continued to remain unexplored in the context of recent boom in free trade and mobilization of resources. Enough stress is given on power generation and utilization of resources in a bid to boost the economy of the country. But there has not been corresponding mechanism commensurate with the equitable sharing of the benefits of state's exchequer accrued through the utilization of both renewable and non renewable resources from the regions rich in natural resources. Results being such lop sided approach and policies have thrown the regions to the vicious circle of perpetual backwardness at both macro and micro level despite the richness of those areas in resources. In addition to the natural resources, industrialization and other factors, which play all important roles in the economy and all round development of a country and a region within a country, the human resource has been added to this list.

Against this backdrop the back bone of a strong economy of a country is its man power. The man power is not to be valued in terms of number. Rather it is to cater to specific needs both in the technical and non technical fields. However the proper use of man power is again conditioned by whether proper infrastructure in terms of industrial institutions, production units or any other technical institutions which help in developing economy are available in the country or not. Under the prevailing situation the proper man power development in the developing countries including our one is more challenging and a holistic approach is apparently lacking and it could be discussed as under :

Basic Education

The prime objective of any welfare state is to undertake proper step to provide the basic facilities of education and learning to its citizens so that they are acquainted with three R's. In fact access to education is one of the fundamental rights of the people. In a democratic set up it is necessary that every citizen is well aware of his fundamental rights and exercise his or her franchise in a fair and democratic manner without any influence and prejudice. Otherwise there is likelihood of being easy prey in the hands of unscrupulous elements during election process. However, basic education may not help eradicate this problem unless there is sufficient development of the economy at the grass root level. Otherwise money and muscle power will continue to haunt the electorates in a country like ours. This sorry state of affairs is still rampant in our country even after more than five and half decades of adoption of democratic electorate system. So, there is need to bring some radical changes of the prevailing education system in our country. The changes at the higher or university level may not help to achieve this goal. A composite approach covering all stages of education is a must to remove the short comings of our education system. A free and compulsory basic primary education preferably in mother tongue should be imparted covering every child of our society. This is likely to help open up the inner faculties of the young minds.

Secondary Education

Education at secondary level plays a very significant role for the growth of a healthy society and in shaping the destiny of a nation. It is a fact that a sizable section of our population gives up their education after the secondary level. Very few of them are engaged in agriculture, industries or in some organized sector. The curricula in the secondary level should be able to meet up aspirations of both present and future needs of younger generations for their healthy growth so that they could contribute something for the country's economy. The curricula should be designed in such a manner that it should fulfil the aspiration and needs of all categories of students.

Screening of Aptitude

With proper counselling and in accordance to their aptitude students should be screened right from the elementary level up to the secondary level and categorized into a number of groups. Curricula should be designed keeping in view the need of each category. While aptitude is to be given priority in adoption of a curriculum for a specific group of students, there is also the necessity to include in the curricula some vocational courses, so that, most of the students engage themselves in some self employment. In addition to exposing the students to the need based vocational courses there should be thrusts in the curricula for motivation and innovation. Those pursuing entrepreneurial courses there should be provisions of lessons on designing, production and marketing of the products. It would help the students to choose the need based curricula with an opportunity to help them start their small enterprise. Of course the government and financial agencies should provide the initial support with proper monitoring for setting up of any such enterprise.

Blending of Courses

Up to the secondary level school curricula should have a perfect blending of self employment generating courses in addition to the core subjects. It should be utility based with facilities for profuse training. The major thrust should also be to acquaint the students with basics of three R's like reading, writing and arithmetic so that one becomes literate in true sense. A student pursuing vocational course in agriculture should also be taught the basics of medicine, health and hygiene so that besides being a successful farmer he should also be able to lead a healthy life. Similarly a student opting a course of handicrafts should also be imparted some lessons on trade and commerce so that he gets his due profit of his own products.

Plus Two Courses

The curricula for plus two level should again be designed on the basis of aptitude of students. A student having literary bent of mind should be given sufficient exposure to the works of great litterateurs of the world. Similar should be the approach on other courses like music, art, dance form, designing, weaving, cutting, knitting, embroidery works, tailoring, nursing, hospitality, tourism, animal husbandry, piggery, fishery, duckery, specialized training on the use of non timber forest products like cane and bamboo, fruit preservation, spice and pickles making, hand made paper, basketry, ropes and cordage, wood craft, furnishers and products of internal decoration, handloom and textile, dyeing and printing, gold and black smithy, metallurgy and alloy making, pottery, plumber, fitter, machine and vehicle repairing, masonary, use of computer, networking, training in hardware and software etc., etc.

However, the facilities for all the above vocations may not be introduced everywhere. A specific course is to be introduced only with an eye to help generate self employment and availability of resources and local demand. The emphasis should be only on to generate trained and skilled manpower capable of engaging in establishing production units of their own through little government support. Or they may be directly absorbed in private and public sector establishments. Once saturation of such man power is reached the courses may be temporarily discontinued and new courses may be introduced on demand.

Opportunities for Higher Education

Beyond plus two level the access to degree and diploma level courses should be extremely limited. The access to higher education should be made available to only deserving students having aptitude for some specific course. Extra care should be taken in screening the meritorious and deserving candidates for higher education. The idea behind the restriction is to discourage and to check the colossal loss of time and resources. Presently our country is flooded with graduates and diploma holders above ninety percent of which are without any proper job and are found unfit to meet the present demand.

Infusion of Work Culture

There has been a disturbing trend in the society that our educated youths have developed aversion to work culture. There is a general tendency among them that they do not like to work in villages. They concentrate in urban areas and often become prey in the hands of unscrupulous elements in the society. This is one of the major factors of growing tension in the society in recent years. However, youths alone may not be held responsible for this sorry state of affair. As noted elsewhere the growing unemployment both in the urban and countryside is the failure of the present education system in developing skill and motivation among the youths. School drop outs and University graduates hang around in towns and cities in search of a suitable job. They are also lured by the apparent cosy and colourful life of the urban areas, which are lacking in the country side.

Access to Higher and Technical Education

Given the present education scenario it is a much debated question whether the door to higher and more sophisticated technical education should be opened for all or not. In the common Indian parlance the scope of higher education and facilities for technical education is extremely limited in comparison to developed countries. In India the percentage of population pursuing higher and technical education is less than ten percent in comparison to developed countries where it is as high as forty percent and even more. Still there is no reason for worry if we look into the scope and usefulness of higher and technical education in our country. While there may be certain gap areas in the field of technical education where we may still require some sophistication in our technical manpower, the picture in the field of conventional higher education is very grim. Presently our country is flooded with man power having highest university degrees. In fact, it has become a serious cause of concern for our society. Instead of solving any useful purpose this lot in the society has been responsible for creating a new group in itself which can well be categorized as bourgeoisie class in accordance with Marxian philosophy. The expectation of this class of society is very high and remains aloof from others with usual aversion to any productive work, following a prejudiced ideology of their own so much so that they alienate themselves from the society. They become a source of social burden as they are often being misguided by others and in their turn mislead the common people creating rift and disorder in the society.

It is not that our society produces leading personalities like Ravindranath, Raman or Einstein everyday. Starting from Plato and Aristotle to our present time there are only handful of seers and visionaries in the society who have revolutionized our society. To bring the truth home we may cite how our country with one billion populations has been able to produce only one Gandhi or Buddha or only four Nobel laureates in last couple of centuries. It is true that in the field of technical education we have progressed a lot in last two decades. But, with only 3-7 percent technical man power produced in the country we have not been able to absorb them all. So, in recent years there has been an exodus of technical man power to developed and other countries from India. This is certainly not a healthy trend with the huge amount of investment involved in establishing the technical institutions and training of technical man power. Our country cannot afford to lose the technical man power for the prosperity of other countries. This brain drain results in an enormous loss of resources for a poor country like ours.

On the basis of foregoing random thoughts on education scenario we need to have some pragmatic and down to earth approach to mitigate the problems of education in general keeping in view the immediate and future needs of the country, which could be summarized as under :

- Extension of facilities of basic education to every nook and corner of the country.
- Introduction of compulsory universal free education in the elementary level preferably in mother tongue.

- Strict and effective counselling and screening from the elementary level.
- Designing of curricula for secondary level on the basis of need and aptitude of students.
- Compulsory vocational and need based education for capacity building.
- Adoption of region specific and resource based courses both at secondary and senior secondary levels.
- Counselling and screening at secondary and senior secondary levels for selection of a group of most dedicated and brilliant students for higher education on the basis of their aptitude.
- Doors for the higher and technical education should be extremely limited so that only deserving students get access to higher education.
- Assuring complete job security for the technical man power both in the government and private sectors.
- Establishment of regional technical institutes of excellence to cater to local needs for effective employment of technical man power.
- Selecting few extremely brilliant students for more sophisticated education and training even outside the country so that their expertise could be utilised for useful purpose.
- Government should provide full support to those a few who select few peruse specialized technical and higher education.
- Ensuring employment to trained and technical man power in industrial and production units catering to the needs of local resources.
- Limiting the doors of higher and technical education to extremely meritorious students whose aptitude and motivation could be monitored from the secondary level onward.
- Avoid mushroom growth of institutions of higher learning to check the deterioration of standard of education and

wastage of resources. This would also check generating a section of jobless frustrating lot in the society.

- Those having genuine aptitude for learning may be encouraged to go for distant mode of education.
- Complete control of arable land, forest and other natural resources under government and organized sectors so as to ensure optimum utilization of those resources. This will ensure employment of trained and technical man power.
- The guaranteed scope of employment in government and organized sectors would lead to quality improvement of trained technical man power.
- While dealing with the subject of the challenges of modern education one should not lose sight of the responsibilities of government and society over the highly educated, trained and technical man power. They should be treated as human wealth with utmost stress on fruitful utilization of this resource on productive purpose and future health of the society. At last, the quality control should be the ultimate aim of whatever policies and programs are undertaken in generating a highly educated, trained as well as technical work force which may ultimately lead to the making of a prosperous and healthy nation.

5

Higher Education in India in the Liberalized Economic Era : Addressing to Threats of Higher Educational Potentials

— M.A. Salam

Education stands at the root to boost up the economy in order to compete with the foreign economy in the liberalized economic era.

Introduction

Clearly education has two effects : Consumption effect and Production effect. Primary education basically serves the consumption need of the society while higher education is oriented to contain the production effect in the form of *(i)* ability enhancement, *(ii)* nourishing the entrepreneurial skill, and *(iii)* skill formation. The ability enhancement mainly establishes the link between the research wing of higher education as the supplying unit of stock of knowledge and the industrial organization as the beneficiary. That is to say information gathered during the research process must be transferred to the students who later in the capacity of an employee in industrial unit must help the decision making units of the industrial organization. The entrepreneur capacity formation makes the stakeholders (students) innovative and well-receptive to understand the varying market conditions. The entrepreneurs are the first liner of economically productive groups. It is their visions about the market mood of near future which decides the future of the industrial units. Hence innovation and forecasting skill are the next important components of the higher education. They must be inculcated in the students. The skill formation tries to link between education and industries through transfer of the technology *i.e.* know how to operate the technology ('Know-How'). Technology does not only refer to machines, it also includes the efficiency of industrial organization in terms of information-decision flow.

Keeping this in mind, the article highlights three aspects of higher education namely *(i)* Papers taught, *(ii)* Contents of papers *(iii)* Evaluation system. The higher education is just like industry which produces variety of outputs for various users (consumers and producers). Similarly higher education system should provide variety of papers for various purposes which must be sufficiently flexible for adapting the changes. Further the contents of paper must address the issues that employers want to get tackled by their employees. Furthermore the answer scripts should be evaluated with due consideration of ability, skill and innovative formations and not the mechanical memorization and reproduction of the paper contents.

This is the vast potency of higher education if the system does work; otherwise it proves boomerang and poses threat to the system.

The paper runs on the following sections :

1. Introducing the Liberalized Economic Era
2. Characteristic features of Higher Education in India
3. Expectations from Higher Education during the post-liberalized phase
4. Questions on Employability
5. Summry and Suggestions.

Introducing the Liberalized Economic Era from the Point of View of Institutional Economics

From an Institutional angle[1], post-independence phase of Indian economy can be classified into two categories : (1) the resource constrained phase from the 1950_s to the middle of $1980_{s,}$ and (2) the demand constrained phase popularly known as post-liberalization phase.

For around three and a half decades of the post-independence economic situation of India was similar to the resource constrained system because :

— low volume of capital stock relative to labor

— little scope for savings due to low size of income and high *mpc*[2]

— overwhelming food shortage

— shortage in foreign exchange[3].

The upshot of these arguments is to make Indian economic situation closer to the situation of a resource constrained system where once the economy embarked on the path of industrialization, demand component does not retard the growth rather it is the supply bottleneck which precludes it. So if the supply bottleneck would be removed *i.e.* by adequate food supply and adequate foreign exchange reserve, the problem of growth would be treated well by market forces.

Simultaneous to this situation we had potential demand components in our economy in the form of :

— Potential market due to large size of population if (i) distribution of output is taken care of (ii) sufficient income is generated;

— Structural change in the mode of production causing progressive monetization and commodification of the economy;

— Pent-up desire and demonstration effect.

Further the constitution has been functioning as an instrumentality for the market economy. The axiomatic proposition of the constitutional contexts are[4] :

— supremacy of individual rights over group rights and State,

— juridical and formal notions law and justice,

— liberal bourgeoisie right to property,

— socio-economic content and substantive aspect of justice,

— charitable and cosmetic approach to uplift the depressed sections,

— greater dependency on the alleged impartial & autonomous judiciary, and

— the adoption of the modern scientific paradigm of development.

Hence primacy was given :

- Fundamental Rights over directive principals of State policies,
- Individual over Group,
- Liberty over Equality,
- Individual property over Collective welfare,
- Procedural and Juridical justice over Socio-economic and Substantive justice.

Therefore, the constitution has been the custodian of the capitalist class interest.

The state being unable to guarantee employment, individual welfare, redistribution of assets, wanted to shed off its responsibility; further state was getting burdened with mounting deficit B/P and fiscal crisis[5]; furthermore, India was uncritical in accepting the western liberal paradigm for modernization. Hence, changes in international scenario were to be incorporated in the forthcoming changes in economic policies. As a result, a package of economic reforms (1991) was introduced under SAP (Structural Adjustment programme).

This is a change from dirigisme political economy to the political economy of liberalization based on the global capitalist market forces *i.e.* a change from resource constrained economy to the demand constrained economy. The NEP (New Economic Policy) has two implications : (1) internal-downgrading planning, downsizing the Raj administration, privatizing public sector, (2) external-integrating the economy with the world economy. In this liberalized era, the characteristic feature of the economy is potential output which is always larger than the actual level of demand at the base distribution of income. Hence growth is largely dependent on factors specific to demand side.

II

Characteristic Features of Education in India and the Agency Role of NAAC

Education in India is the responsibility of the provincial state. The constitution assigns the union government the limited role of co-ordination and determination of standard of education. However, the center through financing and planning the education does have considerable influence. Followings are some prevalent features of our higher education.

— The educational structure in India varies from state to state. The UGC guidelines are not being implemented in toto. Now it is gradually becoming uniform.

— The educational standard also significantly varies from region to region. There is difference in method of teaching, in medium of teaching and in the content of papers.

— There is hardly any match between the syllabi content and prevalent problem of society. Partly it is due to the acceptance of infallible assumptions of ceteris paribus in teaching plan and partly we have uncritically borrowed the theories developed by the west to solve their then contextual problems. This is a serious issue. We like to deal it quite closely.

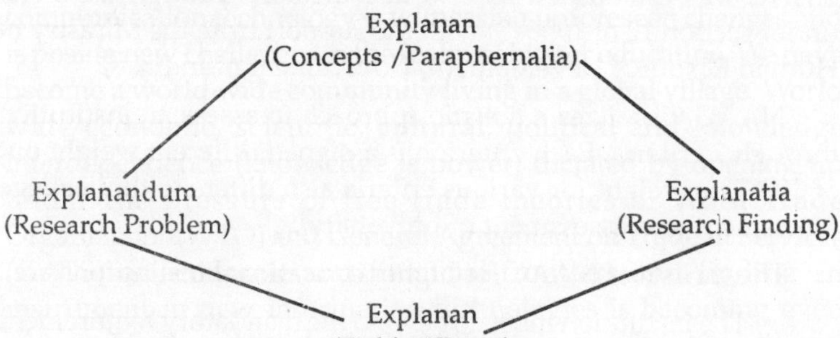

— Gender gap in enrolment exists. But recently the rate of girls' enrolments is rising but still it has to go long way to cover the gap.

- Growth rate of expenditure in higher education is faster than school education. Article 45 of the Constitution says that the state shall endeavor to provide within a period of ten years from the commencement of the Constitution (1950) for free and compulsory education for all children up to 14 years; which has been later extended to 1965 and the age was reduced to 11 years. But still it is far cry. It is postulated that it is possible only when resources from secondary and higher education could be transferred to the primary education. This is possible when the enrolments in higher education must be restricted[7].

— And another problem with higher education is of increasing graduate unemployment. But planners are unable to control or to resist the private demand for higher education because clients are politically turbulent and their parents are influential.

The higher education system found the state as the main and biggest employer of the educated youth. This system functioned undisturbed till 1991. But after 1991 with free trade economy the old dirigisme system started getting halts and breakdown due to *(i)* disinvestments in government sector, *(ii)* entry of foreign and private universities through information technology revolution. Due to liberalization, privatization and globalization in India through GATT and WTO institutions are to be standardized, for they have to become competitive, compatible and accountable. For this reason they are to be assessed and accredited by an agency known as NAAC (Nation Assessment and Accreditation Council). NAAC was established in 1994 at Bangalore through UGC Act under section 12 of 1956 (3) with the support from the Ministry of Human Resource Development, Government of India.

NAAC visualizes a holistic approach to assess an institution through 7 criteria. Each criterion is assigned different weight out of 100. The weight for various criteria also differs within college assessment and assessment of university[8].

The thrusts of NAAC for higher educational institutions are :

— The institution must go beyond the mandatory requirement of affiliating system. It must adopt need based professional and innovative programmes along with the on-going programmes.

– There must be a shift from teacher-centered approach to learner-centered approach. Therefore teachers must be sufficiently equipped with the new concepts and developments to meet the emerging challenges due to globalization. Audio visual aids must be used to improve teaching. Hence students' feedback is necessary in preparing the teaching plan and method.

— The institution must develop R&D wing to undertake the research projects as per local requirements. Consultancy wing must be added. Teachers having worked in the area must provide their information to the units requiring such consultancy.

— Above all institution must be a center for social change and development.

III

Expectations from Higher Education during the Post-Liberalized Phase

Quit similar to the two approaches individuated in the personality of an individual namely the well-being approach and self-agency approach[9]: we have two effects of formal education : *(i)* consumption effect of education,*(ii)* production effect of education. Consumption effect of education has direct impact on standard of living because better and comfortable life is possible due to ever increasing trend of commodity production. Primarily school education is meant for this purpose. Hence expansion of primary education is advocated in almost all education policies. Production effect of education has direct impact on social values associated with growth and development *i.e.* an increasing amount of production of goods & services are possible only through the productive effect of education. The higher education is basically orientated for this purpose. Hence consolidation instead of expansion of higher education is advocated. Since we are dealing with higher education we will limit our discussion here to the production effect only.

One may classify the whole cohort of production into three categories : natural resource, capital, and human resources. Each of them needs improvement for instance land through fertilizers or irrigation; capital through technological advancement; similarly human resources lend themselves for improvement through education. Further the capability of human being can be put under two categories : *(i)* the labour productivity, and *(ii)* the entrepreneurial ability. T.W. Schultz maintains that human's economic capabilities are predominantly "a produced means of production". We can split the total difference in human's earning into two parts namely rental share which is due to the difference in inherited capabilities; share in the form of return to capital invested in people. Difference due to rental share is very meager and therefore homogeneity of labour among 'the classicists'[10] is postulated. Difference due to the return of capital invested in human being is substantial. Ceteris paribus the structure of wages and salaries is determined by the type of education, the employee has received[11]. Here we have the role of higher education in developing both capabilities of human being (labour productivity in the form of skill and dexterity, and entrepreneurial ability in the form of innovative ability and decision-making power). In brief what education does are :

— it makes the working group receptive for invention and innovations;

— it promotes division of labour for consumption of advanced technology;

— it makes the working force to deal with 'know-how';

— it promotes mobility of labour and entrepreneurs on international scale;

— it transforms the social-cultural-political milieu.

Therefore, these, in total, form the expectation about the higher education. Now here quite succinctly we have a look on the demand and supply sides of higher education.

Demand components for higher education : We have following components which form the demand for higher education.

— *Size of population i.e.* ceteris paribus the larger is the size of the population; the greater will be the requirements for higher education.

— *School rate i.e.* the ratio between those who are actually going to school and who are of school age. The higher is the school rate; the larger will be the requirement for higher education.

— *Rate of economic growth and economic development*. Educational is essential factor in growth and development. It is obvious that there is positive correlate between the qualified manpower and economic performance of a society because it is increasingly recognized that use of technology and know-how largely depends on such skilled manpower.

— Further *the salary structure* is determined on the basis of educational qualification and there is substantial wage differential between modern sector and traditional sector; hence this fascinates the students to go for higher education.

Supply components of higher education : The following are the components which shape the supply side of higher education.

— *Time Factor* : Investment in education is relatively long term investment. It requires specific time period to acquire a certificate or degree. It is assumed that the larger is the time period; the better will be the product in terms of quality.

— *Unity* : Like industries we have here both vertical integration and horizontal integration. That is to say there is link across the papers within the subjects and there is link across the years consumed in the study process.

— *Complementarities i.e.* proportions must be observed in component parts for a qualitative product: teacher-student ratio, accommodation, equipments, and administration etc.

These are the factors which determine the institutional efficacy of higher education and therefore, they have strengthened the expectation side of higher education. This was holding good in dirigisme phase of resource constrained economy; because in dirigisme phase the state led development was the prevalent culture; and the state has emerged as the biggest employer; some of the expectations about higher education was well-met. But in the liberalized era this opportunity is drying up which poses question on the efficacy of the system that higher education has hitherto adopted.

This question mainly pertains to the three aspects of higher education namely *(i)* papers taught, *(ii)* contents of papers, *(iii)* evaluation system. That is to say like industry produces variety of output for various users: consumers and producers; similarly higher educational system should provide variety of paper for various purposes which must be sufficiently flexible for adapting the changes. Further the contents of paper must address the issues that employers want to get tackled by their employees. Furthermore, in evaluation part we must not only evaluate the knowledge content of the answer scripts but also ability and skill must be evaluated. This is possible if the two aforementioned changes are first incorporated because the evaluation pattern simply follows the materials in paper content.

IV

Questions on Employability

On the question of employability, it is often posited that quality of education has deteriorated on the one hand and quantity has increased on the other. Consequently the supply of educated youth in labour market has moved ahead of their demand. For deterioration of quality of education, the reasons are :

— Local language used as medium of teaching where there is dearth of suitable textbooks and supplementary literature necessary to achieve competence in the subjects;

— Papers contents are uninteresting for the students partly because they hardly address the local problems and partly there is mismatch between the cognizance level of students and analytical requirements of paper;

— Learning process of students is mostly a matter of mechanical memorization than understanding and hence there is little discussion of intellectual contents of the papers with teachers or with fellow friends. As a rule they go for question-answer type of leaning. Consequently many of them do not go to read textbooks in English available in library.

— In addition, a large majority of students are beset with financial worries which make concentration on academic work difficult.

— Equally there is slackness on the part of teachers who teach the syllabi mechanically without involving their intellectual passion. There is little enthusiasm in leaning of new truths because research is not considered as an integral part of their duty. Further whatever research is done that is usually of unconvincing quality. Attending orientation programme and refresher courses are the recent imperatives.

— There is separation between the educational system and production activities of industries. This separation is mainly due to the poor research quality carried by the educational institutions. There are three ways through which educational system and industries are linked. These are : *(i)* ability formation through knowledge base; *(ii)* entrepreneurial skill; and *(iii)* skill formation.

(i) The ability formation : The link should be : the higher education does the research work and research information affects industries decision. That is to say information gathered during the research process adds to the knowledge stock which is processed and transferred to the students who later in their capacity of an employee in industrial units must help the decision-making unit of industries. In this way the research unit of the higher education must get integrated with the industrial activities. During this process, training by industrial units to the new recruits patches the gap, if it exists between the educational institution (the supplying unit) and industrial requirements (consuming unit).

(ii) The entrepreneurial capacity formation : Further innovations in industries are ever-processing activities to adjust them with varying market conditions. Innovation skill must be inculcated in the entrepreneurial capacity of students during their educational pursuit.

(iii) Skill formation : Furthermore, there is link between education and industries with transfer of technology, popularly known as 'know-how'. To operate the new technology, skilled labours are provided by the educational system.

On the quantity aspects, it is postulated that over production of various educational output (excess graduates, post graduates, doctors, engineers, lawyers etc.) brings the marginal return of higher education low. So there should be clear criterion to limit the seats as per demand factor. Our arguments in this regard are two folds. *(i)* Our system is not the controlled and planned system. We are heading towards market orientated system. Hence, this is not feasible to estimate the demand for various outputs of educational system. It is the market forces which will take care of it. Utmost seats are to be fixed considering the organizational constraints which usually we do. *(ii)* it is not over investment in education which has caused the rising problem of educated unemployment rather it is imperfection of labour market which has given rise to this problem. Hence the appropriate remedy involves in effective manpower policy designed to improve the functioning of labour markets rather than contraction of higher education. Quite succinctly we like to analyze this issue.

In analyzing the causes of the rise in demand for labour by an industrial organization, Marshall considers four elasticities and their relations. These are :

— the demand for labour input increases if the elasticity of demand for the output is low;

— the demand for labour input increases if the importance of labour in the production process is less;

— the demand for labour input increases if the elasticity of substitution between this input with other inputs is low;

— the demand for labour input increases if the elasticity of supply of substitute inputs is low.

Hicks combined then in a mathematical formulation[12] *i.e.,*

$$E = \sigma (\eta + e) + ke (\eta - \sigma)/ (\eta + e) + k (\eta - \sigma)$$

Where E = elasticity of labour

η = elasticity of output

k = relative importance of labour *i.e.,* share of wage in total cost

σ = elasticity of substitution between labour and capital

e = elasticity of supply of capital.

But this reflects the situation for the demand for labour input from one firm or industry, while unemployment is a macroeconomic phenomenon. Prof. Pigou concludes that unemployment is primarily due to bad wage policy which fails to adjust with the changes in real demand function for labour[13]. He argues that the elasticity of the real demand for labour in the aggregate is :

$$Er = \phi'(x)/ \phi(x) . F'(x)/ F''(x)$$

Where F′(x) = the general wage rate

x = total men employed in wage-goods industries

y = total men employed in other industries

$\phi(x) = x + y$ *i.e.*, the number of men employed in the wage-goods industries is a function of total employment.

Keynes has criticized this Pigou's formulation on the ground that Pigou denied the possibility of involuntary unemployment because Pigou assumed that $n = x + y$, where 'n' is the total supply of labour in labour market. This means that labour is in a position to determine its own real wage. That is to say demand for output of the non-wage-goods industries (the rate of investment) obeys this assumption. In other words, in capital market the rate of interest adjusts itself with the marginal efficiency of capital in a manner which ensures full employment. Hence the non-inclusion of the investment in Pigou's formulation for employment determination is the weakness which Keynes[14] has tried to finish in his theory of employment.

Keynes argues that amount of labour (N) that entrepreneur decides to employ depends on *(i)* the amount which the community is expected to spend on consumption *i.e.*, propensity to consume (D_1); and *(ii)* the amount which entrepreneurs expects to devote to new investment (D_2). So that,

$$D_1 + D_2 = D = \phi(N)$$

Where ϕ = aggregate supply function

D_1 = $\chi(N)$ *i.e.* consumption expenditure by the community following the psychological law of propensity depending on the amount of labour employed.

D_2 = $\phi(N) - \chi(N)$ *i.e.* volume of investment.

Hence, volume of employment in Keynesian system depends on three variables namely the aggregate supply of function (ϕ), the propensity to consume (χ), and the volume of investment (D_2).

Keynes argues that the volume of employment is not determined by the marginal disutility of labour measured in terms of real wage as the classicists propose. This is the maximum level of employment as sets by the real wage. The actual level of employment is determined by the propensity to consume and the rate of new investment, and this level of employment is uniquely related to the real wages—not the other way round. 'if the propensity to consume and the rate of new investment result in a deficient effective demand, the actual level of employment will fall short of the supply of labour potentially available at the existing real wage, and the equilibrium real wage will be greater than the marginal disutility of the equilibrium level of employment' (p : 30).

Now it is clear that actual level of employment (N) is a function of effective demand (D_w) *i.e.*, $N = F(D_w)$. It is assumed that effective demand directed to individual industry, say 'r' is (D_{wr}). And (D_{wr}) is a unique function of the total effective demand (D_w).

Then $N_r = (D_{wr})$ may be written as $N_r = F_r(D_w)$.

The elasticity of employment for 'r' industry is

$$e_{er} = \delta N_r / \delta D_{wr} \cdot D_{wr}/N_r$$

The elasticity of employment for industry as a whole is

$$e_e = \delta N / \delta D_w \cdot D_w/N$$

Since there corresponds a unique distribution of effective demand between the product of each individual industry; it does not however, ensure that an increase in aggregate expenditure will affect the effective demand of each industry proportionally because of two reasons : *(i)* individuals as a rule do not distribute the expenditure of their additional income in the same proportion which they were hitherto spending; *(ii)* prices of different commodities will respond in different degree to the rise in expenditure. It means that changes in employment will not follow the changes in effective demand between the commodities. Hence 'if the increased demand is largely directed towards products which have a high elasticity of employment, the aggregate increase in employment will be greater than if it is largely directed towards products which have a low elasticity of employment. In the same way employment may fall off without there having been any change in aggregate demand, if direction of demand is changed in favour of products having a relatively low elasticity of employment' (p. 286).

When increased demand is directed towards a product of relatively low elasticity of employment, a large portion of it goes to swell the incomes of entrepreneurs and small portion goes to the wage-earners and other prime-cost factors.

This is the theoretical analysis of the labour market where we understand that increase in aggregate expenditure and its distribution over the commodities do have effect depending upon the elasticity of employment in the concerned industries or organization. Hence, an integral approach towards the development policy, investment policy, trade policy, and price policy for an effective employment policy is needed to solve the unemployment problem of educated youth.

V

Summary and Suggestions

The paper sums up and suggests the following :

1. With the conclusion of dirigisme phase, the state is downsized in its activities. Hence the higher education is loosing and further expecting to loose *(i)* the initiatives by the state in various programmes orientated for the educational improvements, *(ii)* the state being the main user of higher education products in the form of the biggest employer. Hence, paper suggests that this is the right time to bring changes in higher education system so as to keep abreast with the changes of the liberalized economic era. It suggests changes to be brought in three areas : *(a)* the course structure *i.e.,* it should be made more flexible as per need of time; *(b)* paper content: where issues from the employers' angle must also be incorporated; *(c)* evaluation system which should not be limited to evaluate only the memory power of students, rather it must develop the method to evaluate the ability, the skill, and the decision-making-innovative capacity of students.

2. In regard to the deterioration in the quality of education, paper has highlighted the reasons which must be tackled at both ends namely teachers' attitude towards profession and students' motive for improvements.

3. Further paper highlights that through higher education two qualities of human resources are processed *i.e.,* labour skill and entrepreneurial ability. Hence in view of changes during the post-liberalized era, it is suggested that entrepreneurial ability must be given added weight during the process of human resources by various institutions of higher education.

4. In regard to the quantity, paper strongly recommends that

it must increase because it bears a positive correlation with economic growth and economic development. Educated unemployment is not because of over production of degrees as it is postulated; rather it is due to *(i)* deficiency in aggregate demand, and *(ii)* its misdirection (towards the output having low employment elasticity in the production line). Hence to tackle the problem an integral employment policy is to be evolved involving development policy, investment policy, trade policy and price policy.

Notes

1. Institutional Economics emphasizes that economic performance is a function of both technology and institutions. It stresses upon the organizational structure controlling the economic system. It has two traditions. One is started by Thorstein Veblen (showing progressive role of technology and inhibiting role of institutions). Another is from John R. Commons (acknowledging the progressive role of technology but within the approaches of instructions).
2. Sukhamony Chakravarty (1990) highlights these two points to explain the resource constrained phase of Indian economy.
3. Prabhat Patnaik (1999) emphasizes good shortage and shortage of foreign exchange as the yardstick to understand the resource constrained economy.
4. See Amarnath Mohanty (2004).
5. See Amit Bhaduri and Deepak Nayyar (1996).
6. See Prabhat Patnaik (*op.cit.*).
7. See Mark Blaug (1969).
8. See S. N. Pathan (2005), p. 35.

Criteria	*University*	*College Affiliated*	*College Autonomous*
1	2	3	4
Curricular Aspects	15	10	15
Teaching and Evaluation	25	40	30

1	2	3	4
Research and consultancy etc.	15	05	10
Infrastructure	15	15	15
Student support	10	10	10
Organization and management	10	10	10
Healthy practices	10	10	10

9. See Amartya Sen (1999).
10. See J. M. Keynes (1936).
11. See Mark Blaug *op.cit.*
12. See The New Palgrave (1988).
13. See J. M. Keynes, *op. cit.*
14. See J. M. Keynes, *ibid.*

REFERENCES

1. Bhaduri, Amit and Deepak Nayyar (1996), *"The Intelligent Person's Guide to Liberalization,"* Penguin Books, New Delhi.
2. Blaug, Mark, Richard Layard, Maureen Woodhall (1969), *"The Causes of Graduate Unemployment in India"*, Penguin Press, London.
3. Choudhury, R.A., Shama Gamkhar, Aurobindo Ghose (1990), *"The Indian Economy and Its Performance since Independence"*, OUP, Delhi.
4. Eatwell, John, Murray Milgate, Peter Newman (1988), *"The New Palgrave : A Dictionary of Economics,"* Vol. 2, The Macmillan Press Limited, London.
5. Keynes, J.M. (1936), *"The General Theory of Employment Interest and Money"*, Macmillan and Co. Ltd., London.
6. Mohanty, Amarnath (2004), *"From Passive Revolution to Possessive Individualism? Tracing Trajectory of India's Political Economy,"* Review of Development and Change, Vol. IX, No. 2 July-Dec., pp. 185–220.
7. Pathan, S.N., (2005), *"Quality Improvement Programme in Higher Education through NAAC"*, Intellectual Book Bureau, Bhopal.
8. Patnaik, Prabhat (1999), *"The Performance of the Indian Economy in the 1990's Social Scientist"*, Vol. 27, Nos. 5–6, May-June.
9. Sen, Amartya (1999), *"Development as Freedom,"* OUP, New Delhi.

6

Globalisation and Higher Education in India : Issues and Concerns

—Pratap Chandra Swain

Globalization seeks to integrate the economics, standardize the politics and eliminate political and geographical distances. India cannot afford to remain in isolation in this age of globalization.

In the post cold war era, the world system has undergone unprecedented technological and economic transformations through a complex process of change. In other words, a global economic and technological war is going on among the different countries, particularly between India, China and other developing countries on the one hand, and the United States of America, European Union and many developed countries on the other. This contemporary worldwide process of change is popularly described as globalization, which has stimulated increasing interest in new theories of discourse. As a result globalization has emerged as one of the powerful intervention in contemporary political thinking as well as world wide living pattern. However, the concept of globalization in its contemporary form can be traced back to 1990s. In fact John Williamson coined the term globalization in 1990[1] to explain the integrated approach of the US Treasury Department, the IMF, the World Bank, the WTO the Inter-American Development Bank for making a paradigm shift in the process of development, within a neo-liberal framework. As such Joseph

Stiglitz characterizes globalization as a "consensus formulated between 15th street (US Treasury Department) and 19th street (IMF and the World Bank) in Washington"[2]. In other words, the ongoing process of globalization is based on the above "Washington based consensus" which means "Westernization" in general and "Americanization" in particular.

Significantly, globalization seeks to integrate the economies, standardize the politics and eliminate politico-geographical distances between peoples of the world. It reflects a complex process of interconnectedness in the contemporary political, economic and natural environments. In a broad spectrum, globalization can be described as 'the worldwide phenomenon of technological, economic, political and cultural exchanges, brought about by modern communication, transportation and legal infrastructure as well as the political choice to consciously open cross border links in international trade and finance[3]. However, globalization can be perfectly imagined with the help of its two key engines, *viz.*, 'liberalization' and 'technology'. Within the framework of liberalization as well as sophisticated modern technology, globalization facilitates the heightened mobility of people's ideas, culture, goods and capital across borders.

Globalization has major economic goals on its agenda. The economic globalization is rooted in the principles of neo-liberalism. The contemporary human life is predominantly shaped by the reality of economic globalization, which signifies a market driven world economy as well as the expansion of "corporate capitalism".[4] As such the scholars characterize globalization as "the ideology and policy formulation associated with free market capitalism."[5] Ordinarily, globalization involves a comprehensive process of economic reforms leading to the liberalization of interest rates, trade, inflow of foreign direct investment, privatization, reduction in the role of the state in economic affairs, deregulation, rolling back of subsidies etc. On the whole, globalization leads to the integration of the domestic economies with the international economy. In reality, the distinct impacts of economic globalization can be seen in terms of increase in international trade and flow of capital; development of global financial system; increase in the share of the world economy controlled by multinational corporations; increased role of international organizations such as WTO, IMF etc, in the matters of international transactions; increase of economic practices like outsourcing; reduction or elimination of tariffs and capital control; construction of free-trade zones; harmonization of subsidies and intellectual property restrictions etc.

In the context of the social economic and political architecture of the contemporary world, the on going process of globalization has been all pervasive and irreversible one. A number of political actors and institutions as well as economic players have been instrumental in restructuring the trade and service sectors in globalized fashion. Under WTO, the GATS (General Agreement on Trade in Services) have been formed which consists of 12 specified services including education. India as a developing country has already signed the GATS. Consequently, the public education sector in India, particularly higher education has been opened up. This has generated much scholarly debate and academic interests in the globalization of higher education. The present paper is an attempt to understand the process of globalization in the context of its impact on higher education in India.

Indian Perspective

The process of globalization operates like a trap. The entire world is viewed as a globalized world. A state may or may not be interested in the process of globalization but globalization affects each and every state of the world today. As such India cannot afford to remain in isolation. The response of the Indian state towards globalization has been very much dynamic. In other words, Indian society, polity and economy have gone global in a big way. It has already restructured its politico–economic and developmental framework with a complete departure from Nehruvian model.

During early1990s, India confronted with a severe economic problem *i.e.* the so-called balance of payment crisis. This coincided with the post–cold war phase which resulted in a series of new global political-economic developments. In the meantime, the Narasimha Rao government assumed office. At the very beginning, Rao government made a significant move and invited the advanced industrialized countries to come forward and help India in resolving the balance of payment crisis. It fetched a timely response from the industrialized countries that made India to open its market to the foreign investors for the resolution of economic crisis. This has been a major attempt to integrate Indian economy with the global economy. With this, the government of India ventured to make globalization of Indian economy by drastically changing the Nehru – Indira model of development. At the instance of IMF India undertook the structural adjustment programmes (SAP). In Indian context, the SAP aims at *6Ds* (Denationalisation, Delicensing, Disinvestment, Decontrol, Deregulation and Debureaucratisation) approach. Narasimha Rao government adopted the "new economic policy" in 1991 incorporating the SAP. Based on the Narasimha Rao—Manmohan Singh model of development, the new policy package rejected the old model of state-led economic and social development and chalked out a new path of fiscal discipline, liberalization, globalization, deregulation and privatization of the public sector etc. In fact the new economic policy aims at opening the domestic economy to foreign competition, investment and trade. Precisely, the Narasimha Rao—Manmohan Singh model of development shifted the "focus of attention from the state to market and from domestic to global". Since the new economic policy in 1991, "Liberalization, Privatization and Globalization" (LPG) have been the new policy framework for governance of India. Precisely, the Indian state, in its strategic option for globalization, has made a shift from the state supported capitalism to semi-privatised "free market" capitalism and from self-reliance in economic development to reliance on Foreign Direct Investment and the MNCs.

The Milieu of Higher Education

The modern higher education was started in India as early as in 1817, with the establishment of Hindu College in Calcutta. The British ruler introduced the system of higher education in India on the European pattern. As such India inherited one westernized system of modern higher education from the very beginning. Subsequently, after independence, Indian policy makers modestly tried to Indianise the pattern of higher education. In fact higher education was put in the priority list under 'public education sector'. Thus, a state controlled and state sponsored system of higher education was designed in India, with 19 universities and 591 colleges, immediately after independence. The number of the institutions of higher education were steadily increased to more than 261 Universities/deemed Universities, more than 8361 general colleges and more than 2340 professional colleges in the new millennium. This great advancement made India to emerge as the second largest higher education system in the world.[6]

At present globalization is blowing hot and cold in every sphere of Indian life. It has made a paradigm shift in the regulation of higher education. Under WTO and GATS (General Agreement on Trade in Services) regime, the Indian higher education has been made market oriented. The GATS directive strongly advocates for the drastic cut in the public expenditure on education. Its pattern of higher education is based on the model of University of Phoenix, which is a profit-generating corporation and accordingly listed in the New York Stock exchange. There is virtually no choice on the part of a developing country like India but to accept WTO-GATS model of higher education. The New Economic Policy of 1991, based on the theory of LPG (Liberalisation, Privatisation and Globalisation), significantly affected the higher education. After signing in GATS in 1998 higher education has been identified as a 'non-merit good' and a 'marketable commodity'. The damaging impacts of the process of globalization on higher education of India are in order :

Withdrawal of State from Higher Education

The crux of the neo-liberal agenda, in the form of globalization is the withdrawal of the state from public utility services and handing over hitherto state run service sector like education to the private sector. In other words, the vital areas of public life like education which is traditionally reserved for the state is now transferred to the agencies of civil society which heavily depend on multinational corporations and international bodies for fund. In the wake of the process of globalization the union government as well as the state governments in India are reducing their expenditure on higher education. This is reflected in the plan expenditure and budget expenditure of both the governments every year. It has become a declared policy of the government of India and also the state governments that the recurring expenditure and maintenance grants to the institutions of higher education are to be curtailed. While the allocation for education in the first five-year plan was 7.2% of the total outlay, it has come down to 2.9% in the tenth five-year plan. The expenditure reform committee in its fifth report on

7th March'2000 recommended "there should be a freeze on recruitment of staff in all autonomous organizations at all levels. In addition, an adhoc cut of 10% in the total staff strength should be imposed in all these Institutions"[7]. Following this, the UGC issued a directive allowing the Universities and Colleges to fill up only 80% of their teaching vacancies on temporary basis. In the wake of the withdrawal of the state from the higher education sector, non-governmental organizations, self-help groups and other private bodies have become new managers of higher education in India. These agencies are pushing through the globalized agenda of higher education within the framework of GATS.

Opening up of Higher Education Sector

As a signatory to the WTO and GATS, India has very cautiously started gradual opening up of higher education sector to the private enterprises as well as the foreign universities. There has been phenomenal growth of the private educational institutions including "Deemed Universities" within India in recent years. Significantly, the number of such deemed universities has been increased from around 15 in 1999 to 105 in 2006. The foreign educational institutions in general and those of U.S. in particular are increasingly interested in India. Around 150 foreign Universities, roughly 50 from U.K., 45 from Australia, 30 from USA and the rest from Canada as well as other European countries, are participating in the higher education sector of India. University presidential delegations from Harvard, Yale, Stanford, Carnegie Mellon and Purdue Universities and also few high level delegations from prominent institutions including the Asia society have come to India during the last two years in order to study the higher education situation in India. Interestingly, twenty prestigious U.S. Universities have entered into partnership with Amrita Visha Vidyapeetham for progressive collaboration in higher education and research through e-learning and EDUSAT-India's educational satellite. Further, many other foreign institutions offer twinning programmes which provide approval to the curriculum in India by a foreign university and also facilitates the transfer of academic credit for enabling the students to complete their studies at these universities. In a unique way, the Goa Education Development Corporation Ltd. (GEDCL) is planning to develop an educational estate at Verna in South Goa, which would attract reputed National and International Institutions to set up shop. It is very important that the United States Educational Foundation in India (USEFI) has been playing key role in developing partnership between India and U.S. institutions and also facilitating the entry and establishment of accredited U.S. institutions in India.

The protagonists of the globalization of Indian higher education strongly advocate for bringing foreign Universities to India on the ground that these Institutions would provide opportunities for expansion of access to higher education within India. Further, with the entry of high quality foreign university the Indian students need not go to overseas rather they will undergo same study from their desired foreign educational institution within India. This will ultimately help in keeping Indian Investment within the country. In addition to this, it is argued that the U.S. Institutions, having proficiency in preparing students for the job market, would definitely enhance the quality and relevance of contemporary education in India[8]. In view of the recent developments in Indo-US friendship, U.S. Participation in Indian higher education sector will go on increasing in the days to come.

However, with the increasing participation of the foreign institutions in Indian higher education, the indigenous Indian institutions are getting threatened so far as their survival is concerned. The Parliamentary Standing committee on Human Resource Development, in its 172nd Report on University and Higher 'Education 2006' has cautioned against the entry of substandard foreign educational institutions and also against the maintenance of double standard even by the established foreign institutions in India. Hence the standing committee has suggested for setting up a body to regulate the activities of the Foreign universities. The Ministry of Human Resource Development has already appointed a high-powered committee headed by Prof. C.N.R. Rao in January' 2005 to examine all issues relating to the entry of foreign educational institutions into India and submit necessary recommendations. As a great relief to the public higher education sector, the HRD Ministry, in its 'policy paper on Foreign Direct Investment (FDI) in Higher Education', has clearly mentioned that there should not be any haste in opening the education sector under a multilateral regime without adequate safeguards. The paper rejects the commercial trade based approach of the commerce ministry, which had "restricted itself to a narrow, middle class business process outsourcing (BPO)—IT perspective."[9]

Higher Education as Non-Merit Goods

In the post liberalization era, the World Bank and IMF assume the role of donor for the development of the developing countries like India. These international bodies largely determine the policies and programmes of the government of India. As a result the government has redesigned its policy on higher education as per the sweet wills of Fund-Bank (IMF – World Bank) managers. Taking advantage of the situation, the donor organizations put conditions for the abolition of subsidy for higher education and also for doing away with the practice of permanent recruitments in the universities and colleges. This move is being justified considering higher education as non-merit goods. As non-merit goods the higher education has no externality and it does not benefit the society at large. It only benefits those who get it but not others. Hence, it is argued that the public expenditure on the higher education sector should be reduced and this sector should be handed over to the private enterprises.

Laissez Fairism in Higher Education

In the wake of the on going process of globalization, higher education has been left alone by the state. The union government as well as the state governments insists the universities and colleges to be self-reliant. These Institutions have been advised to raise their revenue from different sources like public contributions, hike in fees, selling or renting their property, undertaking consultancy, and counselling, undertaking R and D projects funded by industries and companies, preparation of educational/research materials like text/references books, audio/video cassettes/CDs etc. Further, the Universities are being encouraged to setup a "company or registered society" and also associate as well as collaborate themselves with the private sector for the purposes of revenue generation. In the process the state has deserted the higher education sector in respect of financial support as well as resources generation. The Indian Institutions of higher education are passing through a very difficult phase as they have been pushed into an ill designed globalized Darwinian world. These Institutions are required to compete among themselves and also with their foreign counterparts. During the course of the struggle for existence, many institutions of higher education in India are facing the danger of dying out.

Marketisation of Higher Education

Under the auspices of the WTO-GATS regime, higher education is treated as a marketable commodity. The University and Colleges have become a part of the market. In a market model Universities/ College subjects that can make and attract money are given priority. The study of traditional disciplines in science, humanities and social sciences has failed to serve the needs of the market. Ultimately, market as well as technology oriented subjects like management studies, fashion designing, modeling, petroleum science, biotechnology etc. have come into vogue. In view of the commodification of higher education the universities Vice-Chancellors, Educational Directors and College Principals are likely to assume the role of 'traveling salesmen' to promote their programme and sale their product. The institutions of higher education are required to show their growth as per the demands of the market economy. Accordingly market mechanism dominates the mindset of the policy makers in higher education. In other words, it is the market which decides the value of any academic subject, utility of subject teachers and above all the standard of a particulars institution of higher education. As the market rules the roost, it becomes a disaster for the social sector in general and the public education in particular. Today higher education is no more a service to the community as it has been degenerated into a marketable commodity. This goes against the ideals of the UNESCO.

Making Higher Education an Industry

In the wake of commercialization of higher education the institutions of higher education work as industrial units. While conducting themselves as industrial units, these institutions are characterized by private ownership as well as control and guided by certain traits such as maximization of profit and appropriation of the same, higher production, work discipline, routinization etc. The private enterprises are coming forward in a big way to take over the sphere of higher education. As a result private universities, deemed universities, private professional institutions are coming up to industrialise the higher education sector. Moreover, the existing universities and other institutions of higher education are being advised to pursue research and teaching for promoting the interest of industry and business rather than the benefit of the society. A possible liaison of university-industry is emerging.

Within the industrial framework, higher education has been reduced to a mechanical process. The universities are largely adopting credit based curriculum, semester system, cafeteria approach and above all mechanical classroom teaching. On the whole, the globalized higher education has lost human face. Like the labour unions in the industries, the teachers are frequently coming to the streets in support of their legitimate claims. But the government remains indifferent towards the demands of the teaching community. This adversely affects the academic life in the colleges and the universities.

De-Professionalisation of Teaching and Mad Craze for Technology

Another serious impact of the process of globalization on higher education is the mad craze for technology and undermining the role of teacher in the learning process. Distance education and e-learning have come into vogue. Audio/Video broadcasts/ICT and related new technologies are being used for running of statewide/countrywide virtual classroom. In the process technologies are used to replace the teacher in the classroom. As a result teaching is no longer a lively experience for both the teacher and taught. The mechanical process of delivery of lectures through audiovisual gadgets and studying through readymade study materials as well as online lessons will never impress upon the minds of the students. In an attempt to de-professionalise teaching, a robot is likely to be used to perform the role of the teacher. Ultimately, teaching and learning will fail to develop as a mutual interactive process thereby spoiling the psychological bond between the teachers and the students. Above all the social atmosphere and corporate life in the universities and colleges will be far cry.

Declining of Equity in Higher Education

The on going process of globalization has made higher education purely market based. The reduction of the state expenditure on higher education has compelled the universities and colleges to hike in fees structure. Moreover, the overseas universities coming to India are more interested in trading higher education than disseminating knowledge. They offer capitalist mode of education and adopt elitist fees structure as a result, the cost of higher education becomes exorbitant and this sector remains beyond the reach of the lower middle class as well as weaker sections of the Indian society. In other words, the globalized higher education is meant only for those who can afford the exorbitant cost but not for all. In the process, higher education looses equity and gets restricted to the privileged sections of the society. In view of the elitist nature of the globalized higher education, it leads to the creation of three different educated classes—those educated in foreign universities, those from costly private domestic institutions and economically weaker sections studying in government funded institutions. This leads to social tension and goes against the very ethos of democracy.

Thus, the consequences of globalization are alarming for the higher education sector in India. The process of globalization has questioned the very efficacy of the Indian institutions of higher education as well as the relevance of the existing educational system of India. It advocates for the global benchmarking in education. In the process, only three Indian institutions rank among the top 500 in the world. The Nobel Laureate, Joseph Stiglitz rightly questions the survival of the Washington consensus—based globalization. He called the year 2003 as disaster for globalization. Infact the process of globalization creates a Darwinian world leading to the survival of the fittest. John Ralston supplements Joseph Stiglitz by saying that "Washington consensus—based globalization has been fast petering out."[10] Making a note of caution, Mikhail Gorbachev observes : "if globalization is allowed to develop spontaneously, we get something like social Darwinism...Without direction it may become a destructible process and the first signs of such destruction are already starting to show".[11]

In order to face the challenges posed by globalization towards higher education, the Parliamentary Standing Committee on Human Resource Development, in its 172nd Report on University and Higher Education submitted on May 22nd, 2006 has identified five important issues in higher education such as access and equity; relevance; quality and excellence; governance and management;

and funding. The union government is expected to come with progressive legislations in order to tackle these issues.

India subscribes to the UN concept of Globalization with a social dimension characterized by equity and fairness. Ideally Globalization in India never ends history and geography. The Indian situation needs indigenous economic reforms with a human face without sacrificing our civilization values. As the Indian vision of globalization entails an emerging one world with great respect to humanity, the policy makers should not blindly imitate the west and adhere to principle of market supremacy. It is appropriate to conclude with Juan Somavia, the Director General of International Labour Organization that "there can not be a successful globalization without a successful localization."[12]

In our plural society, with conflicting values and diverse ethnic identities, we urgently need a class of educated people. As such the higher education should be associated with the process of the social needs of the people rather than the production process of marketable commodities in the era of liberalization and privatization. The civilization values and cultural heritage must guide the educational process. While globalizing higher education in India our policy makers should keep in mind that we had famous centers of higher learning like Takshasila, Vikramsila, Pallavi and Nalanda Viswavidyalayas during the days when there was no university in Europe. Thus we need to retain our noble indigenous tradition of higher education, with necessary fine-tuning, in the age of globalization.

REFERENCES

1. Girish Mishra, *"Nehruvian Model of Economic Development and its Relevance Today"*, in Mainstream, Vol. xi. 48, Nov.16, 2002, p. 14.
2. For details, see, Joseph Stiglitz , *Globalization and its Discontents*, Oxford, 2002.
3. For details see, Muktedar Khan, *www.keepmedia.com/pubs/foreignpolicy/fair* globalization.
4. Henry Kissinger's Lecture, at the Trinity College, Dublin, 12 Oct. 1999.
5. Rober Gilpin, *The Challenge of Global Capitalism : The World Economy in 21st century*, Princeton, Princeton University Press, 2000, pp. 293-324.

6. See, People's Democracy, Vol. X, No. 50.
7. *Op. cit*.
8. See, The Hindu, Nov. 14, 2006.
9. See, The Hindu, Nov. 25, 2006.
10. See, Girish Mishra, *op. cit*.
11. Mikhail Gorbachev, *"Threats of Social Darwinism – An Alarmed World"*, "World Affairs, Vol. 5 (1), Jan-March 2001.
12. *Ibid*.

7

The Quality Package and Higher Education

—Asim Ranjan Parhi

The enthusiasm to access higher education to all without proper institutional, infrastructural, financial and professional back-up is a factor of quality deterioration in itself.

INTRODUCTION

Higher Education in Indian context has been a reservoir of contradiction. Emphasis on world class output in institutions like IITs and IIMs encounters populist and opportunist political reservation policies; enviable infrastructural and competence level struggling with exorbitant free structure and so on. At the other corner one finds the study of Humanities and Social Sciences in innumerable colleges of every state without any target oriented approval or skill based learning. This paper unfolds a few major areas that need to be pondered over and addressed in the scenario of Higher Education in Arunachal Pradesh with special emphasis on the non-technical streams in colleges.

Theorising Quality

Quality in higher education generally refers to the level of excellence at infrastructure, skill, competence of teachers and taught ultimately culminating in the utility of the products. But quality is not always utilitarian. It could be independent of the above things in a particular circumstance; commitment. But this is an idealized concept today. Competition in professional fields has resulted in a global underestimation of general education. The policy makers emphasize on maximum output with meagre resources. In such a circumstance quality has to be diluted with a package, even at the degree courses of the Arts programme as a product of glamour as most professional institutions have done.

MAJOR CAUSES OF QUALITY DETERIORATION

1. Public Outlook

Most of the parents and the general public look down upon the whole set up of 'college', 'Teachers', 'Arts' and so on. They remain ignorant of their worth and scope. For them anybody pursuing a Science stream, professional course is the darkhorse. This has resulted in the mushrooming of incompetent engineering graduates and a sheer wastage of money in those sectors. The public image of the general education can be changed with a certain amount of fee hike that can create a glamour and be utilized in infrastructural growth.

2. Policy Making

The biggest area of concern is our policy makers who are bureaucrats. Bureaucratization of education has spoiled quality to a large extent. A certain state Governor once took exception to the appointment of Principal from Science stream at an Arts College. The educationist Governor was aware of this malady. In most cases the administrative officers dictate terms on policy, planning only to assert a neo colonial power.

3. Fee Structure and Teacher Status

As stated earlier, the fee structure for general education is low and it creates a false impression of the nature of education at that scale. The teachers at these colleges are abysmally ill paid which creates a scope for lack of accountability.

4. Infrastructure

In comparison to any private technical institution, our colleges provide a very insignificant infrastructural help in terms of classrooms, laboratories, library, auditorium, playground and so on. A college with a reputation of 20-30 years also suffers from many such bottlenecks in comparison to a new commercial institution funded by a private agency.

5. Universal Access of Higher Education

The motto of making higher education reach every doorstep is an absolutely erroneous move. It appears to be everyone's business due to an easy entry without any entrance test. Such a move only creates a sense of confusion among the large bulk of students, parents and non-serious approach on the part of the teachers. No one feels accountable and the source (the teacher) scarcely refills itself in terms of new skill ad expertise.

6. Location of Language

Apart from the above characteristics, the most sensitive issue today is that of language. Most of the states flaunt a pseudo pride in their own language resulting in a chauvinistic stance and myopic, sentimental handling of a very pertinent question. We are also more adaptable to any language than the other counterparts. But instead of looking forward in that direction, a large number of colleges in contemporary times have compromised on this position. The importance of English in higher education is simply incomparable and its utility could be ascertained taking into account the benefit that the north-eastern have got because of English, being their medium of instruction. They have excelled in competing others only because of their comfortability in English, their conversation skills and exposure through the richness of the language.

THE QUALITY PACKAGE

Having specified a very small area of the causes of concern, we may harp on the remedial measures and change of outlook separating higher education/college education in our mind rather than as an automatic promotion from the schools. It is said that the institutions of higher education have to provide all round development of the students-intellectual, physical, moral and spiritual: development of the mind, body, heart, personality; disseminate knowledge, promote skills and develop outlook so as to produce young persons who are intellectually alert, physically strong, morally upright, aesthetically sensitive, socially committed and economically self reliant. The only way to do this is to ensure that the quality of higher education is such as fulfils these goals[1]. This could also sound stereotype but we cannot shy away from our limitations, *i.e.* ours is not a purely skill distributing institution like the technical ones. We may have a reservation on the excessive preaching quality of such a goal. It needs a packaging, a decorative face-lift to declare to the world that it is exclusively for the selected few and something coveted, saleable.

REMEDIES IN PRIORITY

1. Screening System

The first thing our college education requires is a strict common entrance for anybody aspiring to get into the college (degree) education parallel to any of the recognized professional courses. But such a position would seriously blur the image of humanities as socialistic and welfarist. The other major hurdle is how to tackle the financial crunch that may arise due to shortage of students.

2. Brand Image

An image of privatization creates a brand. We need to sale our product, courses as a shampoo brand. Values do not vanish if we refuel them by a cosmopolitan, glamorized design. As far as implementation of a given set of objectives concerned, an eminent educationist says : If a given scheme is cast in the 'mission mode' and specific tasks assigned to the members of the team-Government, UGC, University, teachers, students, management and university employees—it is in my view, entirely possible to carry out a nationally important operation. Thanks to this approach, more complex missions have triumphed in India in fields as varied as agriculture and space[2]. It can be traced from this that any course structure, faculty need to repackage, reorient them depending on the time and changing worldview. The Engineering stream has successfully revitalized it with funds from NRIs and other bodies with very high fee structure. And people seem to be running towards those institutions.

3. Funds, Infrastructure

Any institution could garner funds from different UGC Provisions once it fulfils certain requirements. Government and other sponsoring agencies have time and again provided funds for infrastructural aid through MPLAD etc.

4. Teacher Welfare and Research

Once the streamlining of courses, institutions and student enrolment get completed it has to be ascertained that the teachers are extremely taken care of. Raising the salary of teachers has been always a contentious issue. Other sectors in this country always keep on pointing fingers towards it without realizing that a teacher requires a lot of money for pursuing research and procuring books/ journals. It is a 'twenty four hours' profession as far as reading and preparing for the courses is concerned. It is certainly beyond a nine to five job. Once it is settled, the accountability is on them. They need to renew themselves and attend the refresher courses compulsorily, subscribe to some required material. Research is an important segment of academic life. Paul Ricoeur, a French philosopher comments : When research is vigorous it is not only knowledge which moves forward, the entire university is vitalized from top to bottom. Research provides the university with its driving force and its creative stimulus and it protects other forms and levels of education from the dangers of Sclerosis and from becoming ends in themselves, by continually obliging them to adapt and renew their teaching . Research cannot be undertaken without training research workers and without educating those who will themselves become educators (*Espirit*, May-June 1964). But there is another side to most of the social science research. A large number of research projects are repetitive, wastage of money and without any result oriented findings. Yet to develop a work culture we have to take initiatives at least to work in that direction. Any such excuse as stated above only takes us backward. Serious attempt needs to be taken to create an atmosphere for writing articles, conducting seminars with sizeable student participation that could generate independent thinking.

5. Student Accountability

Student indiscipline due to political involvement extends to sporadic social violence. It happens due to free entry of students without skill at the earlier level and lack of brilliance in every aspect. Once a goal oriented, capable group of learners enter into higher education, it might take the shape of quality campus.

6. Curriculum and Evaluation

As such the curriculum in humanities and social sciences is alright along with NSS, NCC and other activities. But every subject/topic has a preface and target. Any single lecture should not ignore that target to be achieved which in turn would decrease paraphrasing and enhance critical thinking. Theories, concepts and analytic power need to be taken to centre stage. Evaluation requires large scale decentralization.

CONCLUSION

Any armchair policy or seminar findings prove ineffective if they do not see the face of reality, that is classroom activity and administrative reform. Suitable measures in this regard can be implemented lessening the class load (number of classes) and strengthening quality. Steps need to be taken in providing as much autonomy as possible to the teacher concerned with more emphasis on academic accountability. Ultimately it is by the focused and pan-Indian effort of the teachers and students, quality education can be the desired achievement in the colleges of Arunachal Pradesh.

REFERENCES

1. See P.R. Dubhashi's *'Indian System of Higher Education'* in University News, Vol. Xxxii, No.8, Feb. 21, 1994 as quoted in *"Maladies of Higher Education"* by M.S. Valiathan in Professional Competency in Higher Education, CPDHE, Edited by N.K. Uberoi, University of Delhi. Delhi, 1995.
2. *Ibid.*
3. Gautam, P. Satya, *"Making Quality Higher Education Accessible in India"*. University News, Vol. 43, No. 41, Oct 10–16, 2005.
4. Kirpal, Viney, *"Quality in Higher Education : A Right of the stakeholder,"* University News, Vol. 43, No. 38, Sept. 19–25, 2005.

8

Quality Assurance in Higher Education in Arunachal Pradesh : Issues and Challenges

—*R.K. Mandal*

In a globally competitive world, India will be a loser in the international educational trade market, if quality and relevance of education are not inbuilt.

Globalization is the emerging reality of the 21st century and the advent of the 21st Century accompanied by tremendous development in science, technology, information and communication technology is witnessing unforeseen changes and is posing new challenges in the realm of higher education. We have become a world wide community living in a global village. World wide economic, scientific, cultural, political and knowledge interdependence (knowledge is power) dictated by opening up under the pressure of free trade theories of Word Trade Organization(WTO) and General Agreement on Trade in Services (GATS) of economic and financial frontiers and finding an instrument in new information technologies is becoming even more securely established. Globalization means integration of economics and societies through cross country flow of information, ideas, technology, goods, services, capital, finance and the people. In another sense it refers to removal of barriers to free trade and the close integration of national economy—"a world in one nest".

In a globally competitive world, India will be loser in the international educational trade market, if quality and relevance are not inbuilt, empowerment and status of the teachers are not enhanced, suitable infrastructure is not available, obsolete curriculum and courses are not properly substituted and revamped, research specially mass action researches are not strengthened and evaluation and monitoring are not inbuilt. Without a world class education, the out flow of students will comparatively become more than the inflow along with more brain drain to brain gain. Thus in a globally competitive world, it is quality of education that can sustain a nation. Quality education will produce knowledgeable persons and in the modern world "knowledge is power."

The Quality Assurance in Higher Education is gaining wider acceptance amongst the stakeholders across the globe. Even though the quality assurance mechanisms in different countries are at different levels of maturity and capacity, there is a broad agreement on need and effectiveness of quality assurance. Of the three factors involved in production : land, labour, and capital, it is labour and more particularly the quality of labour that is the key determinant for a country's competitiveness. It is, therefore, not surprising that there is a strong positive correlation between endowment of skilled labour and the gross domestic product per worker across countries. The quality of higher education enhances a country's capacity for participation in an increasingly knowledge-based world economy and has the potential to enhance economic growth and reduce poverty. Education is an important index of human development alongwith economic growth and empowerment; it forms the core of every social and human development doctrine. Jawaharlal Nehru accepted education as the most important means to bring about social change. His belief was that "It is only through right education that a better order of society can be built up. Education is the most important requisite to open up the individual". Among various levels of education, higher education has pervasive and influential impact on development, since it empowers the individual with necessary skills and competence for achieving important personal and social goals and thereby contributing to the social development. It is widely believed that the state of higher education in a country is an index of its future well-being. Higher education is needed as a vital tool for intellectual, cultural and aesthetic development and means for achieving wider social aspirations. It also has an increasingly crucial role to play in producing change agents for moving the country along the development continuum. The phenomena of liberalization, globalization, and privatization of the Indian economy coupled with revolution in information technology have brought new challenges to higher education.

The dream of India to become a knowledge super power by 2020 will be a mirage unless higher education reaches to the masses and there is technological empowerment of the working class. In the introduction to his work "Buffalo Nationalism" (2004) Kancha Iliah has forcefully presented a case for imparting higher education to the working classes. According to him, the prime cause of India's underdevelopment is the disassociation of intellectual labour from physical labour.

The strategy for bridging the democratic deficit in our way of life through education was outlined by the UNESCO Conference in Geneva on "Quality Education for all Young People". The conference declared : "Promoting quality education and training for all young people between the ages of 12 and 20 is essential to securing a better future and constitutes an essential mechanism for combating social exclusion at the local, national and global levels. As both a basic right and a public good, this education must respond to the needs and interests of all young people with a view to ensuring the realization of their full potential, their successful integration in the world of work, as well as their capacity to participate in active life and as responsible citizens".

The National Policy on Education, 1986 and its Programme of Action, as reviewed in 1992, envisaged improvement and expansion of education in all sectors, a stress in improvement in quality and relevance of education at all levels, alongwith technical and professional education. The strength of a country either in economy or even in defence depends not in having its material resources but only in having its qualitative people. The quality of people is achieved through only the quality of education. The greatest and the most precious asset of a country is its people as it is they who exploit all natural resources and potentials of a region. Thus, the people form the wealth of a nation. The Task Force on Higher Education and Society appointed by the World Bank and

UNESCO in year 2000 suggested that without more and better education, developing countries would find it difficult to benefit from the global-knowledge-based economy.

The present millennium is witnessing phenomenal global changes and no nation can isolate itself from the process. In the process of global changes and development, India has achieved success in various fields *i.e.*, agriculture, industrialization, modernization, urbanization, trade and commerce, transport, communication, science and technology, production and so on. With the result of these phenomenal changes, educations are expanding at every corner in India, as it is assumed as the Human Resource Development (HRD) in the country. However, after independence, the country has become more conscious to educate her people. Therefore, it has introduced various educational schemes and programmes to attain higher level of education and also to achieve socio-economic as well as overall development. But this educational expansion or change has not taken place for everyone and all sections of society. The Scheduled Castes (S.Cs), Scheduled Tribes (S.Ts) and underprivileged people are still lagging behind in all stages of education. Despite constant efforts both by central and state governments to spread the education of S.Cs., S.Ts and other weaker section, the level of education among them is very low in comparison to general castes and other community and this level of education exhibit high degrees of dispersion and disparities. Majority of them are still away from educational accessibility.

Higher Education in India

At present there are around 247 Universities and 96 Deemed to be Universities, more than 16 thousand colleges, 95 lakh students and 4.5 lakh teachers in India. When India became independent, there were just 18 Universities, 500 colleges, 2.28 lakh students and about 25 thousand teachers. These figures shown in Table – 1 give impression that the massive expansion of higher education has taken place after 1947. However, it is not completely true.

Although, enrollment of 95 lakh students appears to be huge but it accounts only far less than 1% of total population of India. The large population either has no access or does not afford to go for higher education. Therefore, the efforts are needed to be made

Table 1
Some Basic Information on Higher Education in India

Sl.No.		*1947*	*2003-04*
1.	Universities	18	343
2.	Colleges	500	16000
3.	Students	228804	9463821
4.	Teachers	<0.24 lakh	4.36 lakh
5.	Budget	55 crores	> 78000 crores

Source : University News, Aug. 14-20, 2006, Vol. 44, No. 33, p. 3.

to provide the access to higher education to as many people as possible. It is required in the interest of our country. Access to education is first and essential step to empowerment of people. In statistical terms, the number of institutions engaged in providing higher education has increased manifold. The numbers of beneficiaries of this educational set up have grown more than ten times since independence.

As many as 80,000 students in the year 2005 went to USA, UK, Australia, New Zealand and Germany for higher education. The trend is increasing. It is because the quality of education in India at par with the quality in foreign countries, is simply not available. Each student has to spend around Rs. 15 lakh per year. Yet they are going. We need to make introspection to build our institutions qualitative and competitive by world standards. This is essential to save our money as well as to avoid brain drain and to achieve the dream of becoming a developed nation by 2020. India can fulfil the aspirations of younger generation, if and only if, it leads in quality in research, innovation, patenting and hi-tech start ups etc. (Naik, 2006).

Popularisations of education among the masses, including higher education, is the key to human welfare. It is generally accepted that an enrolment rate of atleast 20% of the relevant age group (between 17 and 23) is an essential condition for development today. Whereas the developed countries have crossed the 50% mark, India still lags behind at around nine percent of its total population. Again if we say about Arunachal Pradesh it will be around 7.10% of its total population.

Higher Education in Arunachal Pradesh

In Arunachal Pradesh, the real beginning of formal education started during 1947 when two lower primary schools at Sadiya and Pasighat were established with 100 enrolments comprising both boys and girls. Afterward, another primary school was set up at Riga. Since then, there has been rapid development in the field of education in Arunachal Pradesh.

In this State, higher education started first with the setting-up of Jawaharlal Nehru College at Pasighat in 1964. Next Dera Natung Government College was set up in 1979, gradually, Indira Gandhi Government College in 1986 at Tezu, Bomdila Government College in 1987 at Bomdila, Donyi-Polo Government College in 1996 at Kamki, Rang Fra Government College in 1996 at Changlang and Tirap Government College in 1997 at Deomali. Rajiv Gandhi University (previously Arunachal University) was setup in 1984.Thus, there are at present 7 Government colleges functioning through out the State. Besides, there are three private colleges functioning at Itanagar, Ziro and Pasighat. Out of these colleges, Jawaharlal Nehru College and Dera Natung Government College are imparting general education in Arts, Science and Commerce streams while the remaining colleges are imparting education only in Arts stream. In Indira Gandhi Government College, Arts and Commerce are taught. Higher education in Arunachal Pradesh needs a far-reaching structural reconstruction.

In respect of technical education, there are only three technical institutions. One is North Eastern Regional Institute of Science and Technology (NERIST) established at Itanagar in 1986 with limited seats for the State. In order to fulfil technical manpower requirement of this State, Rajiv Gandhi Polytechnic has been set up at Itanagar in under the World Bank Assisted Project. The institute offers technical level diploma courses in Information Technology, Travel Tourism and Hotel Management, Costume Design and Garment Technology, Herbal Remedies and Cosmetology, Automobile Engineering and Electrical and Electronic Engineering. There is only one private Homeopathic college situated at Itanagar. A Horticulture and Forestry college has been set up in 2002 at Pasighat under the sponsorship of Central Agricultural University, Imphal, Manipur. As there is practically no college for studying in medicine, veterinary, agriculture, fishery etc. under government as well as private sector, students are sent to study these disciplines of Higher and Technical education in the institutions of other states of the country. A number of students are sponsored by the State Government through seat quota allotted to this State by different institutions. Regarding Higher Education in the state some issues and challenges are discussed below.

Issues and Challenges : Arunachal Pradesh cannot side track itself from world-wide trends taking place throughout the globe for adopting strategies regarding higher education for its youth. There are various factors responsible for the present day changes in Higher Education. They are enumerated us under :

(i) Liberalization, Globalization of trade.

(ii) Technological advancement particularly in the field of communication network and systems.

(iii) Government's increasing emphasis on Market Economy.

(iv) Increased international labour mobility.

(v) Growing importance of life-learning.

Quality assurance is one of the central issues in higher education today. The serious issues and challenges including teaching, admission and infrastructure are discussed below. Many countries are moving toward instituting more careful mechanism for quality assurance and regulation of degree offered. International efforts are under way in the field of quality assurance, although national mechanisms are necessarily at the heart of a system of ensuring quality and relevance of higher education. Quality assurance in higher education is one of the central issues of the current period.

1. Present Environment : There are many changes and new challenges in terms of how present environment is affecting internalization and how the growing international dimension of higher education is an agent of change itself. Globalization has been regarded as a powerful and pervasive factor for changing the overall environment. Higher education will have to devise for ways dealing with such changing trends in order to get benefit out of them. The national and international dimensions of higher education are therefore becoming increasingly important and at the same time more complex. It is the national analytical judgement on the part of Central/State Governments to frame and follow higher educational policies for itself and other nationals.

2. **Education Delivery Methods :** Fast changing information and communication technology system demand new education delivery methods to be installed to compete with those using especially on line and satellite based methods. How is it possible for the students of Arunachal who are accustomed to follow the traditional method of classroom lecture using only blackboard to compete with the students of other States, who follow modern methods of teaching? Apart from classroom lecturers, more attention has to be given to the accreditation of these programmes and recognition of qualifications for domestic and cross border education.

3. **Skill Based Vocational and Professional Educational Institutions :** It is the need of the hour for the development of Arunachal Pradesh. This policy would assist unemployed educated youth to find the relevant jobs in their related field of specialization. At the same time this will also provide opportunities for self-employment.

4. **Industry Based Education :** Arunachal Pradesh is endowed with natural resources. The State is presently looking for industries to be established so as to generate income and provide employment. Technology intensive knowledge should be imparted by the professional institutions so as to establish different types of industries in the State where the educated persons get job as per their eligibility. Education without utility is meaningless not only that it will also be harmful to the society.

5. **Higher Education in Arunachal Pradesh Suffers from Many Problems :**

(i) There are insufficient teaching and non-teaching staff in colleges.

(ii) Poor library facility, coupled with no cataloging system, untrained staff and non-computerized, is seen in every college.

(iii) Explosion of student population in D.N. Government College and J.N. College whereas very few students are enrolled in other colleges. The class rooms in D.N. Government College are unable to accommodate the strength of existing students.

(iv) No transfer policy of teaching and non-teaching staff exists in real sense.

(v) Class room teaching persists with conventional method. There is no use of computer with internet, video conferencing, overhead projector, etc.

6. Quality is Systems Improvement : It is an unending journey. It requires a deliberate and persistent attempt in a systematic way. Quality does not come by chance or by accident. The quality in system is every one's job, from top to bottom. People work efficiently in such institution where systems are good. It stands on the following aspects :

- Quality is a continuous improvement *i.e.,* slowly and steadily.
- Quality comes when the teachers are passionate.
- Quality comes through the strategy of better Human Resource Development.
- Quality comes when every teacher succeeds in igniting the minds of students.
- Quality is empowering teachers.
- Quality comes through better teamwork with better co-operation from top to bottom.
- Quality comes when every one works in a systematic way.

Today what we see is not only in this state but throughout the country. The youth of a nation where truth has been the keyword, a part of the national motto Satyameva Jayate is brimming with falsehood, fraud and dishonesty. If students are even partially interested in improvement a way out of the darkness of unknowing into the light of understanding. This will come with the apprehension of our need to awaken and grow; commitment to learning and growing and practical application of ethics and values which may lead to a transformative experience. But it is essential that the soil should be prepared at the level of school which can be richly cultivated in the higher education. Higher education is steadily worsening ethical values in students and there is a dire need to deliberate jointly and to seek solutions. Values may be social, religious, ecological or ethical. Ethical values include one's capacity to be one's own self, to harmonize the contradictions within and to be of service to other. Higher education can enhance qualitatively by giving depth to each curriculum and emphasizing those values of life which are beyond the phenomenal subject and add eternity to education, "Education is not limited to the imparting of information or the training in skills. It has to give the educated a proper sense of values", wrote Radhakrishnan. Students in higher education prepare to take place in administration, industry, commerce and other vital areas of civil life. In the absence of some kind of ethical enlightenment, the specialized knowledge may be used to cause harm to the self or to the society. Therefore, in order to overcome physical, mental, social, moral, national and international crises, higher education must give preponderant place to inculcation of ethical values, even if these constitute a hidden aspect of the curriculum. We, the Indians expect that Higher Education should intend to inculcate in the young students the quality of self-reliance, self potential and self confidence through awareness of the social, intellectual and moral environment, problems of the Indian Society. But it is a bitter truth that common people are badly treated sometimes by the literate people. That is why; today it is high time and essential to insert certain topics in almost all disciplines of higher education to build moral character so as to bring all round development of Arunachal Pradesh. This is a new challenge of higher education particularly in Arunachal Pradesh. Today, students of higher education are self-centered, mad after fleeting promise of pleasure, full of conflicts and therefore dysfunctional. All kinds of ethical value whether related to self like self-esteem, self-respect, self actualization, or interpersonal like tolerance, forgiveness, concern, or social like patriotism, equality and co-operation are conspicuously lacking even in the so-called highly educated young generation. The fire of competition has defeated co-operation just as material gains have replaced misanthropy, as insensitivity stamps minds instead of compassion. To get rid of these problems, ethical values can be cultivated by citing examples from lives of religious and spiritual leaders alongwith extracts from scriptures of the world that are of a universalistic nature. The detached atmosphere of an academic institution can be used to study the deepest ideologies with an open mind.

Ethical values need to be emphasized in higher education because they lead to actualization of innate capacities and elimination of all non-essentials from life. The enlivening influence of high ethical values can promote a flow of creative ideas and all thoughts, emotional states and actions can channelise into a constructive direction. Vivekananda believed that the means of work are as important as the end—if the means are ethical, the end is bound to be productive.

7. Recruitment Policy : The World Wide Web, looming as the cornerstone of the information age has revolutionized methods of learning. Knowledge comes almost knocking at our doors with just a click of the mouse. However, the role of the teacher has become even more crucial in making that available to students which is beyond texts. Our humble entry into the worldwide orbit decidedly expands the scope of our firm commitment to the creation and sustenance of a climate congenial not only to cognitive knowledge but also knowledge which is founded on ethical values and moral standards of import in every walk of life. Students are sublimely influenced by the character and conduct of their teachers. As transformative intellectuals, teachers must address themselves to individual students when they need direction, recognizing the heterogeneity of the class. For example, if he/she spots an over ambitions pupil who wishes to rise at the cost of beheading his/her peers, the teacher should train the student to keep ambition within ethical bounds.

Moral character of students, which will lead him through out his lives, depends upon the moral character of the teachers. That is why; recruitment of teachers especially in higher education must be done very carefully. The candidates aspiring for lectureship must be judged psychologically by a psychologist before recruitment. When entire life of student and the well being of the country depend on the teacher, why is a special strategy for recruitment of lecturer not taken? There is proverb that last is good, all are good. Therefore, teachers of higher education must be unique. Teacher will be like 'Parash Pathar' which will turn the lives of the students into perfect noble persons through teaching. Teachers, in fact, play a more vital role in the society than the administrator at the highest level. Administrators keep on changing and their actions do not have any direct bearing on common men. Teachers on the other hand are role-models for the new generation. Their actions do not only affect everyone but have a bearing on future. It is, therefore, imperative that something should be done to improve the method of recruitment (Jajri 2006).

8. Caste Based Quotas in Higher Education : Reservation in public sector education is a particularly Indian practice enshrined in the constitution, a legal form of affirmative action designed to provide greater opportunities to communities and social groups that have been traditionally deprived and excluded. While the quotas in public sector education that are allocated for Scheduled Castes (S.Cs) and Scheduled Tribes (S.Ts) are now taken for granted in most discussions, the current debate is around the recent decision of the ministry of human resource development to provide quotas for backward castes in all institutions of higher learning funded by the Central Government.

Those who oppose the policy of reservation operate primarily with the following arguments :

- It does not address the basic problem of inadequate expansion and poor quality of public education at elementary and secondary levels.
- It militates against "merit" and allows degrees and qualifications to be awarded with less than deserving aptitude and performance.
- It is "inefficient" compared with openly competitive and therefore implicitly "market-based" systems.
- It creates perceptions of "victimhood" and democratically undesirable identity politics.
- Inequalities within the specified communities allow a "creamy layer" to take advantage of the reservations and benefit unduly while depriving the rest of the community.
- The rigid and inflexible nature of the instrument of reservation does not allow for more creative modes of affirmative action.
- It privileges caste-based discrimination and therefore ignores other and possibly more undesirable forms of exclusion.
- It compresses the notion of social justice into only reservation, instead of encompassing broader socio-

economic policies such as land reform and other asset redistribution, strategies of income generation, etc.

There is certainly some relevance to each of these points. Certainly one would deny that the system that has operated in India thus far has been inadequate not only in addressing these issues, but even in achieving the goals set in terms of filling the allocated quotas for SCs and STs in public education and employment. It is also true that caste-based quotas are relatively crude and blunt instruments to address a very complex socio-economic reality (Jayanti Ghosh, 2006).

The author thinks that as entire development of a nation depends on the quality of education, education should be kept outside of reservation. Admission and recruitment of teacher in educational institution should strictly be considered only on the basis of merit. Only "merit based selection" can ensure to maintain quality of higher education. To bring the backward classes including SCs and STs into the main stream of the nation, government can bear entire economical burden of the SC/ST students so that they cannot feel any want during their study in educational institutions. Again government can give allowance to the poor family from where the student has come to take education. In the state, the 40% of the total population live under BPL. They are mostly living in rural areas. Their Son/daughter engaged in jhum based cultivation are their livelihood. Jhum is a labour intensive and low productivity based cultivation. That is why, they cannot afford to send their son/daughter for higher education. Those who afford their son/daughter for education should be given allowances. The most common argument against reservations is that they will affect quality and undermine "merit". But the supposed contradiction between reservations on the one hand, and merit and efficiency, on the other, is a false one.

We all agree that there is a huge demand for higher education in the country, and that good quality in higher education is extremely under-provided. Therefore, there is severe rationing for places, especially in the best institutions. The question is, therefore, not whether we should have rationing or not, but which form of rationing is the best in the prevailing social circumstances. If we accept that intelligence and talent are not the monopoly of any particular social group but are normally distributed across society, then this means that the current system is inefficient since it is effectively picking up candidates from only a small section of society instead of the whole population. It is elementary logic that this would give sub-optimal results for society. This is an argument on social efficiency grounds, which is quite separate from other arguments about creating a more democratic and inclusive education process in general. Caste-based reservations are often critiqued on more sophisticated grounds as well. One criticism is that they promote unhealthy forms of identity politics that distract from more substantive and critical social issues.

In context of the current system of reservation, the author opines in this way that the basic issue, of course, is that the roots of discrimination go so deep that social and economic disparities are deeply intertwined, although in increasingly complex ways. In this imperfect world, none of the proposed solutions is perfect either: The choice is between imperfect instruments with different degrees of effectiveness. That is why we still need reservations for different groups in higher education – not because it is the perfect instruments to rectify long-standing discrimination, but because it is still the most workable method to move in this direction. And most of all, because the nature of Indian society ensures that without such measures social discrimination and exclusion will only persist and be strengthened.

9. Examination system : In our university examination pattern, there is a frequent possibility of errors arising from erratic marking on answer books. It has been practically observed that :

(i) The standard of marking varies from teacher to teacher.

(ii) Again, the standard of marking varies from same teacher in two different points of time.

(iii) Some teachers are more liberal than others in evaluating answer books.

(iv) Some of teachers are interested to evaluate as many answer books as possible within a minimum time to get maximum remuneration. This practice is always a disadvantage to the brilliant students.

(v) Sometimes, some numbers of answer books are evaluated by university teacher and some of same papers are evaluated by collegiate teacher. There must be a possibility of differentiating in marking.

In such a manner, examination papers are quite failure to test the ability of the students to catch the facts, interpretation and application of knowledge.

How to overcome these problems : The following steps may be suggested :

(a) Every answer book may be evaluated by two teachers without writing the marks on answer book. If the two marks differ beyond 15, the answer book will go to third examiner and two nearest marks will be considered and taken average.

(b) If possible, single paper may be evaluated by single examiner.

(c) Re-evaluation will be considered on student's demand.

The author thinks that

(i) In most states, the teaching skill and level of knowledge of a teacher is not taken into consideration in assessing performance of a teacher. Generally, the qualifications, programmes attended and papers presented and publications are taken into consideration. Unfortunately, skill in teaching has been overlooked at the time of selection of higher education teachers of different categories or at the time of promotion to a higher post.

(ii) There is a need of major shift of attention to make education as a priority sector in respect to higher education as well as primary education. The development of education urgently requires a shift in focus to bring out intensive educational programmes to achieve higher level of education.

(iii) There is a need of quick implementation of strong and effective education policies in the state. For this, a monitoring body should be constituted under the supervision of high cabinet level and action should be taken against the persons and officers who show any negligence.

The policy maker has to develop the higher education by equalizing the syllabi as national standard so that our students can compete with the outside students in the job market in order to be employed in the outside of the State.

Again, the State Government has to create more and more jobs in the state so as to engage the higher educated persons because, unemployment problem can give birth of another problem.

(iv) The authority should innovate such type of higher education which may help the educated persons to be self employed. In all the institutions of higher education, job oriented vocational courses should be imparted. For competitive examinations at state and national level, the student should be provided special coaching at all the centres of higher education.

(v) Higher proportion of the State's budget needs to be spent towards the development of higher education.

(vi) As education among schedule tribe suffers due to acute poverty, unemployment and lack of awareness, however, the younger one should be provided full financial supports and scholarships and older one counselling and guidance.

(vii) It is also essential to create a congenial atmosphere in the State. For this, government and people's participation is equally required.

(viii) Quality of teaching can be improved only when teachers get feedback regarding their teaching. This can be ascertained only through inspection of classes. Inspections may be carried out by Director, Principal or other officers.

(ix) Provision should be made to give minimum facilities to the students to get healthy environment in the college campus and admission will be regulated according to the capacity of the college.

Many years ago, Gurudev Rabindranath Tagore had suggested teaching skill test for selection of higher education teachers. The NET conducted by UGC needs to reconsider its strategies for recognizing good scholar. But the good scholar may not be good communicator *i.e.*, may be a bad teacher. For selection of teacher, class teaching should be given more weightage. The methods of recruiting teachers may be reorganized to ensure merit, objectivity and conformity with spatial and functional requirements. The pay and service conditions of teacher should be commensurated to attract talent to this profession.

The whole study demonstrates a very complex scenario and suggests that there is a need of change of people's mind and attitude and put collective efforts to improve education level of schedule tribe in the state. The realization of dream may be possible, if the government takes strong and effective steps in the implementation of state's education policies with this assumption that education is the essence of human beings and the best contraceptive to socio-economic development.

Last but not the least, the author thinks that today's people of the State requires that type of education which must be equipped with the skills needed to face the challenges of 21st century. This requires that the education providers or the higher authority of education has to study the changing needs of the students from time to time. The challenges ahead are for the policy makers of higher education who should take initiative to serve the hitherto neglected interests of students.

I strongly believe that the effective and dedicated teachers have profound impact on the success and lives of their students. The quality of academic standards is inextricably linked with the quality of inputs received by the students and the quality of education of any country depends on many factors and one of the crucial factors is teacher competence. The teacher competence in turn depends mostly on their own capacity as well as quality of training and other support provided to them.

Without educating girls, the state can never brings all round development as women constitute a half of its total population. The State should enforce women's empowerment through higher education by providing facilities such as bearing total educational expenses coupled with healthy environment in colleges like separate rest room for leisure period in co-education colleges and separate girls' college, etc. Female literacy, particularly in rural areas, in our country is extremely low, the drop-out rate among girls is very high. Girls are normally burdened with household chores. They are deprived of education and exposure to the outside world and therefore, they remain ignorant and superstitious. There is a need to convince the illiterate parents for girls' education vis-à-vis motivating these parents for adult education programmes. Female students can interact with such girls and persuade their mothers for their enrolment in colleges/schools. Cognitive empowerment of women carries her to self-confidence and self-reliance i.e., psychological empowerment which can lead to further social action or economic activity that stimulates political and economic empowerment. Different academic strategies and other plans are drawn out for this purpose. Training and education for empowerment of women in the state result in individual empowerment and social transformation whereby, women have more control over their lives and more of an effect in the changing society to eliminate and reduce gender bias and discrimination. President *A.P.J. Abdul Kalam*, said "empowering women is a prerequisite for creating a good nation, when women are empowered, society with stability is assured. Empowerment of women is essential as their thoughts and their value systems lead the development of a good family, good society and ultimately a good nation".

REFERENCES

1. Agarwal, Pawan (2006), *"Higher Education Policy"*, EPW, Nov. 11-17, Vol. XLI, No. 45, p. 4645.
2. Dongaonkar, D. (2004), *"Higher Education in India : The Varies Dimension"*, University News, 42(21).
3. Ghosh, Jayanti (2006), *"Case for Caste-based Quotas in Higher Education"*, EPW, Vol. XVI, No. 24, p. 2428 – 2432.
4. Jajri, H.A.S (2006), *"Higher Education : Maladies and Remedies"*, University News, Oct. 23-29, Vol. 44, No. 43, p. 2.
5. Joseph, Thomas (2006), *"Higher Education in the changing Global Scenario"*, University News, April, 03-09, p. 2.
6. Kale, R.K. (2006), *"Higher Education and Development of the Nation"*, University News, Aug. 14–20, Vol. 44, No. 33, p. 2-3.
7. Mishra, P.N., Singh, A.K. and Tripathi, B.K. (2006), *"Human Resource Management : An Emerging Area of Research in Institutions of Higher Learning"*, University News, Vol. 44, No. 35, August 28—Sept.' 2003, p. 1–6.
8. Mahapatra, P.C. (2006), *"Opportunities and Challenges to Higher Education,"* University News, Vol. 45, No. 01, January 01-07, p. 1.
9. Motiram (2006), *"Scheduled Castes' Education in India : Issues and Challenges,"* University News, March 27–April '02, p. 1-5.
10. Mohanty, Sunil Behari (2006), *"Does the Nation Need a New National Policy on Education for High Quality Higher Education?"*, University News, Vol. 44, No. 38, Sept. 18–24, p. 6 -7.
11. Naik, B. M. (2006), *"Quality Assurance System in Higher and Technical Education: Can we afford to ignore it?"* University News, July 24–30, Vol. 44, p. 10.

9

Privatisation and Quality Assurance in Higher Education

—*Utpal Talukdar*

Higher educations are subject to higher pressures due to the mounting demand and, bigger gap and possible allocation of resources from public fund, with the centre and state governments' constraints to allocate more funds towards the same.

Introduction

Since independence, higher education in India has had an extremely fast growth rate. 'India' has now the 3rd largest higher educational network in the world with 256 Universities and 11089 Colleges with a total enrolment of 74 lakhs and an annual expenditure of more than 100 crores. With the advent of globalization and the transformation of education as a tradable commodity, the sector of education has undergone a sea-change. 'Quality' has become the catchwood. It is the need to assure quality in higher education that prompted the University Grants Commission (UGC) to establish National Assessment and Accreditation Council (NAAC) as an autonomous body on September 16, 1994, under section 12 CCC of the UGC Act of 1956, (3). The NAAC's objectives are assessment and accreditation of HEIs (institutions of higher education), assisting Institutions to develop own procedures, techniques and modalities for self-evaluation and enduring optimized use of resources of the Institutions.

In this regard privatization plays dual role of quality assurance as well as reducing the financial constraints in higher education. Higher Education is being subjected to higher pressures of demand and cause quaintly, bigger gap and possible allocation of resources from public fund, with the Centre and State governments finding difficult to allot more funds, a financial crisis is looming large in the higher education sector. It is faced with a dilemma of satisfying the growing aspirations of the youth for university education, on the one hand, and government's inability to meet with its meager resources, on the other.

Privatisation—Future Scenario and Challenges

In our increasing independent and competitive world, where Communication and technological innovations have no boundaries, nations can thrive only on healthy, literate and well-trained population. Efficiency and investment in education must have the highest priority. Preparatory discussions on such aspects of self-financing courses be initiated because if we fix target for expansion of self-financing courses, there will be no more pressure on the entire higher education system in the country. Self-financing should be demand as well as performance driven.

The Indian higher education has some challenges before it. It should be :

- Cost effective
- Relevant to the country's need
- High quality and
- Self supporting.

Under the difficult economic situation and political constraints, restructuring and revitalizing the entire system of Indian higher education would be difficult challenges both to resolve and to find resources. In future, the private sector has to play a great role in the provision of high quality programmes that are more appropriate in terms of quality and relevance to the India's rapidly changing market pressures in the form of technologies and work organisations. Indian scenario, in favour of greater resource diversification and greater self-financing of publicly funded colleges and universities, is getting in clear focus.

Privatisation and Quality Assurance in Higher Education

Based on the reflection that on Quality Criteria and parameters and the possibilities and merits of various best practices under the NAAC parameters of Quality, private Institution of higher learning has been forced to maintain the quality and standards. In this regard a private Institution of higher education in Arunachal Pradesh—Saint Claret College, Ziro has established the internal quality assurance cell in recognition of the relevance and significance of Institutionalization of monitoring mechanisms for quality sustenance and enhancement, as advocated by NAAC. Though the NAAC has made IQAC mandatory for Institutions following their first accreditation, the Saint Claret College, mandates it for itself, in tune with its uncompromising commitment to quality and excellence. The Institution has adopted following measures under NAAC parameters of quality.

Criterion I—Curricular Aspects

- Institution has drafted its Mission Statement, Hierarchy of Core Values, a 7-point Objectives.
- Through Prospectus, Handbook, TOP, and SOP, communicate them systematically to all constituencies.
- To suit the Institution's Mission and Objectives, the college has introduced PESEC programmes, DCA, Additional Units, Term Exams, CHEP, Associations etc.
- The Range of programme is not great. Add-on Courses try to compensate them.
- Feedback on programme is sought from lecturers and additional units are created.
- Staff Exchange Programmes with other Institutions.

Criterion II – Teaching-Learning and Evaluation

- Well conceived Academic Calendar.
- Departmental Planning and Benchmarking.
- Innovative Programmes: Zero Hours; CHEP Hours; SCALE; Departmental Fests; SCCZ Quiz Hour; Additional Units - Unit '0' and Unit 'A+'; Library Hour; DCA etc.
- Question Banks

- Academic Journal with Weekly ATRs.
- Audio-Visual aids.
- Student Assessment Procedures : Monthly Assessment Tests, Three Term Examination, Continuous Internal Assessment Report with Grading and Percentile Ranking, Monthly Attendance Bulletins, Term-wise Attendance and Examination Marks Report for Parents, Individualized Mentoring.
- Staff Recruitment : From diverse states, based on UGC Parameters, Departmental Verification of the Applications, Interview and demo class.
- Quality Assurance and enhancement through IQAC.
- Open and Participative Mechanisms: Senior Claretine Council Meetings, Monthly Core Claretine Council Meetings.
- Teachers forever encouraged for academic updating and professional development.
- Faculty Evaluation by students and peers.

Criterion III – Research, Consultancy and Extension

- Research and Publications mandated by service rule and promotional criteria.
- Computer Literacy for the Staff and Computer facility in the Staff Room.
- Consultancy is encouraged.
- PESEC Extension Programmes, CASA interventions in the community, NSS Unit.

Criterion IV – Infrastructure and Learning Resources

- Sufficient number of classrooms, Library, Computer Lab, Geography Lab, Anthropology Lab, Staff Room, Auditorium, Food Court.
- On-Campus Hostel Facility for 100 girls and 30 boys.
- Incremental growth to keep pace with the academic growth is facilitated.
- Optimal use of infrastructure by evening courses, summer courses.

- Library open from 8.00 am to 8.00 pm; Computer Lab facilities open for staff, students, and outsiders.
- Sports facilities as of now; football, volleyball, badminton, table tennis, other indoor games.

Criterion V – Student Support and Progression

- Detailed information to students through prospectus, handbook, SOP.
- Scholarships offered to meritorious students, besides Governmental Stipend for APSTs.
- Hostel facilities, Transportation facilities of students.
- Support services through personalized mentoring, career guidance reference books, remedial through study circles and peer teaching.
- Job-oriented add-on course like DCA, DTP course.
- Alumni Association.
- Student Evaluation of the staff and the college facilities.

Criterion VI – Organization and Management

- Academic and administrative planning are realized through various offices by the management.
- Organizational structure : Provincial Council, North East Delegation Council, Governing Body, Advisory Council, Management Committee, Core Staff Council, Senior Claretine Council, Junior Claretine Council, HoDs and Co-ordinators, Students Animators.
- Quality Assurance through IQAC.
- Government through principle of participation and transparency, by means of SCC and Monthly Core Staff Council Meeting and discussions.
- Self Appraisals, Peer Appraisal, Student Appraisals for the Staff.
- Budgeting and auditing procedures are regular and standardized, following the Province norms.

Criterion VII – Healthy Practices

- Social Responsiveness of the Institution through

employment oriented add-on courses like DCA, DTP, CASA Days, and Scholarships.

- 'Danyi Reela' School Fest for promotion of traditional tribal culture and language.
- Value-based education through CHEP, SOP, CASA etc.
- Annual TOP, SOP, FEP.
- College Week 'RESONANCE'.

Suggestions

After the discussion on the issue regarding privatization and quality assurance, author makes the following suggestions for the furtherance of excellence in HEIs. Every Institution of higher learning should establish Internal Quality Assurance Cell (IQAC), which monitors the initiatives under the seven criteria of quality. Every Institution should develop clear Mission Statements and Objectives. It is beneficial to have a 'Vision Document' for a seven year period, based on which yearly action plan can be chalked out and implemented. Institutionalization and Documentation of the systems and process is a must for validating initiatives and making sure its continuity and sustainability.

There is an urgent need to revamp the teaching-learning processes and evaluation. Since the academic standards of entering students are generally poor, it is essential to introduce bridge courses and remedial teaching. It is useful to have a diagnostic test immediately after admission to identify students who would need special coaching and provide for the same. And the students who are of great potential can be given enrichment courses too. However, care has to be taken in order to avoid any harmful labeling or branding which could be counter-productive.

Adoption of innovative teaching methods is an absolute necessity. Enhanced teaching aids, use of audio-visual accessories, language labs, computer applications in traditional subjects, etc will go a long way in preventing the student absenteeism and facilitating greater appreciation of classroom teaching. Unless teaching/learning is made fun and play, student-folk rarely gets attracted to the classrooms.

Infra-structural development is a must for ensuring quality. While nurturing its own colleges, the government should provide financial assistance for basic infra-structural needs of the private colleges too, as they are functioning at geographically and structurally handicapped conditions. Providing such assistance can only hasten the drive towards excellence and quality.

To have quality measures and quality assurance, the governments, the managements, the staff and the students – every stakeholder in education – should join and play their parts with great commitment. Such synergy is indeed, possible and the latest trends that are seen in the state are promising.

REFERENCES

B. Donald (1990), Higher Education—Cass ell Educational Limited.

Altbach, P. G. (1987), *Higher Education in the Third World, Themes and Variations*, Radiant Publishers, New Delhi.

Mohanty. J. (2000), *Current Trends in Higher Education*, Deep & Deep Publications Pvt. Ltd., New Delhi,

Paulson, V.V. (2005), *The Need of the Hour in Higher Education in Arunachal Pradesh*, The Arunachal Times, Itanagar.

Sethi, J.D. (1987), *The Crisis and Collapse of Higher Education in India*, Vikas Publishing House Pvt. Ltd., New Delhi.

Das, B.C., Gogoi K.P (Nov. 2002), *"Relevance of Higher Education Today"*, *Edutracks*. Neelkamal Publications, Hyderabad.

Lewis, R. G., Smith, D. H. (1998), *Total Quality in Higher Education*, Vanity Books International, New Delhi.

Stella, Antony (2004), *Best Practices in Higher Education*, Report of the National Conference organized by NAAC , Bangalore.

University News, June, 1994.

University News, December, 2000.

University News, November, 2002.

University News, December, 2002.

Journal of Higher Education, 1998, Vol. 21.

10

Education as a Key to Women Empowerment in Arunachal Pradesh : A Perspective

—Debashis Neogi

In order to achieve equitable and inclusive human development, women need to be equally empowered like men counterparts for which increase in women literacy is the first concern.

Introduction

The history of evolution of mankind is not as simple as is understood in common parlance. More complex, however, is the process of development of this mankind. From time immemorial, the civil society has been continuously subject to such developmental interventions. Scientific experiments, social revolutions and economic reforms – all have a single agenda at their core – progress of this mankind. However, these are not the sole determinants of the advancement. Infact, the extent, to which the society is able to translate such changes to their every day living, counts more. No society is perfect by birth. A progressive society is always sincere to accommodate those changes, which are deemed necessary in the ever-changing time frame. At the same time, these changes are not often welcome by the orthodoxies. These are the shocks. The real test of the society lies in its shock absorption capacity. Such capacities are, in turn, evolved from the fundamental ethos – which also forms the backbone of the societal structure. The society's capacity to incorporate the better and develop, ultimately, determines its future prospect. In this sense, the process of capacity building is crucial. Here lies the importance of education. As a matter of fact, education is considered as the only effective instrument of capacity building. There is always a high degree of correlation between the attainment of education and the level of development. The notion is true both at the macro level as also at the micro level.

If education plays a pivotal role in designing the course of development, it is the women folk that form the primary element of the development process. Due to the historically accorded status and also because of the socio-cultural prejudices, women in general are identified as the vulnerable section of the society. The deprivations of women are significantly visible in various macro indicators like education, health, employment etc. In different spheres of life they are also subject to a lot of hurdles, which are necessarily gender specific. But they are the mothers, daughters and wives, without whom no home and no society can exist. So, sincere effort is urgently required for the emancipation of women from all distress. However, the pre-requisite in the process is their empowerment and the initiatives for empowerment should, obviously, begin with education.

Unfortunately, the global scenario in women education is disappointing. As per UNESCO estimate for 1995, it was found that the extent of gender disparity was wide spread. The worst affected regions were South Asia with 37% female literacy as compared to 63% literacy of their male counterpart. For the Arabian states, these figures were 44% and 68% and for Sub-Saharan Africa these were 47% and 66% respectively. All these regions are identified as the less developed ones. Excepting the developed countries, and Latin America and the Caribbean, the enrollment of female in school is lower than the male at all the age groups. According to UNESCO, "the largest single category of persons denied equality of education opportunity in world today" is female. In India the male-female gap in literacy rate, though decreasing, is still high. It was 18.30% in 1951, which increased significantly to 26.62% in 1981. But since then it is falling and now in 2001 the figure is 21.70%. The female literacy is alarmingly low. As per 2001 population census, it is 54.16%. In Arunachal Pradesh, the rate stands at 44.24%. Comparing what it was in 1971 (3.71%), remarkable improvement is achieved in female education in the state. But there is still a lot of ground to cover.

The significance of women empowerment has gathered momentum over the years. It is also reflected in the recent Union Budgets of the Government of India. The initial years of planning in India had opted for development on the basis of trickle down theory. However, in reality the fruits of development did not trickle down and the weaker section of the society, including women, remained excluded. Taking note of the adverse state of health and education among women, the Government of India, besides its large number of ongoing projects, has decided, to provide a substantial budgetary support to these gender related issues. The 7th Five Year Plan had adopted the Women's Component Plan (WCP) to initiate a mechanism for identifying and monitoring the schemes, directly benefiting women. In the 9th Plan, provision was made for allocating unconditional minimum quantum of funds for the women welfare related schemes run by the different Ministries/Departments. The WCP was the precursor of Gender Budgeting. The 10th Plan went a step further when it decided to launch Gender Budgeting. In 2004–05, the Ministry of Women and Child Development, Government of India had adopted "Budgeting for Gender Equity" as a Mission Statement. Finally based on the recommendations of the Ashok Lahiri Committee on 'Classification of Budgetary Transactions', the Government of India has introduced a statement on Gender budgeting in Union Budget 2005–06. It included 10 demands for grants. The unabated importance of gender sensitivities is again reflected in the Union Budget 2006–07, when the number of demand for grants increased to 24. The Gender Budgeting is, now, well institutionalized in India. The Draft Approach Paper to the 11th Five Year plan aimed "Towards Faster and More Inclusive Growth" (Planning Commission, June 14, 2006). Its objective is to include the excluded and it gives stress on 'Gender Balancing'. All these steps echo the concern of the nation for women, for their overall development, and thus empowerment. The Government has recognized that education is the primary step towards women's empowerment. The policy of the Government gives stress on of removal of illiteracy among women and all the hurdles towards their access to education. Sarva Shiksha Abhiyan, the flagship scheme of the Government of India for universalisation of elementary education, is specially focused towards the underprivileged sections of the society, including the girl child. Schemes of residential schools for scheduled caste girls in backward areas and the provision of scholarships to the scheduled caste and scheduled tribe students with special emphasis on girls, implemented by the Ministry of Social Justice and Empowerment, have added further impetus to women's education. The proposed scheme of Kasturba Gandhi Swatantrata Vidyalaya, the residential schools for girls will take the elementary education for girls in India a step further. Beside basic education, enough emphasis is also given for higher education of women. In India, at present, there are as many as 1578 women's colleges. Along with this, there are five universities exclusively for women. Today the importance of education in capacity building and empowerment is no longer any unfamiliar notion. If basic education forms the preliminary step of women's progress, the higher education is, perhaps, the best medium to ensure social, economic and political empowerment of women in India. When one talks about women empowerment, the topic involves a large number of issues like economic opportunity, social equality, political representation, participation in governance, property right and personal right. The agenda is always to remove the gender-based asymmetry in all the events.

Social Empowerment

In India, for a long time, the five-year plans have been trying to address the women's problems. But empowerment simply through provision of a few income-generating schemes has definitely been insufficient to ensure a better quality of life for the women. Today women are subject to frequent domestic violence, sexual harassment and social subjugation. Empowerment will lead them to learn to protect themselves from such evils. In fact, the Constitution of India has made provisions to assure gender equity. Article 14 talks about equal rights and opportunities in political, economic and social spheres. Article 15 prohibits discrimination on the basis of sex. Article 15(3) enables affirmative discrimination in favour of women. Article 39 provides option for equal means of livelihood and equal pay for equal work. Article 42 provides just and humane conditions of work and maternity relief. Article 51 (A)(e) mentions fundamental duty to renounce practices, derogatory to women's dignity. Besides, there are a number of women specific Legislations like Immoral Traffic (Prevention) Act, 1956; The Maternity Benefit Act 1961; The Dowry Prohibition Act, 1961; Indecent Representation of Women (Prohibition) Act, 1986; The Commission of Sati (Prevention) Act, 1987 and Protection of Women from Domestic Violence Act, 2005.

What the women need is to understand their rights and become aware of these legal provisions. The only possible way to sensitize women in this regard is through imparting education to women. Of course, one can think of the role of higher education in this 'real empowerment' process. An educated woman – an empowered woman can take note of the legal options available to her and take adequate measure to safeguard her dignity in the society.

As today's daughters are tomorrow's mothers, they must understand the advancement of medical sciences and reap its benefit to the maximum extent. They must have thorough knowledge regarding safe sex. It is only through women's awareness, the deadly deceases like HIV-AIDS can be wiped out from the society. The would-be mothers should be aware of the safe process of delivery while giving birth to a child. Unlike the past practices, today, the best place of maternal delivery is the authorized health centers where the services of doctors, trained nurses and midwives are available. After becoming mother, the responsibility of mother further increases, as she, now, will have to be cautious for the health and hygiene of her child. The infants need to be vaccinated regularly. Here also the level of awareness of the mother is crucial.

But unfortunately, on many occasions, the tribal women of Arunachal Pradesh seem to be lacking such awareness. Still a significantly large number of births in the rural parts take place at home without caring for the safety and hygiene of the mother and the baby. In spite of intensive counselling by different government and non-government agents even in the remote areas, every year many children are left out of the 'free' vaccine programmes. Lack of any formal education is grossly responsible for such social ignorance. To get rid of such deficiencies we have to ensure cent percent female literacy. In fact, more than literacy, emphasis should be given for imparting quality education to the womenfolk.

Economic Empowerment

The Second World War, the partition of the nation and the famine—the concurrent occurrence of these events has brought in some real advancement to the Indian women. The economic crises had compelled the female members of the family to break all the social barriers and go out of the house in search of some decent jobs, beside their male counterparts, only to provide financial support to their families. However, there can be no denying the fact that to get social status on the equal footing with male, female need to have access to decent job and become self-reliant. The Government of India has initiated a number of self-employment schemes, especially for women. If we consider the case of Arunachal Pradesh, the women folk of this predominantly rural state are skilled by birth. In the tribal society, along with their male counterpart, the women are also engaged in income generating activities. They weave beautiful clothes, prepare handicraft items with bamboo, cane and stone. They also make brass-made traditional ornaments. However, their talents and skills are under utilized as majority of them are uneducated and are unable to explore the business potential of the products they produce. Today, when employment opportunity in government sector is squeezing day by day, women, like men, must inculcate the spirit of entrepreneurship in them. They can, thus, be engaged in gainful self-employment.

Women, in the unorganized sector, face with various difficulties. They do not have access to credit. They work as the wage labourers and so they are poor. The World Bank Report (1991) has mentioned that the women are the central to the success of poverty alleviation efforts in short run, medium run and long run. For this, women empowerment should be in proper direction. One of the effective ways is to organize women into groups. The New Industrial Policy of India has enough ingredients to encourage women in industrial activities. It has redefined 'Women's Units' as those units in which women have majority share and management control and has provided with some special facilities including concessions for the women entrepreneurs. The Self Help Groups (SHGs) of women try to develop the entrepreneurial ability among the rural women. But, the most serious problem, which many of the SHGs face today, is inefficient management of finances and inability to understand the market. As a result, on many occasions, the members of the groups fail to repay the credit. As most of them are illiterate, they are unable to understand the ethics of business and credit. This, in turn, brings the business prospect of the group to low ebb. Education, however, can make the much-needed difference here. Since an educated woman is an empowered woman, she can utilize the spirit of SHG to the fullest extent and eventually emerge as a successful woman entrepreneur.

In Arunachal Pradesh, like in the other rural parts of the country, the women are mostly engaged in household work. Besides, they also look after the cattle and help the male members of the family in cultivation. Like other hilly regions, the female members of the family are more active here. As per 2001 population census, in Arunachal Pradesh, about 39% of the total workforce is female. Out of that 30% is engaged in cultivation; 2% is agricultural labourers, 0.41% is working in household industries and about 7% is other category's workers. Unfortunately, majority of these women are illiterate. As a result, they are quite ignorant about the scientific advancement in agriculture. Often, the efforts of the extension workers also go to astray due to their inability to grasp the preaching of these extension workers. If women had received at least the basic education, the outcome would have been different all together. The reflection of education could enrich the quality of life of these rural women.

The National Policy for Empowerment of Women 2001 has given stress on abolition of illiteracy among women. It has also decided that all the impediments in the way to their access to basic education, their participation in vocational, technical and professional education should be removed. The Government of India has ensured elimination of discrimination on the basis of sex in various vocational and professional educational courses. The educational institutes are also encouraged to design the courses for capacity building of women to enable them to take up jobs in the vast globalized market.

Political Empowerment

Mikhail Gorbachev, the President of erstwhile Soviet Union once remarked "the status of women is a barometer of the democratism of any state, an indicator of how human rights are respected in it". However, women, in a country like India, are still identified as one of the weaker sections of the society. For a long time the rate of women participation in India's political processes is low. Because of the typical characteristics of the men-dominated society, the women often do not have any decision making power in the power politics. Barring a few cases, the number of women contesting in the electoral proceedings in India is significantly low. The low participation rate in governance and administration has resulted in inadequate attention given to the core issues of women welfare. At this point it must be mentioned that the low level of education among the women can not be overlooked. The inadequate education is held responsible for such plight of the women folk of the country. However, their exclusion from the political activities has generated resentment among the women. Since the eighties the issue of women empowerment has started to emerge as an important component of the development priorities in India and the political empowerment of women has become a buzz-word among the policy makers. The 73rd and the 74th Constitutional Amendment Acts introduced in 1992 have ushered in a new era for the Indian women. The reservation of one-third of the total seats for women in all the elected offices in both rural and urban local bodies has further strengthened the democracy in India. Efforts are also there for reservation of 30% of seats in the State Legislative Assemblies and in the Parliament. By ensuring women participation in governance, the Acts have paved the way for efficient redressal of women's problems. It has also been effective to let the women be aware of their legitimate rights.

Even though sincere efforts on part of the Government has opened the door for political empowerment of women in India, its outcome depends much on the capacity of woman to understand her responsibility and deliver goods in desired direction. Here again lies the importance of education. Education not only leads to acquiring of knowledge, but also makes one matured enough to understand the policy matters and take wise decisions in governance. However, of late, a change has started to become visible in women literacy across the entire nation. Arunachal Pradesh is also no exception to that. Without getting indulged into the debate whether it is the political empowerment which has encouraged the women folk to pursue education or it is the other way round, it can be claimed that it has really improved the status of women in the society. The women participation in governance, at least at the grass root level, is highly promising. The number of women in the Panchayat Raj Institutions in the state at present is really impressive. At the Gram Panchayat, it is 2597 against the male number 3934. In Anchal Samities, the total number of women is 572 with that of men being 1073. Among the Zilla Parishad Members, 46 are women, while 92 are men. Out of the total number of District Chairpersons, 6 are from female category as against 8 from its male counterpart. This is a landmark in the development history of women in this border state. Such an increased political consciousness has changed the socio-economic lives of women in Arunachal Pradesh. Now, the women folk are well aware of their surroundings and the demand-supply nexus in the market driven economy. As a result, the educated, empowered mothers motivate their girl children not only to become literate, but also to pursue higher education and contribute to the society.

Conclusion

In the words of Dr. A.P.J. Abdul Kalam, the President of India, "Empowering women is a prerequisite for creating a good nation, when women are empowered, society with stability is assured. Empowerment of women is essential as their thoughts and their value systems lead to the development of a good family, good society and ultimately a good nation". The need for education in overall empowerment of women is not any new concept in India. Long back, Eshwar Chandra Vidyasagar, Raja Ram Mohan Roy etc. had pioneered renaissance in India. They recognized women education as an instrument to end the subjugation of women to male domination. A lot of reference regarding the role of education in women empowerment is there in the Indian literature. For instance, 'Kamal' in Sarat Chandra Chattopadhaya's novel 'Shesh Prashna' was highly educated. She had dared to ignore all the social prejudices and went ahead. The character 'Sucharita' in Rabindranath Tagore's famous novel 'Gora' is an ideal example of education led women empowerment. 'Ghare Baire', another novel of Tagore, has mentioned about a husband, who had keen interest in his wife's education and did not even hesitate to arrange tuition to teach her English and hired an English lady for that purpose. Again, in Asha Purna Devi's trilogy, the characters 'Satyavati', 'Subarna Lata' and 'Bakul' not only became educated by their own zeal, but were also able to spread the spirit of women's education and women empowerment among their kith and kins.

Undoubtedly, over the years, tremendous advancement is noticed in women's education and women's empowerment across all the sections of the Indian society. But the advancement has not been collective. Still we find the Roop Kanwars and Sati system in our rural parts. Till now, whatever progress we have managed to secure are mainly confined to the urban areas. The Dalits and other lower caste people in the rural parts still lack proper education and as a result, nothing significant has been achieved in their empowerment, notwithstanding innumerable attempts – sincere indeed, made by the Government in this direction. There is an urgent need to find the causes of low female literacy level among the scheduled castes and scheduled tribe population of our country and accordingly choose the suitable measures for their upliftment.

The issue of women's education and women's empowerment has assumed further significance in a state like Arunachal Pradesh. Given its geo-political identities and strategic sensitivities, it is an urgent requirement here to widen the 'development net' across all the sections of the tribal society. The women in this part of the world are more laborious, more skilled and more competent to look after their families. What they lack is quality education. Though over the years, more and more girl child are coming to schools, attention must be given to ensure their participation in the higher education. Beside one university, seven Government Colleges along with a few privately run colleges are there in the state. But the rate of participation of women in higher education is not uniform. Sincere effort is required for even spread of the spirit of higher education. Though provision of some relaxations, like readmission of failed girl students to the undergraduate courses, are there, some extra incentives are still required. In this regard, the establishment of an exclusively girls' institution for running courses from class I in elementary education to the final year at the undergraduate level will not be a bad investment. The institute should be a residential one and should provide the best of the facilities to mould the talents of the tribal girl students both in curricular and extra curricular activities. It can again be a good platform to launch the careers of these students in academics, in sports or in cultural activities. The residential education system will also prevent early marriage of the girl children, which, apart from restricting population explosion, will have a far reaching impact on the overall development of Arunachal Pradesh.

REFERENCES

1. Ghadially, Rehana (eds.) (1985), *Women in Indian Society*, Sage Publications, New Delhi.
2. George Zeidenstuen (1987), *Women and Development*, World Development Report, No. 6 & 7.
3. Indira Hirway and Anil K. Roy, *"Women in Agriculture and Rural Development"*, Indian Journal of Agricultural Economics, Vol. 54, No. 3, July-September 1999, pp. 251–271.
4. Chadha, G.K. and P.P. Sahu (2002), *"Post Reform Setbacks in Rural Employment, Issues that Need Further Scrutiny"*, Economic Political Weekly, Vol. 37, No. 21, May 25-31, pp. 1998–2096.
5. Various Official Reports of Government of Arunachal Pradesh.
6. Various Official Reports of Government of India.

SECTION—III
Normative Dimensions

11

Compulsions to Commitment : The Value Dynamics of Higher Education

R.B. Tripathy

There is a need to prepare a report that would to identify teachers who are not up-to the mark as examiners and have been ruining the live of the students by marking neglectfully or ignorantly.

Higher education managers have been attracting adverse comments relating to impropriety, corruption, incompetence. In reply to all these allegations, we academicians tend to sit in ivory towers and never feel we are under public scanner. Heads, resting on shoulders, belong to people, but ideas which work in their heads are of ruling class. Paper bullet is more effective means of controlling masses than the bullets of the gun. When heads of the people can be filled easily with ideas of ruling classes, where is the necessity of breaking them? This is a paradox, definitely an illusion. This drives we stakeholders of higher education to adhere to changing dynamics of higher education. Conforming to the objectives the author prefers examination system and science education as preferred value dynamics of higher education.

View presented is product of author's empirical analysis. Examinations conducted by University is life changing gamble. The results are quite unlikely to be an indication of either their academic caliber or actual performance in examinations. They may simply reflect the examiner's ignorance, callousness or prejudices, which would be impossible to pin down under the existing review system. Hence these examinations have the arbitrariness and opacity of destiny itself, and stoicism remains the best policy, even if it that means a radical upsetting of career plans. The vulnerable, and shameful, tradition is required to be changed.

If fee is paid to the university for a service and it is not rendered, it is time to invoke consumer act. Examination is a major component of syllabi curriculum. The sanctity and value attached the systemic progression of examination as a system remains under constant evaluation throughout the country. Students pay fees to the university for the proper evaluation of their feedback through types of examinations. Often issues like appointment of examiners, scrutinizers and guidelines for them, setting of question papers, allocation zone, evaluation and re-evaluation of answer scripts, tabulation, and declaration of results come for academic public discussion, keeping in view anomalies in examination system. When students ask for rechecking of answer scripts, only error in tabulation of marks obtained is looked into.

The question fee is paid for rendering a service for which the payer gets a certain service or benefit from the service provider. If deficiency in service rendered is detected, a consumer can address the consumer forum for redressal. It is time for enlarging the ambit of consumer forum act and help consumer fight shoddy services provided by universities. There is a need to prepare a report that would identify teachers who are not up to the mark as examiners and have been ruining the lives of students by marking neglectfully or ignorantly. Let the student inspect his answer script (as it is already in practice in some universities of India) with teachers chosen by him out of the panels fixed by university, if he suspects some foul play. This will ensure quality control and make examiner serious to do justice with answer scripts. Of course the question will follow, if a teacher cannot mark scripts properly how come he will be allowed to continue to teach at all. Of course this will generate good public academic debate and will lead to value-dynamic in higher education. Let us be committed to change our colonial mind-set.

There is increasing evidence of plummeting interest in science. Universities find hard to get faculties of right kind. Core science is considered unproductive and thereby neglected. Out performance in core science is not bad, but not enough to be competitive. There is a need of serious introspection of our standing in the world in the field of core science education and scientific research. More serious thought is required at all levels of higher education which improves the basics of science education with specific policy frame work. This needs period specific and context specific planning. There is a greater responsibility on academics and planners in science education to find out ways and means to attract students to core science education and scientific research. Majority after +2 level prefer engineering, medicine and management as they have better prospects in the era of globalization. The decreasing interest in science, no doubt, has affected the quality of science education. In an age, when science education undergoes high specialization with new expansions, student's intake in terms of quality is quite alarming. With disinterested lot, often existing faculty find it difficult to cope with nation's commitment. Therefore, it is high time for us to start with new commitment to enrich potentials of science education through debate, discussion and effective planning. In this sense bearers of higher education and planning have to undergo serious introspection to judge right kind of science in times to come.

In 1948, the Sarvapalli Radhakrishnan Commission on University education said "Democracy on its very life depends on the high standard of general, vocational and professional education. Dissemination of learning, incessant search for new knowledge, increasing efforts to plumb the meaning of life, and provision of higher education to satisfy occupational needs of our society are the vital tasks of higher education".

We have concentrated too much on Professional education at the cost of vocational, general and scientific education. We need to amend and invigorate it so that it becomes an effective tool for the making of a just, vibrant and advancing society. Therefore the National Knowledge Commission projects expression, excellence and inclusions the three principal objectives. I order to do so, it recommends an increase in the number of universities from the present 370 to as many as 1500 by the year 2015, and the setting up of unto 50 national universities as exemplars of excellence.

So it is imperative that our undergraduate education needs an overhaul. Some welcome steps have already been taken with the start of Indian Institutes of Science Education and Research (IISER's), which give a five-year comprehensive M.Sc. in science. The curriculum they have devised is a composite one inclusive of languages, humanities and social sciences, increased hands on work, and opportunity to do research projects. The Department of Science and Technology is indeed launching a sustained national programme called INSPIRE (Innovation in Science Pursuit for Inspired Research). This scheme targets a spectrum of age groups-right from ten to thirty two years. (See "New ideas to invigorate science education", The Hindu, July 2007).

Higher education institution has started stagnating academically but expanding demographically. This demographic expansion creates a kind of illusion in so far as it masks the steady decline in quality behind the increase in quantity. Hence there is a tremendous demand for a composite curriculum. The undergraduate education, which is mostly single field oriented, needs re-orientation in the state level undergraduate educational institutions, making it oriented towards research/application/fieldwork. The idea of exemplar of excellence needs to be executed out from the base level of education in a state leading to ultimate conversion to higher education. This is possible when education is depoliticized and debeaurocratisied. It is time to be alert.

12

Professional, Technical and Value Education for Socio-Economic Development

—Anil Choudhury

The knowledge is available in abundance, but it is without the moral fiber that binds its use and the ethics that guides its application. Thus professional and technical education without values resulting in its dehumanization.

The education infrastructure is the backbone of any country, which supports the human resource development. "*Human resource*" development is the key to all other developments. In order to develop quality human resources with values privately managed Technical and Professional Government institutions or private institutions controlled by Government can play the leading role.

Professional and technical colleges are the main thrust of the strategy in Higher Education. Higher Education should reinforce its role of services to society for Socio-Economic development, especially assisting in the elimination of poverty, intolerance, violence, illiteracy and environmental degradation. The objective of education is to train and condition the mind so that an individual can function effectively and efficiently. Character building was an essential part of the educative process in ancient years, when *Gurukulas* existed. The Guru was responsible for character building of student and in turn students have to acquire the knowledge and skills along with the ethics of how to use it.

Human values along with technical, professional, and behavioural skills can be fostered through value based formal education, thus linking values with knowledge.

In the present world of electronic and computer communication, education is impersonalized and is acquiring the characteristics of a commercial commodity. The Information Technology and Computer based distance learning have shrunk the role and personalized influence of the *"Teacher"*. The knowledge is available in abundance, but it is without the moral fiber that binds its use and the ethics that guides its application. Thus, dehumanization of professional and technical education may happen if value education is not imparted. No real internalization of values can be achieved unless the learner agrees with it. The only key in this is *"Communication"*; it can be developed with the co-operation. Value education teaches the student that knowledge and skills are not the only requisite to succeed in life, but a positive attitude and a human way of action. Therefore, professional and technical with essence of value education is the key for Socio-Economic development.

Analysis of the Education System

- In our education system getting a pass in the exams is the priority, not learning. Even institutions fail in teaching various arts, and common sense. The present higher and technical education system should be reinforced with the essence of value education.
- Transfer of values is essential but it is very difficult. The communication is the only key for conveying the values; therefore it can be given more emphasis in the curricula of professional and technical programmes.
- Human values can be fostered through personality development programmes.
- Curricula and educational infrastructure should be built such that learning ambience should be created in institutions of higher learning.
- The curricula is backbone of education system, its review is required periodically and scientifically.
- Our *culture* and our *educational system* to name but two

factors do not only inhibit the flowering of entrepreneurial talent rather they positively discourage it.

Inculcating the Entrepreneurial Skills among Educated and Technical Youth

Alternate Options to Provide Better Education

- Vocational education system at school level with strong support and involvement of industrial houses should be introduced.
- After identifying the talents/strengths appropriate career options should be provided to youths as it is done in European countries.
- Vocational training centers should be strongly supported by industries.
- Entrepreneurship based curriculum at the root level should be introduced.
- *Privatization* should be used as an alternate delivery system to provide better education.
- Government should work only as a nodal agency for policy making and setting of quality standards in education at any level.

As our present education system is unable to provide appropriate career/vocation option and is unable to identify strength of youths, there by, we are losing the important resources. Every institute/school should have the *Entrepreneurial Skill Development* centre instead of establishing such institutions/ organizations separately because there is a communication gap between such separately established institutions.

An example here :

The Rajiv Gandhi Polytechnic established under Tech. Ed. III project of MHRD with six diploma programmes gives more emphasis on self employment and the curricula have also been prepared accordingly. These programmes are need based and suitable for taping natural potentials. This is just a start. It still requires some specific steps and concentration.

Environmental/Cultural Factor : Having a good number of naturally talented technocrats is not enough. Environment and culture factors are also equally important. These factors are :

1. Government policies, rules and regulations for setting up of enterprise.
2. Providing land shed, power, water etc.
3. Supply of raw materials.
4. Getting Licenses/import licenses.
5. Providing common facilities.
6. Granting tax relief or other subsidy.
7. Providing information.
8. Advertisement of various schemes of entrepreneurships etc.

On all counts of economic indicators "*India is shining*", just imagine where we can be if only we resolve our education related problems?

13

The Attitude of Parents Towards Higher Education for Girls : A Case Study of Deomali Town of Arunachal Pradesh

—*Hage Hassang*

Education can provide immense opportunities especially to the weaker section and downtrodden women to organize themselves for achieving their common economic goals. Education to women in India can help them to handle their economic problems systematically and effectively.

Introduction

Women have been subjected to the tyranny and oppression of a patriarchal order for centuries and most of them are suffering from the same even today. Though there are women who have distinguished themselves in various spheres of activity, education of women has not been one of the main concerns of the society. In spite of equal opportunities, the girls studying in colleges are outnumbered by boys. Illustrating the inequality of sexes in the field of education, the International Commission on Education (1996), states that "a respect for equity demands a special effort to do away with all inequality between sexes in the field of education. Gender inequality lies at the root of the lasting situation of inferiority that effect women at every stage at their lives. Education in general and higher education in particular is an insurance against economic need. Access to the higher education both technical and professional will guarantee economic leading to social status and hence empowerment to women." Efforts have been made by the government in this regard yet women in most of the cases cannot avail themselves of these opportunities, because of various factors like illiteracy, poverty and social convention. Almost half of the women in our country still remain illiterate. In Arunachal Pradesh women in general and tribal women in particular lag far behind their male counterparts in education.

Objective of the Study

Parents have a great role to play in the education of their children, Swami Dayananda once stressed on the duty of parents as regards education of their children in the following manner. "To give their children the highest education possible, to instruct them in the ways of truth, to make them refined in character and manners, in short to devote all their wealth, body and mind to accomplish this object is the paramount duty, the highest virtue, and the glory of parents". The specific objectives of this study are :

1. To examine the nature and extent of male, female disparity in literacy in Arunachal Pradesh, and
2. To highlight the attitude of parents toward higher education for girls,
3. To examine the economic background of parents.

Methodology

This paper is based on primary sources of data collected through questionnaires. Fifty parents are selected randomly from Deomali town of Tirap District for interview. The questionnaire was canvassed among people of different educational levels, income, linguistic and religion groups settled in Deomali from different parts of Arunachal Pradesh. The questionnaire was designed to find out what effects certain parameters have on the attitude of respondents. Views were deliberately sought on certain programmers of education which have traditionally been considered to be the sole heritage of men.

The study is presented in two sections. The first section includes the background note on the status of women education in the State. The second section deals with the discussion, findings of the study and the conclusions.

SECTION- I

Educational Status of the Women in Arunachal Pradesh

Education in Arunachal Pradesh came very late. Till independence the State had only 4 primary schools and literacy less than one per cent. A modest beginning was made after independence despite formidable constraints like inaccessibility of territory, people's unawareness of the need of education and traditional dependence on children for domestic and field work. With increasing emphasis through successive plans, commendable progress could be made over the past few decades. Literacy rate in the State increased from 7.23 percent in 1961 to 20.79 percent in 1981 and 54.34 percent in 2001. In spite of this, the situation is still gloomy in women education and the rate of dropout for girls in the State is very high. According to 2001 Census, male and female literacy rates in Arunachal Pradesh were 65.07 percent and 44.24 percent as against all India rate of 75.81 percent and 54.16 percent respectively. Thus, male-female discrepancy in literacy in the State was recorded 20.83 percent, highest among the North Eastern States (Table A.1). District wise, the highest male-female discrepancy in literacy was recorded in West Kameng and Tirap district 34.4 percent, and the lowest was found in West Siang 17.06 percent and Upper Subansiri 17.32 percent (Table A.2). In fact, there were general aversions to female education (especially in higher education) as most of the villagers were poor. Number of Scheduled Tribe girls studying in the colleges and university is much lower then the male counterpart. The male-female discrepancy in enrolment was recorded 33.27 percent in colleges and 30.91 percent in university during 2001-2002 (DES, Government of Arunachal Pradesh, 2001)

SECTION – II

Discussion and Findings of the Study

On the basis of attitudes reflected in the sample survey all the respondents are classified into two main categories : *(i) Category A,* those with an income up to Rs. 10,000 per month having formal education up to the higher secondary or high school level, and *(ii) Category B,* those with monthly income more than Rs. 10, 000 and formal education up to the university level.

Table A.1
Comparative Data of Literary Rate of Arunachal Pradesh with other States of North-Eastern Region (1991–2001)

State/Country	*Population*	*Total Literacy Rate*		*Literacy Rate (%)*				*Male-Female Discrepancy*	
				Male		*Female*			
	Persons	1991	2001	1991	2001	1991	2001	1991	2001
Arunachal Pradesh	109117	41.59	54.74	69.12	65.07	29.69	44.24	32.43	20.83
Assam	26638407	52.89	64.28	61.87	71.93	43.03	56.03	18.84	15.9
Manipur	2388634	59.89	68.87	71.63	77.87	47.60	59.70	24.03	18.17
Meghalaya	2306069	49.10	63.31	53.12	66.14	44.85	60.41	8.27	5.73
Mizoram	891058	82.27	88.49	85.61	90.69	78.60	86.13	7.01	4.56
Nagaland	1988636	61.65	67.11	67.62	71.77	54.75	61.92	12.87	9.85
Tripura	3191168	60.44	73.66	70.58	81.47	49.65	65.41	20.93	16.06
India	1027015247	52.2	65.38	64.1	75.85	39.3	54.16	24.8	27.70

Source : CMIE February, 1996 and Census of India 2001, Series—13, page. 15.

Table A.2
Literacy Rate of Arunachal Pradesh, District wise—2001 Census

District	*Population*			*Literates*			*Male/Female*
	Total	*Male(%)*	*Female(%)*	*Total*	*Male(%)*	*Female(%)*	*Discrepancy(%)*
Tawang	34705	50.93	49.07	11589(33.39%)	63.15	36.85	26.3
West Kameng	74595	57.16	42.84	38488(51.59%)	67.20	32.80	34.4
East Kameng	57065	50.37	49.63	18548(32.50%)	65.09	34.91	30.18
Papum Pare	121750	52.67	47.33	72021(69.15%)	59.15	40.85	18.3
Lower Subansiri	97614	50.39	49.61	36025(36.90%)	60.16	39.84	20.32
Upper Subansiri	54995	50.68	49.32	22623(41.13%)	58.66	41.34	17.32
West Siang	103575	52.27	47.73	52015(50.21%)	59.05	41.99	17.06
Upper Siang	33148	53.83	46.17	13409(40.45%)	64.55	35.45	29.1
Dibang Valley	57543	54.36	45.64	28131(48.88%)	52.94	37.06	15.88
Lohit	143478	53.84	46.16	64899(45.23%)	63.67	36.33	27.34
Changlang	124994	52.49	47.51	52116(41.69%)	63.80	36.20	27.6
Tirap	100227	51.34	47.66	33736(33.65%)	67.24	32.76	34.48
East Siang	87430	51.62	48.38	44196(50.55%)	58.33	41.67	16.66

Source : Statistical Abstract of Arunachal Pradesh, 2001, Published by Directorate of Economics & Statistics, Govt. of Arunachal Pradesh, Itanagar.

No clear correlation could be established between the attitudes and factor like sex, mother tongue and religion. *Category A* respondents are people with a rural background drawn from Deomali or nearby areas, whereas *Category B* belong to the educated middle class with an urban background drawn from different parts of State.

The main finding of the study is reflected in the following Tables :

Table 1
Surveyed Household's Preference for Higher Education of Their Children

Category	*No. of Respondent*	*Son(s)*		*Daughter(s)*	
		Yes	*No*	*Yes*	*No*
Category A	33	33 (100)	—	24 (72.72)	9 (27.27)
Category B	17	17 (100)	—	17 (100)	—

Note : *(i)* Figure in parentheses indicates percentage of total.

(ii) Dash implies data not available.

As indicated in above table 72.72 percent of the respondents in *Category A* are in favour of higher education to the girls and rest 27.27 percent of the respondents do not want to send their children after higher secondary mostly for economic reasons. Many parents especially those with income less than Rs. 1001 per month feels that they cannot just afford to send their children to college. However, all respondents of *Category B* agreed that girls should be given higher education to gain economic and cultural advantages.

Table 2
Category-wise Preference for Higher Education of their Daughters

Category	*No. of Respondents*	*Educational Level*			
		Higher Secondary	*Under Graguate*	*Post-graguate*	*Ph.D.*
Category A	33	9 (27.2)	22 (66.66)	12 (6.06)	Nil
Category B	17	—	6 (35.29)	11 (64.70)	—

Note : *(i)* Figure in parentheses indicates percentage of total.

(ii) Dash implies data not available.

Table shows that maximum percentage about 66.6 percent of *Category A* respondents wanted to educate their daughter upto undergraduate level. However, their preference for higher education (post-graduate) is very low only 6.06 percent. In contrast to this in *Category B*, 64.70 percent of respondents were in favour of education for girls' upto the postgraduate level. They however did not favour girls go in for a Ph.D. degree. They think tnat Ph.D. degree is not necessary for them.

Table 3
Reasons for not Sending Girls for Higher Education (Post-graduate)

Sl. No.	*Reasons*	*No. of Respondents*	
		Category A	*Category B*
a.	Be mixing with boys	—	1 (16.66)
b.	Be mixing with people belonging to others caste?	1 (3.22)	1 (16.66)
c.	Possibly neglect her husband/children?	2 (6.45)	—
d.	Not make use of her degree later in life	4 (12.90)	2 (33.33)
e.	Become 'Modern" and reject family tradition and social customs	8 (25.8)	2 (33.33)
f.	Any other reasons	16 (51.61)	—
	Total	31 (100)	6 (100)

Note : *(i)* Figure in parentheses indicates percentage of total.
(ii) Dash implies data not available.

Majority of the respondents in *Category A* feel that girls are inevitably going to leave them in course of their marriage naturally, so they (parents) do not show interest in their education. On the other hand, 25.8 percent of the respondents say that daughter would become 'Modern' and reject family tradition and social customs and neglect religious duties. About 12.90 percent of parents say that daughter would not make use of her degree later in life, 6.45 percent expressed their views that if daughters were allowed for higher education (post-graduate) she would possibly neglect her husband/children. Options given by respondents of *Category B* is somewhat different, about 67 percent feels that girls would become 'Modern' and reject family tradition and social customs at the same time they are of views that girls may not make use of her degree later in life. Further 34 percent of respondents say that girls would be mixing with people belonging to other caste or boys which may lead to inter caste marriage.

Table 4

Opinion for Continuing Education after the Marriage of Girl Children

Particulars	*Options*		
	Yes	*No*	*Can't say*
Category A	4(12.12)	29(87.87)	—
Category B	6(35.29)	—	11(64.70)

Note : *(i)* Figure in parentheses indicates percentage of total.

(ii) Dash implies data not available.

It is observed from the Table that 87.87 percent of the respondents in *Category A* were opposed to girls continuing their education after marriage. They believed that husbands should have higher educational qualification than their wives have. They felt that if their daughters were highly educated, it would be difficult to find suitable matches for them.

Category B respondents showed a relatively more liberal attitude in this matter. About 35.29 percent of the respondents were in favour of girls continuing their education after marriage. They believed that it would boost her social status. Again next 64.70 percent of the respondents were of the view that it was preferable to leave it to the choice of the husband and his family.

Table 5

Preference for Education of Son/Daughter (In Case of Financial Constraint)

Particulars	*Option*		
	Son(s)	*Daughter(s)*	*Can't say*
Category A	30(90.90)	3(9.09)	-
Category B	8(47.05)	6(35.29)	3(17.64)

Note : *(i)* Figure in parentheses indicates percentage of total.

(ii) Dash implies data not available.

Financial status of the family can play an important role in determining the education of their children. As shown in the Table, *Category A* has shown strong preference for son's education under financial constraints. About 90.9 percent of the respondents choose to spend on the education for their sons and rest 9.09 percent for their daughter. They considered the education of their sons a necessary investment and expected them to contribute to the family income. However, there was a mixed response from *Category B*, about 35.29 percent of the respondents favoured daughter education rather then sons and 17.64 percent favoured offering equal opportunities to their sons and daughters if forced to make a choice.

Table 6
Preference for Education of Son/Daughter
(without any Financial Constraint)

Particulars	*Options*	
	Both Son(s) and Daughter(s)	*Son(s)*
Category A	25(75.75)	8(24.24)
Category B	17(100)	—

Note : *(i)* Figure in parentheses indicates percentage of total.
(ii) Dash implies data not available.

If there are no financial constraints, 75.7 percent respondents of *Category A* would prefer to give equal opportunity to both son(s) and daughter(s) for higher education. Whereas 24.24 percent of respondents say that they would prefer son(s) education on the ground that it would add to family income and make him/them independent financially. In contrast to this, all respondents of *Category B* says that they would give equal opportunity for higher education to both son(s) and daughter(s). Thus, a *Category B* respondent shows a more liberal attitude in these matters in comparison to *Category A* respondents.

It is clear from the Table 7 the maximum number of the *Category A* respondent (37.5 percent) were in favour of education for sons in engineering branch and daughter in Humanities (58.35 percent). All respondents did not favour girls going in for engineering education. All opinions reflect the influence of the traditional attitude that girls are not suitable for the engineering profession.

Table 7
Parents' Preference for Their Children's Branch of Education

Branch	*Category A*		*Category B*	
	Son(s)	*Daughter(s)*	*Son(s)*	*Daughter(s)*
Engineering	9 (37.5)	—	6 (35.29)	2 (11.76)
Science	5 (20.88)	3 (12.5)	5 (29.41)	4 (23.52)
Humanities	6 (25.0)	14 (58.33)	3 (17.64)	2 (11.76)
Commerce	1 (4.16)	2 (8.33)	1 (5.88)	2 (11.76)
Medicines	3 (12.5)	5 (20.83)	2 (11.76)	7 (41.17)

Note : *(i)* Figure in parentheses indicates percentage of total.

(ii) Dash implies data not available.

However it is significant to note that no such opposition to others was expressed by the respondents.

Category B respondents however had shown their willingness to pursue their daughter in engineering branch. About 11.76 percent respondents favour girls going in for engineering education, 41.17 percent in medicine branch and 23.52 percent on science education. However it is significant to note that the preference for girl's education in Humanities is much lower, only 11.76 percent in comparison with 58.33 percent in Category A.

Conclusion

All parents favour educating their daughters, though they differ on the degree and level of education. However, those with lower incomes and formal education only upto the higher secondary or high school level (Category A), show a markedly distinct attitude from the rest with higher income and formal education upto the University level (Category B).They prefer to educate their sons rather daughters, if the choice was forced upon them under financial constraints. Whereas, only 47 percent of Category B respondents subscribe to this attitude. All parents believe that higher education imparts social and economic advantage and increases the prospects for a better life. However, Category A respondents exhibit conservative attitude in favour of higher level of education (post-graduate). On the other hand, Category B respondents shows a more liberal attitude and they would like their daughters to go in for higher education up to the post-graduate level. However, they think that a Ph.D. degree is not necessary for them. On the question of continuation of studies after marriage, the majority of the respondents prefer to leave the question to the choice of the husband and his family.

From the above discussion it can be concluded that the status of girls education especially of higher education is not quite encouraging which is a matter of great concern for Arunachal Pradesh. The main reasons are the indifferent treatment and lack of whole hearted support and guidance from the parents. Therefore, the attitude towards education has to be changed and they should get equal opportunity for getting education. Parents should be given informal education so that they could experience the value of learning or gaining knowledge. Efforts should be made by organizing awareness campaign to motivate the parents as well as the girls. Besides, to promote equality for women through education a deliberate, planned and sustained effort should be made so that the new value of equality of sexes (through socialization process) can replace the traditional system of inequality ingrained in the patriarchal social order of domination.

REFERENCES

1. Biswas, N.B. (1996), *Development of Education in Arunachal Pradesh.* Arunachal University Research Journal, Vol. 1, 37–47.
2. Choudhury, J.N. (1982), *Arunachal Panorama,* Directorate of Research, Govt. of Arunachal Pradesh, Shillong, Daya Publishing House, Delhi.
3. Government of India (1986), National Policy on Education, Ministry of Human Resource Development, New Delhi.
4. Government of Arunachal Pradesh (2001), Statistical Abstract of Arunachal Pradesh, Published by Directorate of Economics and Statistics, Itanagar.
5. Karup, A.M. (1992), Extent and Problems of Tribal Education, B. Chaudhury (Ed.) Tribal Transformation in India, Vol. IV, 205–212.
6. Kind, M.E. (1994), Economics of Gender and Education Choice, In Husen T., Postlethwaite T. (ed) 1994. The International Encyclopedia of Education, Vol. 4, Elsvier Science Ltd. Oxford, England.
7. Schultz T.P. (1993), Returns to Women's Education in Developing countries, World Bank, The Johns Hopkins University Press, Baltimore and London.
8. T. Mibang, P.T. Abraham (2003) Eds. *Arunachal women and Education,* Himalayan Publishers, Itanagar.

14

Student's Perception of Quality in Higher Education : A Case Study

—Madhuparna Bhattacharjee

The development of modern technology and fast changing communication scenario as well as media has enabled education to offer both unprecedented richness of content and the capacity to deliver it.

Introduction

In an increasingly interdependent world and competitive atmosphere, all countries will have to vigorously pursue policies to optimize comparative factor endowments. The rapid technological changes as well as ever-increasing knowledge boom, while making transaction seamless, have reinforced the process of global integration. Further, the battles of this century will be fought and won with the "power of ideas". Societies will increasingly become knowledge based and promote knowledge-based performance-oriented activities and industries.

In this context, the State of Arunachal Pradesh has a distinct advantage with enormous natural resources along with a population profile concentrated in the younger age group, where many new opportunities can be fully optimized, for which, equipping our human resources with required skill and knowledge becomes an essential condition.

Education, as we all understand, is the process whereby society passes on the acquired and accumulated knowledge and experience of the past generations to its youth in a systematic and abridged form, so that it can start where past generation have ended and move ahead from there. The development of modern technology and fast changing communication scenario as well as media has enabled education to offer both unprecedented richness of content and the capacity to deliver it. Under this circumstance, only if we could break free from the limitations of outdated curriculum and outmoded delivery systems, we could utilize opportunity to close the education gap that separates the world's most prosperous communities from their poorer cousins living in this region.

Being at the apex of this educational pyramid, higher education has a key role to play in the system as it provides people an opportunity to reflect on the critical social, political, economic, cultural and spiritual issues that humanity is facing today.

Traditionally, higher education has provided the wisdom and expertise, which equips young people for their future roles in the society as leaders. This remains valid, since higher education must uphold education and values, which moulds socially responsible citizens. But today, the university sees its functions as going beyond this to include the use of acquired knowledge in order to directly or indirectly enhance the material well-being instead of human well being at large in terms of happiness and comfort of the mankind.

Higher education is now regarded as an institution not only for developing knowledge and training young minds, but also for dissemination and practical application of such knowledge for the welfare of humanity at large.

Along with this, in the context of higher education gaining international dimension, universities are expected to be sensitive to the local, national and global expectations. These dimensions of changing conditions and emerging trends—starting from mass higher education of comparable quality to new models of management and performance evaluation have brought both quality and standards of higher education to the forefront. The need to move from ensuring minimum standards towards assuring higher standards is apparent.

Today, performance evaluation, accountability and higher standards have become watchwords in any discussion on revamping higher education. Hence, the countries are being pressurized to ensure quality of higher education at a nationally comparable and internationally expected standard. It is with this conception that the NAAC was set up. (National Assessment and Accreditation Council, India).

Concept of Quality in Higher Education

The concept of "*quality*" is contested as to what counts as quality? In general, there are two scientific strategies for attempting to measure quality. Most common is the one that deals with choice of indicators, measured subjectively as well as objectively. The subjective approach emphasizes the role of perception, both in terms of expectations and current circumstances.

The methodological rigor associated with the concept of quality is impressive, but there is clearly no consensus on a specific statistical measure that best comprises a standard scale of quality. There is always a nagging question of the cross cultural validity of objective indicators since they ignore variations in beliefs and values concerning what are important. This is because; values, expectations and perceptions of 'good' or 'bad' vary between cultural groups. It may be as difficult to define a universal scale of quality as it would be to define universal scale of beauty. This is not to imply, however, that minimal requirements in terms of basic standards can not be identified. Such criteria may be considered necessary but not sufficient for judging quality as high or low, good or bad.

While objective indicators of quality may be useful scientific tools for legislation and policy makers wishing to measure the efficacy of the system, they generally obscure important variations in the concept of quality. (Barlett and Brown). This can be understood by a layman from a simple statement such as this—"Rose is beautiful". This is a universal truth. Nevertheless quality may mean different things to different people, who, therefore, demand different quality outcomes and methods in order to assess quality. Deriving therefore from the earlier statement we may like to add that "Red rose is beautiful and not the black rose."(Emphasis from researcher's point of view). Barnett (1994) agreed that what counts as quality is contested. Harvey and Green (1993) described quality as a relative concept. Quality is relative to the user of the term and the circumstances in which it is involved and applied.

Thus, it means different things to different people. This also raises the pertinent question – whose quality are we talking about? (Harvey and Green, 1993, p. 10).

Here, our concern and assertion is about the quality in Higher Education. There are a varicty of stakeholders in higher education including students, employers, teaching and non-teaching employees, government and its funding agencies, accreditors, valuators, auditors and assessors, (including professional bodies). (Burrows and Harvey, 1992). Each of these stakeholders has different views about quality, influenced by one's own interest in higher education. First, for a committed scholar, the quality of higher education is its ability to produce a steady flow of people with high intelligence and commitment to learning that will continue the process of transmission and advancement of knowledge. Second, to the government, a high quality education system is one that produces trained personal as scientists, engineers, doctors, teachers, architects, etc. and judged to be required by the society in general. Third, to an industrialist, a high quality educational institution may be one that generates output as graduates with wide ranging flexible minds ready to acquire skills and be able to adapt to new methods, new skills and needs of the corporate world.

Each of these aforementioned view points represents a valid expectation of higher education from each category of stakeholders and about what they think of quality. Thus a valid and acceptable measurement is required and the standards to be applied will surely be different for each of these notions of quality.

This idea resonates with Barnett (1994) who conceives the view that as the threshold connection between different conceptions of higher education, different approaches to quality and the identification of different outcomes are termed by him as ***performance indicators***, *i.e.* PIs. Behind the various notions on quality of higher education or what constitutes quality, there lies, whether explicitly formed or held tacitly, a view as to the ends that higher education should serve. In turn, these prior conceptions will generate different methodologies for evaluating quality, and in particular will call for alternative sets of outcome measures. *(PIs)*.

Subscribing purely to these ideas of Barnett, this researcher of Dera Natung Government College, Itanagar, felt the need to generate a research oriented study involving the student community in this instant case.

Nevertheless, Barnett's arguments on higher education are conceived as the production of highly qualified manpower, the graduates are seen as products whose career earnings and employment will relate to the quality of education that the learners have received. When higher education is linked to training for a research career, the *PIs* (hence forth will be used as PIs) then becomes the research and development output of staff and students.

The third conception relates to the efficient management of teaching provision. In this view, the PIs are efficiency indicators, such as completion rates, unit costs, student–staff ratio, and other financial data. Further, when higher education is conceived as a matter of extending life chances, the focus is on the participation rates or percentage growth of students from less represented backgrounds, including adults, private or part-time students and physically challenged students.

The above stated conceptions of Barnett, though four different categories, are sometimes overlapping conceptions of the purpose of higher education. Each one of these categories can be put to separate category having its own definition of quality and with a distinctive set of PIs that are associated with it. Common in these four conceptions is the view of higher education as "black box".

None of the above conceptions seem to indicate an interest in higher educational process, or the quality of the learning achieved by the learner. Most of us in higher education even ignore as to what goes on in the 'black box' and our focus is simply on input and output measurements. Burnett (1994) later contrasts these four conceptions with a set of another four conceptions of higher education, which focus on the quality of student experience. The first among them is about exposing students, or initiating them into the process and experience of pursuing knowledge. The second is related to the development of student's autonomy and integrity. The third values the cultivation of general intellectual abilities of students to form perspectives and vision beyond the confines of a single discipline. The final conception of higher education is about the development of critical reasoning.

Prompted by similar kinds of increasing concerns for quality in higher education in India in general, and in the state of Arunachal Pradesh in particular, a brief study was conducted in the month of November 2006, at Dera Natung Govt. College, Itanagar to measure the influence of higher education on student's academic, social, political, economic, spiritual and personal growth. The purpose of the study was to assess whether the institution where they are enrolled is upto their expectation and aspirations, assessed in terms of their experience in the college and the kind of education they received or are receiving. The empirical investigation adopted an approach of assessing quality of higher education (college) using data collected from a group of students belonging to different streams about their subjective experiences during the college years and their perception of value of the educational experience.

This method was thought suitable because, not only are colleges/universities required to graduate students with demonstrable capabilities to turn simple data into information and knowledge and to share this knowledge by documentations and other methods as a source of innovation for the future, but they are also required to demonstrate quality through positive student feedback on their educational experience. Data was collected from a cross section of the student population belonging to professional and non-professional course, juniors-seniors, males-females, boarders in the hostels and day scholars.

A structured questionnaire was used for eliciting information about the students' background, college/university experience and learning outcomes. The questionnaire was adapted from the 'college student experience questionnaire' (CSEQ) (Pace, 2005).

The body of this research attempts to put a generalized causal model which includes measures of institutional features as well as quality of effort; and also the combined influences of the institutional environment as perceived by the student and the effort expended by the student lead to student growth and development.

Further, the idea that institutions of higher education are founded on process of enabling growth and development of students in holistic sense, incorporating social, emotional and cultural development as well, warrants attention to the measurement of quality as a kind of 'transformation'. (Harvey and Green, 1993).

Database and Methodology of the Study

The CSEQ used for the present study is a 47 item instrument built around the idea that college/university experience is a coherent whole that requires a facilitative campus environment and student effort. The CSEQ measures college/university experience related to background information of the student, college activities such as library, computer and information technology, course learning, writing experience, experience with faculty, art, music, theatre, campus facilities, clubs and organizations, personal experiences, student acquaintances, scientific and quantitative experiences, topics of conversation, information in conversation, opinion about the overall amenities in the college, the general college environment, and the estimate of gains in acquiring knowledge.

The college located in the capital township is a government sponsored institution having a jurisdiction over more than 1500 students in the undergraduate courses. A random sample was of 100 students from the above mentioned categories belonging to the streams of Arts, Commerce and Science was drawn and the schedule administered. A quick examination of the characteristics of the sample indicated that respondent students are curious to know the outcome of the study. (Since this research project is underway, all results at this stage will not be revealed for obvious reasons). Simple tables and ratios are employed for deriving the result.

RESULT AND DISCUSSION

In this section, brief analyses of the findings have been provided to understand the behavioural, individual, and subjective responses by the respondent students.

1. Process and Mode of Entry into the Courses

The process through which students are enrolled in an institution indirectly reflects the quality of the incumbents. If the students opt for the course out of interest or because it offers greater job opportunities, one can expect them to be keen learners and intensive users of all facilities for their own benefit. Moreover, the overall quality of higher education depends on the quality of its receptors. Table 1 below gives a general picture on why the students chose their respective courses.

Table 1
Reasons for Choice of the Course

Reasons	*General Undergraduate Courses (in percentage)*	*Professional Courses (on Campus/ off Campus)*
Based on interest and marks obtained in the last examination	65%	86.56%
Employability	56%	27%
Fathers advice	0.03%	8.06%
Friends/Seniors advice	0.8%	8.89%
Counselling	0.18%	2.00%

Source : Field Survey, November 2006, DNGC, Itanagar.

It is revealed from the data shown in the table 1 above, that on an average nearly 65% of the students responded that they are interested in their chosen subject and about 25% replied that they chose the subject because of its employable scope in the state government services, private organizations etc. The scope factor ranks very high for the professional courses. It is also revealed that very few students have followed the advice of parents, peers, faculty or any counselling prior to selection of their subjects.

Data collected on life chances and ambition of the students reveal that majority of them dream of a social/political activist in the state politics or prefer a teaching job. When asked about the mode of selection procedure for entering college, majority of the respondents feel that the type of selection followed currently is inappropriate and many of them suggest prior counselling as a must for selection of subject combination and in case of professional courses the selection should be through a process consisting of entrance test, group discussions, counselling and interview. The students of Non professional courses, about 80% suggest that selection should be done through counselling and a simple subject test. These processes naturally ensure selection of genuinely interested students which enhances class room atmosphere and who obviously struggle to get the most out of the existing situation.

2. Quality of Teaching

Teaching is the process through which various cognitive, soft and transferable skills are imparted and receptivity of the learners could be analyzed. The success of any education and training component depends to a great extent on the quality of teaching. Efficient delivery and attentive reception are the pillars of success of education system. In a higher education set up, the teacher has to be 'a real guide by the side' rather than 'a sage on the stage' and lead the students to learn to practice the skills than just passively listen to the delivery of the lecturers. For the purpose of the present study, the respondents were asked to rate teaching as very good, good, fair and not satisfactory, and other aspects of teaching component such as teachers organizational capacity to deliver, teachers communication skills, motivational skills, class presentation skills, innovative ideas sharing, interaction skills etc. The results are furnished in Table 2 below.

Table 2

Quality of Teaching (in %)

Category of Response	*Undergraduate*	*Professional*
Feel teaching is very good	25.56%	35%
Feel teaching is good	35.00%	47%
Feel teaching is fair	39.44%	18%
Feel need of change in teaching technique	75.08%	82%
Feel teaching need to be interactive	98.00%	95%
Feel need to induct scientific method	65.00%	85%
Feel lack of applied orientation	55.00%	74.7%
Feel lack of seminars and assignments	45.00%	45%
Feel teachers not accessible easily	78.86%	45%
Need of remedial teaching	97.05%	100%
Innovative ideas sharing by teachers	40.00%	33.34%

Source : Author Field Survey.

Nearly 26% of undergraduate and 35% of professional courses students have reported teaching to be only very good quality. Not surprisingly, 75% of undergraduates and 82% of professional courses students suggest for a change in the teaching techniques. 60-85% students from both courses suggest the adoption of scientific methods, applied orientation, and adoption of interactive learning methods, 45% of undergraduates and professional course students suggest seminars and assignments, and demand focusing on application part of the knowledge. Interestingly, 78% of undergraduate and 45% of professional course students reveal that the teachers are not easily accessible. Similarly almost all suggest the need for remedial teaching to complete the prescribed syllabus. There is also very little emphasis on the use of modern audio visual teaching aids, and teachers generally do not share innovative ideas in the subject concerned. The above discussion (though not final analysis) leads us to believe that teaching is not of an expected quality; there is lack of emphasis on the practical application part in the teaching, and generally audio visual aids are not used in class room teaching.

3. Nature of Curriculum

In the arena of higher education students expect to receive the needed inputs for improving their skills and widening as well as deepening their knowledge. In this context a course structure that provides a rigorous training to the students is perceived to be more qualitative. Hence the students were asked to rate their course structure and course work according to level of difficulty or rigorousness. It is revealing to find that majority of the students feel that their course is of medium rigor. This reflects that not only the course structure but also the course work needs to be made rigorous with practical orientation which would ultimately lead to applied knowledge, skill of problem solving, leadership capabilities and team work abilities. This is also an indicator of student's involvement in the learning and doing process. However, as revealed from the data practical orientation is absent and 56.5% of the students suggest inclusion of projects, tutorials and assignments as compulsory component in the curriculum. They also pin pointed that the curriculum structure is of medium difficulty, and not practical as well as career oriented. This gives rise to a pertinent question that the curriculum needs revision from time to time with more specification and is not upto the expectations of the students.

4. Evaluation Process

The effectiveness of teaching and learning procedure is tested in the evaluation process. In fact, the quality education is defined as the one, which provides an individual with an enjoyable, stimulating and challenging environment in which one's knowledge is furthered and is tested against nationally and internationally recognized standards. The evaluation process therefore should be done not only against the standards but also has to be a continuous process. Thus the system of evaluation adopted currently in the study area is therefore viewed as inappropriate by the students in general. They argue against the internal house tests and suggest for other appropriate methods of evaluation based on students' background and participatory capabilities in the class room. They also suggest for a more accountable and transparent method of evaluation. This can ensure objective assessment of the performance of students and provide credibility to the system.

5. Infrastructure for Higher Education

Apart from a rigorous course work, effective teaching and objective evaluation, the infrastructure facilities available for learning and their effective use by the students affect the quality of education to a large extent. These facilities include library, laboratory, computers and internet facility, counselling and career guidance, health, hostel, sports and games facilities, other interactive recreation like creative art, theatre, music etc.

The view on availability and use of all infrastructures are presented in the following section. Nearly 45% of students have used the library as a quiet place to read or study materials they bought with them. A majority of 65% feel that the library atmosphere is not conducive and have never done a reserve reading to read assignment materials other than text books in the library. Majority of students generally use the library reading space for conversations during long gaps between their subject periods. Majority of students do not have any idea of use of index or data base to find material on some topic. Majority of students never made a judgment about the quality of information obtained from the library or other sources and 45% of students never asked a librarian or library staff for help in finding information on some topic or subject specific reference.

A large section of students nearly 85% have never used World Wide Web or internet to locate information related to a course. The students also generally never used a computer to analyze data (statistics, forecasting, etc.) related to their course. 55% of students never interacted with their own class fellows, 45% of them never used the campus garden to relax or study by themselves, 15% of them generally never participated nor attended a cultural or social event like college week, fresher week, and association picnic in the campus or other campus location. A great number of students offering science and geography as their major course have never used a campus learning lab or centre to improve study or academic skills (reading, writing, practical exercises etc.). 65% of students feel rejected on any event organized by the student governing body. Majority of them never attended a campus club meeting or student government group meeting. It is revealed from the study that 55% of students report inadequate library and laboratory facilities and equipment there in.

(i) Hostel Facility

Hostel facility is a vital component as this ensures in-house learning opportunity for the learners in higher education. For a smooth and uninterrupted study the quality of hostels matters greatly and it also has an impact on the over all quality of learning with team management skills. The nature of hostel facility in the instant case is reflected in the following section.

It is found that nearly 27% of the total regular enrolled students reside in the campus hostel. However, majority of them reported inadequate living space, about 70% of them reported unhappy because of non conducive atmosphere for studies in the hostel, majority of them feel the absence of any library or reading room in the hostel as well as nutritious food quality.

(ii) Employment Information and Career Counselling

The students are well aware of a college career counselling cell working to provide information about studies and employment, working on the campus. Despite various programme conducted by the career counselling cell, nearly 60% of respondents have never visited/availed the services of the cell. A large number of students, who do not use the service, may be due to lack of awareness and inadequate service provisions of the bureau.

Conclusion by way of Recommendation

Based on the analysis, one may conclude that the perception about quality changes from person to person. Society, government, parents, providers, employers and students have their own perception about the quality of higher education. Higher education which is meant to provide advanced knowledge, technical skills, and prepare a pool of manpower for socio-economic development of country as a whole and the state in particular, should be put to the litmus test of quality. The present paper sought the opinion of students about the quality of higher education they are receiving. On the whole it may be argued that due to wrong selection process, even the disinterested may enter the course thereby diluting the interest of other students too. The course structure is not rigorous enough to provide necessary skills to the students or involve them more completely in the learning process. The teaching process is also outmoded using predominantly 'chalk and talk' method with little or no practical orientation. The evaluation system is perceived to be not objective and not transparent and not preparing the students for NET, SLET or other competitive type of examinations.

A lot of infrastructure has been developed on the campus but has not been able to keep a pace with the growth in student numbers. Thus, the lacunae lies with the system, the existing delivery mechanism and also the users who generally have not developed a sense of belongingness, attitude of responsibility and accountability on their part for effective use of the facilities in an optimum level which matters a lot for the quality of the system. For example, though the career counselling services are available to the students, a majority of them have not yet visited the centre and almost all students who have not made use of this facility are not aware of what this facility means.

Based on the above discussion and the personal experiences of the students, it is also revealed that in general the students never experienced the use of mathematical terms to express a set of relationships nor have they compared the scientific method with other methods for gaining knowledge and understanding.

Based on the above discussion and the looming resource crunch following suggestions can be offered to improve the learning facilities and quality in higher education :

- Multidisciplinary curriculum must be developed along with diversification in the streams to cater to the needs and fulfilment of expectations of learners, teachers, parents, employers and society in general. Offering a choice based interest oriented subject along with credit base would be a step in the right direction.
- Context specificity and inquiry-oriented experience must be reflected in the curriculum. Learner's participation in the generation and dissemination of knowledge must be the focus of constructivist curriculum.
- Problem solving abilities through problem solving activities must be developed through experimentation, case studies and simulation exercises and projects.
- Students need to be motivated to give clear succinct oral and written presentations during their university examination to improve their communication and literary skills. These would foster their creative skills.
- Widen the access of the students to research programme as a privileged opportunity for apprenticeship and participation in the higher education.
- Appropriate and effective feed back mechanism for the students must be established in this age of right to information. (*e.g.* returning corrected answer books, responding to students queries compassionately on the evaluation procedure, student evaluation of teacher etc.)
- Examination should be designed in such a way that at least some portion of it evaluates the student's insight into the subject.
- Hostel facilities need to be upgraded to include a separate hostel administration along with reading room, common room, and intercom telephone, proper dining facilities along with the facility of cyber café and PCO on campus.
- Wide publicity and orientation need to be given to the students at the entry level about the facilities and amenities

available on campus and off campus. (*e.g.* NICNET facilities, library facilities, potable water availability, reprography facility etc.)

- Assessment of the teachers by the students must be made mandatory and should be practiced for making teaching more effective and accountable.
- Along with the regular curriculums, the centre of learning may introduce Entrepreneurship development cell (EDC sponsored by DST as DST Project) in every colleges in order to give first hand knowledge and training to the students.

REFERENCES

1. Barnett (1992), *"Improving Higher Education : Total Quality Care"*, Buckingham, SRHE/Open University Press.
2. Bagalkoti, S.T. (2006),*"Students Perception of Quality in Higher Education : A Case Study*, pp. 7–13, University News, Vol. 44, No. 46, AIU.
3. Barnett (1994), *"The Idea of Quality : Voicing the Educational"*, in Doherty, G.D.(Ed.) "Developing Quality in Higher Education", London, Routledge.
4. Green (1994), *"What is Quality in Higher Education? Concepts Policies and Practices"*, in Green.(Ed.), What is Quality in Higher Education? Buckingham, SRHE and Open University Press.
5. Harvey, L. and Green, D. (1993), *"Determining Quality, Assessment, and Evaluation in Higher Education"*, Quality in Higher Education, 18(1), pp. 9–34.
6. Maureen (2001), *"Measuring Quality and Performance in Higher Education,"* Quality in Higher Education, Vol. 7, No. 1.

15

Role of Education in Development of Nation

—Milorai Modi

Higher Education helps the individual to achieve certain level of perfection. It also empowers the individual with necessary skills, knowledge and training and creates competence in manpower which in turn helps the development of society and nation.

Present society is being evolved into a knowledge-society and economy is becoming knowledge-based economy. Certainly without education, such changes are not possible; therefore, today higher education is directly linked with economic development of the nation and the society. Higher Education helps the individual to achieve certain level of perfection. It also empowers the individual with necessary skills, knowledge and training and creates competence in manpower which in turn helps the development of society and nation. Hence, higher education system is the determining factor for progress and development of nation. In 1998, the World Conference on Higher Education organized by UNESCO adopted a resolution. In the preamble of the resolution, the importance of the higher education was stated, "Without adequate higher education and research institutions providing a critical mass of skilled and educated people, no country can ensure genuine endogenous and sustainable development and, in particular, developing countries and least developed countries cannot reduce the gap separating them from the industrially developed ones. Sharing knowledge, international co-operation and new technologies can offer new opportunities to reduce this gap. Higher education has given ample proof of its viability over the centuries and of its ability to change and to induce change and progress in society. Owing to the scope and pace of change, society has become increasingly knowledge-based so that higher learning and research now act as essential components of cultural, socio-economic and environmentally sustainable development of individuals, communities and nations. Higher education itself is confronted therefore, with formidable challenges and must proceed to the most radical change and renewal it has ever been required to undertake, so that our society, which is currently undergoing a profound crisis of values, can transcend mere economic considerations and incorporate deeper dimensions of morality and spirituality". At this background, achieving academic excellence and quality education has obviously become the main challenges of higher education in India today.

In India, traditionally the learning system was fenced into small section of the people and was carried on largely through family line. The introduction of English education, particularly from the nineteenth century brought a meteoric progress in education. But, overall provision of educational facilities remained very inadequate till the eve of independence. However, after independence, particularly in last few decades India has made astronomical advancement in various fields. It has successfully demonstrated her determination and devotion, enhanced and developed in many areas by bringing new revolution like green revolution, white revolution, pink revolution etc. The progress made by India in information technology and biotechnology are also equally impressive. Further, due to economic liberalizations, India has been the second fastest growing economy in the world over last few years. Despite these progresses, when we talk about quality education in India, it is still far behind in comparison with the developed nations.

Arunachal Pradesh

In Arunachal Pradesh higher education is yet to be developed in true sense. Therefore, roles and responsibilities of the teacher and its leaders in Arunachal Pradesh are more as the whole society is looking towards the teaching community to take the state in the right direction by producing highly qualified and competent people, which in turn will help socio-economic progress of the state. Arunachal is a poor state; largely it depends on the central assistances. The state has very little scope for industrial and other business development, mainly due to difficult terrain, lack of infrastructural development and lack of quality and qualified human resources, and other bottle-necks. Though we have resources like hydro power, however, it requires crores of rupees which local tribal population does not have capacity; it is to be explored by multi-national companies or corporation like NEEPCO, NHPC etc. Other sector is horticulture where local tribal people can invest. But this sector too is facing many difficulties such as lack of market, communication and transportation and many more. So, for self-reliance and self-dependence the state has to be based on tertiary sector. Nevertheless, Arunachal has to go a long way in improving the qualitative and quantitative dimension of higher education which is directly related to socio-economic development of the society and single most potent means of social mobility, from poor to respectable status in society.

In India, Kerala is such a state where about twenty-five per-cent population are working in other (foreign) countries, therefore, its Foreign Exchange Remittance is two time double than its Annual Budget allocated by the central government. Hence, Arunachal has to go along the line of Kerala by giving importance to education, particularly higher education. For that qualitative and quantitative education system is urgently required. Education, as a basic right and a public good must be responded to the needs and interest of all people with a view to ensuring the realization of their full capacity, potential and intelligence to participate in every activity of life as a responsible citizen. Also, it must respond to the need of the time and situation. Now, it is generally accepted theory that an enrollment of at least twenty-five percent of the relevant age group in higher education is an indispensable condition for socio-economic development. And, in present day, it is a customer driven market rather than industry driven market and education is no exception to this phenomenon. Therefore, all the stakeholders, particularly, employers have become quality conscious. In Arunachal, if government will not make a sensible and responsive (to present situation) education policy immediately, even the job created by the multi-national or PSU/corporations in power sector and other areas will go to outsiders. Because these companies will simply go for quality; and Arunachalees have to settle with only group D & C services, which are not for prosperity, rather it is for survival. It is also said that by 2020 India will be the highest producer/supplier of human resources in the world. If Arunachal has to get some share and to transform state's human resources into asset, it has to give top priority to higher education and invest at least 10% of the Annual Budget of the State.

Therefore, quality and responsive education policy will be the catalyst to cope with the changing scenario; however, the most important prerequisite here is an emphasis on quality education. The higher education system in the state is by and large good but there are still certain areas in which reformation seems quite imminent to ensure quality education. For instance, the appointment of Principal on seniority basis without considering quality and qualification, the scheme for career advancement and associated incentives for teachers and payment of stipend to students are apparently inadequate to spur educational advancement and excellence of teachers and students.

The principal is the leader of the institution/college, as a leader they are not only administrative head but also academic head. Therefore, principal must be academically sound, qualified and interested in academic activities. Today, in fact, the principal is having multi-faceted new roles to play. They are expected to uphold the highest standards in professional commitment, interpersonal skill, emotional maturity and academic integrity. Therefore, even appointment of Principal at the verge of retirement is not healthy system because, it is very challenging job. It requires initiative, innovation, strategic planning and problem solving. The demerit of appointment of Principal on the seniority basis is that by the time they are appointed, they are burnt-out or wean-out; rather, they are busy with preparation for pension. It has been seen, therefore, many a time that in crucial period principals take long leave to avoid heavy duty and institution is to be run by in-charge, again as an in-charge they avoid to take important decisions and responsibility which effect the efficiency of the institution and system.

The institutions where systems are good, people tend to work efficiently and sincerely. Quality comes when the leaders are passionate, when leaders succeed in igniting the minds of faculty members and students and through strategy of better human resource development. Quality improvement is not one-shot affair but a long journey. Hence, the appointment of Principal for the colleges of Arunachal Pradesh must be as per UGC norms/rules *i.e.*, open competition with minimum qualification of Ph.D. and ten years of service (Reader Cadre).

Education system is influenced by many factors *viz.*, faculty, curriculum, examination and evaluation system, infrastructure etc., and for imparting quality education, faculty plays the most vital role because other factors are sterile or non-active. It is faculty or teacher who activates the other components in educational institution. For that, again, teacher's continuous self learning like undertaking higher studies, research and attending seminars/ refresher course for updating one's own knowledge and skills is a must. 1966 Education Commission also observed that "of all the different factors which influenced the quality of education and its contribution to national development is the quality, competence and character of teachers are undoubtedly the most significant". Today, all over world, educational institutions are gearing up to provide training, refresher courses and higher studies like M.Phil./ Ph.D. and post-doctoral studies that will help to improve the quality of faculty, and which will be distributed (knowledge) in a manner that is useful to end users. The National Policy on Education (NEP) 1986 calls for overhauling the teacher education system and made important recommendation for continuous enhancement and upgradation of a conceptual clarity, practical skills and competencies of faculties in their respective specialized subjects in order to ensure a quality education.

Rabindranath Tagore once said, "A teacher can never truly teach unless he/she is learning himself/herself. A lamp can never light another lamp unless it continues to burn its own flame". These lines of Tagore legibly divulge that self learning and continuous learning process is must for quality and effective teaching. Thus, quality improvement of higher education of the state largely depends on promotion of faculty by bolster up and providing incentives for pursuing higher studies, attending/organizing seminars and workshops, undertaking research projects, writing paper in journals etc. The encouragement and recognition of teacher's contributions, timely giving information about the latest and various academic opportunities to faculties are also imperative.

The recent initiative taken by the Director of Higher and Technical Education, Govt. of Arunachal Pradesh to recognize the good teachers (college teacher), by giving 'best teacher award' is a good step towards the improvement of quality education in state, because 'a little praise goes a long way for most of the people to keep them proud. Individuals are like flowers, which need watering regularly without which they wither. People become mediocre without encouragement and by abandonment. If maintained, proudly they deliver the best' (Naik, 2006).

Even the appointment of Reader should be according to UGC norms; it should be promotional and make separate cadre so that all teachers of colleges will strive to achieve through hard work, which in turn would lead to development of quality education in the state.

Further, the criteria for the payment of the stipend of students should be both attendance and percentage. Of course, at this stage, we can not write off the payment of the stipend to students considering the socio-economic condition of the tribes of the state but stipend should be something like that of scholarship. Therefore, it should be made into two slabs. For the students who have got seventy-five per cent attendance but have failed to secure forty or forty five per cent should be given a stipend, say, @ Rs. 260/- or Rs. 280 p.m., and to those students who have got seventy-five percent attendance and have secured forty or forty five percent should be given a stipend say, @ Rs. 320/- or Rs. 350/- p. m. Forty per cent sounds very little but to secure forty per cent, any average student has to do some work and in the process it will improve the quality education. This will also create a healthy academic atmosphere and stir up sense of competition amongst the students.

The real wealth of a nation is its people; therefore, a qualitative and progressive education system will definitely bring quality education in the state, in turn, it will ensure better quality of life to people by bringing about an acceptable level of socio-economic development. It will also address our social evils and help in strengthening the liberal and secular fabric of tribal society of Arunachal Pradesh. Since, education can uplift the person socially and economically, there is urgent need to take measure to improve higher education which is directly related to socio-economic development of the society and the nation.

REFERENCES

1. Peter, K.V., Mohan Kr. B., Raj Mohan K., Bhasharan, C. and Mono Mhan C.B., *"Incentive Schemes and Career Management in Higher Education"*, University News, Vol. 44, No. 24, June 12–18, 2006.
2. Patil, M.R. and Arolkar, *"Faculty Development : an avenue to Quality Enhancement in Higher Education"*, University News, Vol. 44, No. 25, June 19–25, 2006.
3. Naik, B. M., *"Quality Assurance system in Higher and Technical Education: Can we Afford to Ignore it?"*, University News, Vol. 44, No. 30, July 24–30, 2006.
4. Kale, R.K., *"Higher Education and Development of the Nation"*, Vol. 44, No. 33, August 14–20, 2006.
5. National Policy on Education : 1986, MHRD, New Delhi.
6. Programme of Action 1992, MHRD, New Delhi.
7. UGC Annual Report 2003-04 and 2004-05.
8. Krishna, V. V., *"Reflection on the Changing Status of Academic Science in India"*, International Social Journal, 168, UNESCO, Paris.

16

Role of Teacher as a Catalyst of Change

—*Ajay Kumar Mishra*

With fast track changes in economic and industrial development there is bound to be mounting demands on education that would be a foil for the demands of highly diversified human resources.

Introduction

Recent years have seen great changes taking place in the field of higher education. They have not only influenced techniques and methodologies of imparting education but in certain ways have even challenged the very purpose and objectives of higher education. There is no doubt that the technological revolution and the emerging and ever shifting needs of society demands major change in our outlook on the role of higher educational institutions. This is also because of the most compelling facts of our time that at the moment we are living in an era of rapid change.

As we have already entered into the new millennium, the world community is experiencing unprecedented change in many respect and we too are the part of the same. New developments in science and technology, competition, media revolution and internationalization are revolutionizing the education sector. They also make new demands and pose fresh challenges to our established educational system and practice. The rapid advances in technology have brought about a knowledge revolution. It has made education a key factor to professional success, heightened the importance of research and innovation, opened up possibilities for new methods of teaching, new modes of educational delivery system and new aids to research and also brought to focus the pivotal role of higher education for human resource development.

These changes argue that the time has come when the colleges and universities have to reappraise their role and functions in order to meet the emerging challenges of new time and to avail the future opportunities. We are also steadily shifting to a fast track of economic and industrial development which leads to mounting demands on education and call for a highly diversified human resource. If we talk in terms of Human Resource Development it can broadly be defined as the "sum total of the knowledge, skills, and aptitudes of the people inhabiting the country"[1]. In a broader sense, it includes the initiative, resourcefulness, capacity for sustained work, right values, interests and attitudes, and other human qualities conducive to higher output and accelerated economic growth.

Higher education is the main instrument for development and change. It has the important task of preparing leaders for different walks of life—social, intellectual, political, scientific and technological. Universities and colleges function as the focal centre of higher education. The intellectual dynamism, resourcefulness and economic prosperity of a country or society are reflected in the quality of higher education. The ideological climate required for a better quality of life and pace of development is created by the universities and the colleges and the intelligentsia nurtured by them. The role of higher educational institutions in social transformation, nation building, scientific development by training and developing better human resources much needed by the country cannot be emphasized.

Goals of Higher Education

The higher education has undergone rapid development in the Post-Independence era. Presently, the institution of higher education in our country is able to produce all the manpower needed for the country's economic, political and social development. Despite this the fact remains that the system has

1. Mehta, M. M., Human Resources Development Planning (with special reference to Asia and far East), The Macmillan Co. of India Ltd., 1976, p. 1.

not been able to accomplish the goals of higher education. The goal of higher education is not to award degrees only on the basis of indifferent instruction and dubious and unreliable system of evaluation. The goal rather is to develop the younger people of the state in such a manner that they not only have a satisfying personal life but can also make a worthy contribution to the progress of the society to which they belong. The institutions of higher education, therefore, have to provide all round development of the students—intellectual, physical, moral and spiritual development of the mind, body, and heart. Personality disseminates knowledge, promotes skills and develops outlook so as to produce young person who are intellectually alert, physically strong, morally upright, aesthically sensitive, socially committed and economically self reliant. Then alone can the institutions of higher education fulfil their purpose. The only way to do this is to ensure that the quality of higher education is such as fulfils these goals.

Quality of Higher Education

The quality of higher education depends on the following :

- quality of content and technique of education.
- the quality of teachers.
- the quality of infrastructure and
- the quality of students.

Content of Education

The quality of education depends on the content of education. It must fulfil the standards of excellence. The pattern of courses, their curricula and syllabi, should be well designed. The course should have relevance to the world in which we live and they should also keep pace with the progress of knowledge in every discipline. The students of our institutions of higher education must have access to the new frontiers of knowledge in all fields. Our Boards of Studies and Academic Councils are responsible for designing and syllabi. They should be ever alert and dynamic. They should introduce new disciplinary and interdisciplinary courses bearing in mind the twin aspects of expansion of knowledge and the demands of the employment market.

Quality of Teachers

Quality of education is not only related with syllabi and curricula it also depends on the quality of teacher. A good teacher has to be a student all his life. He has to be devoted to scholarship and must also have the capacity to transfer the knowledge. A teacher has to be a good communicator. He should be able to stimulate the minds of the students and invoke in them an abiding interest in the subject. Today we have a variety of new techniques including the computer technology and electronic media for dissemination of knowledge. We have also today academic Staff Colleges where we are given orientation and refresher courses. These courses should introduce the teachers to innovative techniques including assignments to the students, tutorials, problem solving sessions, individual and team studies, practical project work etc. I think that all these modern methods of teaching should be availed of.

Quality of Students

When the concept of higher education is reduced only to passing of examination and obtaining degree, when teachers are not committed and where academic atmosphere conducive to the pursuit of scholarship is not available, the students tend to lose their interest in studies and look upon the college years as only a waiting period till they get some job on the attainment of a degree. They tend to induce in superficial studies, irrelevant activities, indiscipline and even campus violence.

Quality of Infrastructure

The lack of atmosphere of knowledge is made worse by the lack of physical facilities. In comparison to other parts we do not have such facilities available in our library and laboratory. Both are needed to be strengthened in many ways. The hopes of providing needed infrastructure facilities are dashed to the ground by the severe financial crunch faced by higher education in our country. The resources provided for education in terms of the percentage of GNP or budget of the Government has gone down.

Role of Principals

In an age of liberalisation, the role of Principals of colleges is very crucial. They have to be efficient managers. They have also to play the leadership role. They are the coordinators of the activities of all the teachers and staff in the colleges. They have to promote and stimulate both the teachers and students for commitment to scholarship. The leadership role of the principals will go a long way in institution building. They have to promote both curricular and co-curricular activities. For the latter a number of schemes like the NSS and NCC are available in the colleges. The principals must see that these schemes fulfil the purpose for which they are designed. Promotion of sports and cultural activities should be such as to promote the participation of all the students in one such activity or another.

To carry out a programme of action successfully, a fundamental requirement is the unity of objectives. Every one involved in the education must accept the objectives, understand the goals that are set and strive towards their fulfilment. The results achieved by an individual or a group should be measured not by their individual performance but by their contribution to the overall objectivities. Where such a unity of objectives is missing, the implementations of programmes will fail.

Managing Quality in Institutions of Higher Education

Higher education is in a flux throughout the country and the world. In almost all countries presently, there is an increasing pressure on the higher education system to equip the students with not only the expertise derived from traditional academic programmes, but also the sufficient range to transferable skills to enable them to play more diversified and effective roles when they enter employment. Therefore, the institution of higher education need to have a very clear understanding of what they are seeking to achieve through their academic programmes. The last quarter of twentieth century has brought fundamental changes in the conditions of countries and states affecting higher education as well. In the post-modern era, higher education has moved from a restricted concept to mass access and that too in a pluralistic system. It has more relevance as a public service something comparable to health and this has brought into picture newer controls through funds provided by government. This has changed the interrelationship between the institutions of higher education, government and society.

Quality Evaluation Process in India

The Indian higher education scenario has now moved forward for assessment and accreditation of institution of higher education.

In this connection particularly two organizations are already in action *i.e.* National Board of Accreditation of All India Council for Technical Education and the National Assessment and Accreditation Council (NAAC), an autonomous organization, with an agenda for apprising and assuring quality in arts, science and other disciplines. This assessment process started in Arunachal Pradesh too and now it is on the verge of completion.

NAAC'S Assessment and Accreditation Process

The process of assessment and accreditation by NAAC is of two types : institutional and departmental (subject-wise). Institutional accreditation studies the functioning of the institution in its totality with its central governance structure and the working of all its departments/centres. However, departmental accreditation focuses on the functioning of a department, considering it as an independent entity with emphasis on the subject *per se*. Though, the manual to be followed by the institution varies according to the type of accreditation as well as the type of institution, the methodology of NAAC's process, which is a three step process, remains the same. The main three stages in the process of assessment and accreditation are :

Stage-I Preparation of self-study report by the institution and its submission to NAAC;

Stage-II Validation of the report by a visit of the peer team; and

Stage-III Final assessment of the NAAC based on the report of the peer team.

Today, NAAC has succeeded in creating considerable awareness among academics, educationists and managers of education on the need for efficiency in operation and for quality in academic functioning of institutions of higher education.

Professional Development of College / University Teachers

Owing to declining standards of Indian Higher Education System, the question of quality assurance becomes critical. One factor that has been identified to improve the standards relates to teachers' education. The document of Plan of Action-National Policy of Education (1986) emphasizes that "it is proposed to organize especially designed Orientation Programmes in teaching methodologies, pedagogy, educational psychology, etc. for all new entrants at the level of lecturers.... and to organize Refresher

Courses for serving teacher at least once in five years." As a consequence of the above the UGC introduced a centrally funded scheme of Academic Staff Colleges (ASCs) in 1987.

The Orientation Course sensitizes the participants in areas like social context of Higher education, methodology of teaching, management issues, psychology, environment and distance education. The Refresher Courses are discipline based and are conducted in collaboration with the respective departments of the Universities or specialized institutions. The scheme of ASCs is regularly monitored by the UGC. Apart from the above a teacher should also be engaged in Research Work and they should be ready to contribute in their respective fields particularly in short courses, Seminars and workshops.

Performance Appraisal of a Teacher

Performance appraisal of a teacher is a matter of great debate. The performance and quality of the functions of any institution is determined by a varity of factors, some of which are external to the system while some are internal. If we talk in terms of assessment and accreditation, institutional improvement, institution efficiency, etc., it is of central importance to understand the teachers' contribution to all this. The best way is to do an appraisal of the performance of the teacher against the background of his/her description. Performance appraisal carried out scientifically encourages goal setting among the individuals in any organization. In my opinion if once an individual is assigned responsibilities and is also given the authority to perform certain tasks, he or she becomes answerable for proper performance of the assigned responsibilities. Assessment is done in order to ascertain whether an individual has performed his duties fully understanding his role prescription. On similar lines, in an educational institution, teachers' performance appraisal may entail an assessment of teachers' work and critical examination of their style of discharging their duties. Teachers' competency and their effectiveness are the fundamental issues under evaluation. If we all the teachers community, take teachers' appraisal positively, the appraisal can be viewed as a means for :

- developing professional skills and knowledge;
- wider participation in and better targeting of in service training;

- dealing constructively with short comings;
- gaining grater confidence;
- improving morale;
- better professional relations and communication within the institution;
- better planning and delivery of the curriculum;
- better career planning;
- better informed reference.

With all these positive aspects, it should not be rejected by the teaching community. It can also be said that the whole concept of appraisal is surrounded by misinterpretation, which has made 'Performance Appraisal' debatable issue. Starting with Radhakrishnan Commission, all the others that followed like Kothari Commission and the National Commission for Teachers in Higher Education as well as the Pay Review Committees, headed by Professors Sen, Malhotra and Rastogi have expressed concern about the need for performance appraisal of teachers. However, major impetus to Performance Appraisal was given by the National Policy on Education (NPE), 1986 and Programmes of Action 1986 and 1992.

The UGC Report "Towards new Educational Management" (Gnanam A., 1990) stressed : "The society has invested precious resources in building up the institutions of higher learning. It is entitled to demand that the members of the academic community individually and collectively be made accountable in concrete visible terms" Today, most of the educational institutions have started applying some mechanism or the other for the performance appraisal of teachers.

The Role of Teacher

The teacher is the principal agency for implementing educational programmes at various levels. Although, his main role is and will remain teaching and guidance of his pupils, he has to promote research, experimentation and innovation. They are to play a pivotal role in extension and social service. This is also the responsibility of the teacher to guide and inspire his students, to enrich his discipline and to inculcate good moral values, which are inconsonance with our cultural heritage and social objectives.

This also involves the transmission of knowledge from one generation to another and extension of the boundaries of knowledge through research, investigation and enquiry. If we all being a teacher accept a progressive outlook on education, we also have to understand the social environment and community needs. What I have observed in Arunachal Pradesh while working as a teacher in the college that the most important factor in educational reconstruction is the teacher—his personal qualities, his educational qualifications, his professional training and the place that he occupies in the educational institution as well as in the community. The reputation of a college apart from other thing invariably depends on the kind of teachers working in it. We should have a genuine interest in youth and an understanding of their psychology. We must be able to contribute to scholarship and advancement of the frontiers of knowledge.

The importance of the role of the teacher as a catalyst and a change agent has become more critical today than ever before. A teacher has to teach his students not only the art of learning but also the art of living and working in a society which they must create as an embodiment of their cherished ideals and realized goals. Thus, education is the only means, which can enrich the nation and improve our society. Without the blessing of education, society could not progress and social and economic development could not be achieved. In the context of rapidly changing global economy, it is imperative that the teachers update their knowledge and skills and be conversant with new technologies and tools for use in the classroom. Lifelong education has become the key factor for succession in a world where information is power and knowledge a dominant factor.

REFERENCES

1. Alder Man Geoffrey (1996), *Audit Assessment and Academic Autonomy*, Higher Education Quarterly, Vol. 50, No. 3, pp. 178–192.
2. Altbach, P.G. (1993), *The dilemma of change in Indian higher education*, Higher Education, 26, 3–20.
3. Ben David, J. (1968), Universities, in Sill, D. (Ed.), *Encyclopedia of Social Sciences*, 16, 191–199.
4. Bourke, P. (1986), "*Quality Measures in Universities*" (Canberra: Commonwealth Tertiary Education Commission).

5. Deshmukh, K.G., (1988), *Universities and Higher Education in the 21st Century*, University News, Vol. 36, No. 28.
6. Government of India (1950), *University Education Commission, 1948-49 Report, Part-I, GOI*, New Delhi, 747 pp.
7. Government of India (1966), *Report of the Education Commission (1964–66) : Education and National Development*, SGOI, New Delhi, Part, I 692 pp. Part, 11, 372pp.
8. Government of India (1985), *Challenge of Education : A Policy Perspective*, GOI, New Delhi, 199pp.
9. Government of India (1986), *National Policy on Education*, 1986, GOI, New Delhi, 29pp.
10. Government of India (1989), *Towards on Enlightened and Human Society*. Report of Committee for Review of the National Policy of Education, 1986, GOI, New Delhi, 409pp.
11. Government of India (1992), *Programme of Action, 1992, National Policy on Education*, 1986, Revised 1992 (Reprinted by UGC), New Delhi, 250pp.
12. Government of India (1997), Government Subsidies in India : Discussion Paper, Department of Economic Affairs, Ministry of Finance, 20pp.
13. Powar, K.B. (1995), "Higher Education in India : Historical Perspective, Present Status and Outlook for the Future," University News, Vol. 33, No. 6.
14. Report of the UGC Committee : Towards New Educational Management, Gnanam Committee, 1990.
15. University Grants Commission, Annual Report, 1996-97.

SECTION—IV
Positive Concerns : Planning the Action

17

Reaching out the Unreached : Higher Education in Arunachal Pradesh through Distance Mode at Perspective

—*M.C. Behera*

The private sector in educational institutes has urban bias. To face these challenges distance mode of education has emerged as a viable alternative with its flexibility, non-formal nature and potential for accessing to diverse courses.

Our young minds have to be ignited.
This ignition is more powerful
compared to any resource on the earth,
under the earth, above the earth.

Dr. A. P. J. Abdul Kalam,
University News, March 2, 1998, p.11.

In recent years, there has been a great expansion of the Universities and institutes running post-graduate, under graduate, diploma and certificate courses in conventional and non-conventional subjects through distance mode. In fact, there is a shift in the mode of delivery of education over the years in our country. There is a journey from *Gurukul* mode to distance mode through formal mode, a journey from the 'stage of craft' to that of technology.[1] The formal mode, however, has certain variants like class-room system and private and correspondence system. In other words, the formal mode consists of regular, private and correspondence modes of delivery. It is the need for private and correspondence modes that has been evolved into Open and Distance Learning (ODL) System. However, unlike private and correspondence modes, distance mode incorporates some features of regular mode like face-to-face contact of teachers and learners through contact and counselling programme and interaction and communication through use of ICT (internet, computer, Video-conferencing, DVD, multi-media, etc.). Understandably, there is a shift from *instruction* to *self-study*, from the indispensable role of *teachers* to the availability of a set of *resources* with teachers as facilitators.

NEED FOR AN ALTERNATIVE MODE[2]

We are living in a knowledge society. The level and range of development of human resource is directly related to the level and field of knowledge of human beings. It is because the level of knowledge is linked to specialisation and qualitative aspect of human resource, contrary to mere literacy index. And knowledge in different fields enlarges the choices of individual. Human development, the catch word of development discourse, is directly linked to qualitative human resource which is nothing but accessing of a greater portion of population to higher and technical education. At the same time, accessing to different fields of knowledge at higher and technical level enlarges human choices. Knowledge thus acquired is indicative of human development because human development[3] indices revolve around economic growth, education and health. Higher and technical education directly fulfils the requirements of education, contrary to mere literacy level, in human development, ensures quality, improves skills, widens understanding, enhances competencies and enlarges choices for gainful employment and thus increases per capita income which is the measure of economic growth. Awareness through education and a better standard of living improves the health condition. Obviously, knowledge in terms of higher and technical education has the key to human development.[4]"

Access to knowledge is not a freedom of choice given the socio-economic conditions of people, especially rural and tribal people. Even in rural and tribal areas the gender factor plays an important role in accessing higher education to aspiring female population (see Table 2 for appreciating gender gap). In this era of

Table 1

Percentage Distribution of Area of a District and Population to the Total of the State

Districts	*Area(Sq. Km)*	*Density of Population*	*percentage of Area*	*Population*
Dibang Valley	13029	4	15.46	5.26
Kurung Kumey	8818	5	10.53	3.87
Upper Siang	6188	5	7.39	3.04
Upper Subansiri	7032	8	8.39	5.04
East Kameng	7422	10	8.86	6.79
Lohit	11402	13	13.62	13.08
West Siang	7643	14	9.13	9.46
West Kameng	4134	14	4.94	5.21
Tawang	2172	18	2.59	3.55
East Siang	4687	19	5.60	7.96
Changlang	4662	27	5.57	11.42
Lower Subansiri	1317	42	1.57	5.08
Papum Pare	2875	42	3.43	11.10
Tirap	2362	42	2.82	9.14
Arunachal Pradesh	83743	13	100.00	100.00

Source : Begi, J., *op. cit.*

Table 2

Urban-Rural Gap in Literacy Rates in Arunachal, 1981-2001

	1981	*1991*	*2001*
Urban-rural gap in male literacy rate (%age points)	38.30	30.99	27.5
Urban-rural gap in female literacy rate (%age points)	40.05	36.92	32.60
Urban-rural gap in total literacy rate (%age points)	41.94	34.57	30.5

Source : Human Development Report of Arunachal Pradesh.

globalisation, nation states formulate policies to be taken care of by market forces. There is a decline in government spending in making public and merit goods available to the mass in order to ensure economic growth with social justice. Private sector is taking over activities which were once considered under the domain government sector, as a matter of principle, to ensure levelling ground keeping the Constitutional provisions in view, for a growth with distributive justice. In emphasising on private sector, perhaps, there is emphasis on economic efficiency through competency and competition.

We are aware of rural-urban, regional and individual inequalities, not in terms of accessing opportunities to resources but in terms of differences in resource ownership. On the face of this unlevel ground, MNCs enter into different sectors of economic and social development. They use sophisticated capital intensive technology and whatever labour force/IT personnel they employ, they select them from a highly competitive job market to which poor and weaker sections have little chance of entry. The education which would have given this opportunity of entry to this section has become inequality breeding agent. Higher and technical education is increasingly getting privatised, the elite section having access to such education has a greater market value in terms of quality human resource than the poor and rural youth of government school products.

Higher education however has not come to the desired level of expectations. On the one hand there is a greater demand for qualified professionals in the field of information technology, business management, genetic engineering, etc. due to the growth of industry and liberalisation of the economy. There are also new avenues like promoting border trade, cultural tourism, etc. Obviously, there is a demand for higher and technical education. On the other, in spite of demand for and availability of higher and technical institutes both at private and government sectors, a large population has less access to higher education. Only 7% of the eligible age group of 17–24 years has access to higher education in India contrary to about 80% in developing countries. India, however, has set a target of achieving 20% participation of eligible age group in higher education to realise Vision 2020.

Precisely, the development of knowledge-based economy, the rapid expansion of the telecommunications industries and the globalisation of business and industries have all brought pressures for an alternative to formal system of education[5].

But challenges are many in the face of shortage of infrastructure, competent teachers, good laboratories, etc. Moreover, the allocation of funds under higher education in the state budget is declining over last few years. Higher education is becoming expensive with urban bias as institutes of higher and technical education are concentrated in urban centres and has a bias for upper stratum of the society. The constraints of higher education can be put as under[6]:

(a) Full time and long study periods leading often to uncertain achievements.

(b) Non-availability of seats in educational institutions.

(c) Non-availability of such institutions in geographically difficult terrains.

(d) Failure of having obtained the required qualifications for entering a particular university course.

(e) Courses and educational programmes not relevant to the existing social needs.

(f) The highest paid teachers are reaching fewer selected students.

(g) Benefits of higher and better education continue to be enjoyed by a privileged few.

(h) High per capita cost of education.

(i) Faulty examination system.

It is in this context that ODL system assumes significance because of its flexibility, not in terms of admission, examination procedures or time relaxation[7] but importantly in terms enlarging choice for a wide range of courses in a cost effective manner. Moreover, it does not have geographical barriers, it reaches to the unreached in terms of geographical distance, to isolated students, by accessing them to study materials, on line interaction, and multi-media sources. Considering from all sides, it can be maintained that distance mode can cater to the educational needs of the weaker sections better than conventional regular mode whether it is in government sector or in private sector. ODL is not a system for weaker sections only, it is considered to be supplementary to regular mode (lateral admission, involvement of teachers in course material preparation, availability of good quality course materials, reducing pressure on government exchequer for maintaining and expanding infrastructure) and most significantly a new stage in the evolution of education using diverse and sophisticated educational technology and transporting knowledge to people than transporting people to the place of knowledge[8]. Distance education in fact takes education to people, but does not distance the people from people for education. The UGC Scheme of Distance Education (1983) mentions the following rationale for setting up the Distance Education System[9].

(i) to provide a system of student-centred self-paced learning;

(ii) to provide a flexible, diversified and open system of education;

(iii) to develop by providing wider access to higher education to persons of all ages and sex particularly to working persons and to economically or otherwise handicapped and persons residing in remote areas;

(iv) to provide means of upgradation of skills and qualifications; and

(v) to develop education as a life long activity so that the individual can refresh his/her knowledge in an existing discipline or to acquire knowledge in new areas.

Under this backdrop the paper examines the higher education scenario in tribal state of Arunachal Pradesh keeping human resource development in view and argues for a systematically planned distance education mode for accessing higher and technical education to aspiring youths who otherwise remain deprived of.

WHAT IS DISTANCE EDUCATION ALL ABOUT?

The beginning in Distance Education in India was first made in 1962 at Delhi University for UG courses. The main objectives of launching correspondence course were[10]:

(i) To provide an efficient and less expensive[11] method of educational instruction at a higher level in the context of national development in India;

(ii) To provide facilities to pursue higher education to all qualified and willing persons who had failed to join regular

university courses due to personnel and economic reasons or because of their inability to get admission to a regular college; and

(iii) To provide opportunities of academic pursuits to educated citizens through correspondence instruction without disturbing their present employment.

Latter on several Universities were set up in various parts of India. Open University concept got strengthened through introduction of Indira Gandhi National Open University (IGNOU) in 1985. However, the first Open University namely, Andhra Pradesh Open University (presently, Dr. B. R. Ambedkar Open University) (1982) marked the beginning of the movement of Open Universities. Some of the open Universities in India are Kota Open University (1987), Yashwant Rao Chavan Maharastra Open University (1989), Dr. Babasaheb Ambedkar University, Ahmedabad; Nalanda Open University, Patna; M.P. Bhoj (Open) University, Bhopal, Netaji Subhas Open University, Kolkata, U.P Rajarshi Tandon Open University, Allahabad and Vidyasagar University of Distance Education (1994), etc.

Distance education is a new stage in the evolution of education which has emerged because of the changing nature of jobs which now require continuous renewal and updating of knowledge and skills (UNESCO, 1995). Throughout the world higher education is undergoing a paradigm shift from an instruction centred formal mode to a learner centred integrated network model which is based on access to learning resources and on student initiative[12]. Precisely, distance education is a mode of education where a student is separated from the teacher from space and time. Viewed from this angle, 'self-study' is distance learning'[13]. General features[14] of distance learning are as follows :

(a) non-formal in nature;

(b) capable of serving educational needs of every adult learner;

(c) capable of offering learning facilities at or near home; and

(d) open in its approach.

Desmond Keegan[15], however, has given more elaborate features considering different definitions of distance education as follows :

— the quasi-permanent separation of teacher and learner which distinguishes it from conventional face-to-face study;

— the influence of educational organisation both in planning and preparation of learning materials and in the provision of student support service which distinguishes it from private study;

— the use of technical media, usually print, to unite teachers and learners to carry the educational content;

— the provision of two-way communication so that students may benefit from or even initiate dialogue;

— the possibility of occasional meetings for both dialectic and socialisation purposes; and

— the participation in an industrialised form of education which, if accepted, contains genus of radical separation of distance education from other forms.

Functional Utility

1. In distance education, a prescribed course of study in broken up into a number of modules, which are posted to students, who has to work on the materials, sent to them. They obtain further guidance and clarification through writing back to the diffusion centre and through attending periodic contact classes which are organised near their places of residence.
2. A second form of distance education is one which uses not only the posted materials, but also the electronic media like radio, TV, computer, etc.

Model of Distance Education

A conceptual planning tool was developed by University of Maryland College for the University system of Maryland Institute for distance education.

(1) Planning issues are common to all models

(a) *Logistical Support* : The students should have access to supports like overnight delivery, priority mail, electronic files transfer and fax.

(b) *Student support :* There must be easily accessible, regularly interacted with the authority about academic matters.

(c) *Faculty support :* Personal Contact Programme (PCP) should be done regularly by the experience faculties.

(d) *Evaluation.*

(e) *Laboratories experiences.*

2. *Planning issues unique to the distributed class room models*

There are three models.

Model A—Distributed classroom : Class sessions involve synchronous communication; Students and faculties are required to be in a particular place at a particular time.

Model B—Independent learning : There are no class sessions; students study independently following the detailed guidelines in the syllabus.

Model C—Open learning and class : Students come together periodically in groups in specified locations for instructor led class sessions through interactive technologies. Presentation of course content is through print, computer disk or videotape etc.

Generally models A and C are used in ODL System.

Traditional Mode vs. Distance Mode : The mode of delivery of education in traditional system is a tripolar process of interactions with study materials, learners and teachers at three poles. But in correspondence course the role of teacher is absent, there being a bipolar correspondence between study materials and the learners[16].

The two modes are shown in Chart-1.

But in distance mode, the teacher is in-built in study materials[17] and in the enlightened management[18] which consists of professional training of academics and administration involved in distance system, use of ICT and multimedia in delivery system[19] and collective functioning and team work. Course materials under

Chart : 1 Correspondence vs. Distance Mode

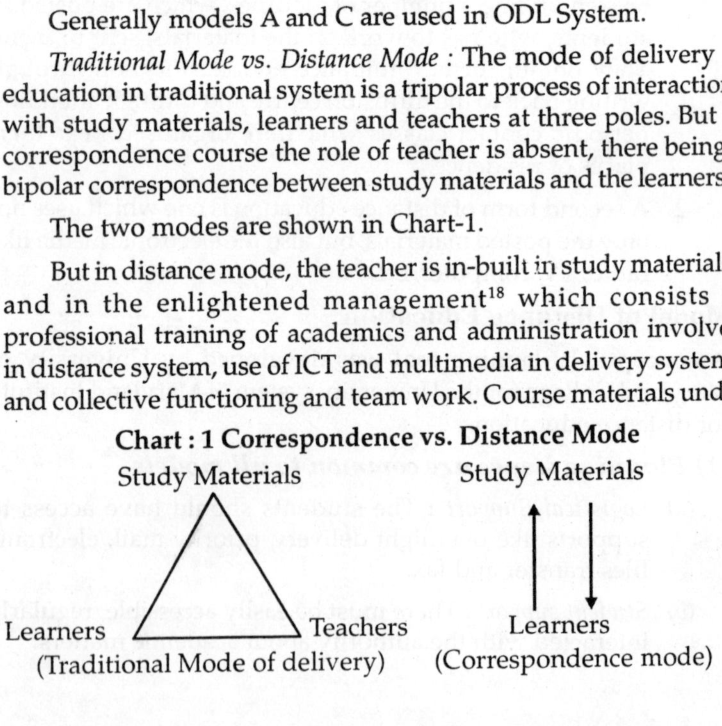

distance mode are prepared in self-instructional format and delivered in both hard and soft copies. Use of Video-conferencing and online interaction in delivery mode provides an ambience of virtual class room situation. Contact and counselling programme, evaluation of assignments with comments for improvement and compulsory assignment writing not only fill in the gap of the absence of teacher in the distance mode but make the teaching-learning process more learner-centred by involving more of student participation.

Distance Mode : Emphasis on Difference[20]

An efficient system of education has two components: interaction and self-study. The essence of distance education is 'self-study', though 'interaction' exists with a difference. Distance mode emphasises on this difference through multi-channel instructional system which comprises :

(a) study material popularly known as lecture scripts;

(b) teaching for short duration to maintain personal contacts, *i.e.* Personal Contact Programmes; counselling sessions, induction;

(c) student Assignment, *i.e.* response sheets;

(d) electronic media: broadcasts on selected topics through Radio; telephonic contact with instructor, Video, teleconferencing, computer, aided instruction, etc.;

(e) study centres;

(f) personal guidance: casual visit by the students to meet the faculty; and

(g) hands-on experience for courses.

This is also shown graphically in Chart-2.

Challenges

Distance education suffers from dishonesty of the persons and institutes which want to make money by issuing certificates. Such fake institutes are being banned by the Supreme Court time and again. Even the UGC withholds recognition to courses offered by such fake universities and institutes.

In order to maintain standard and ensure quality of education, permission of Distance Education Council, New Delhi to run the

Chart-2 Dimensions of self-study

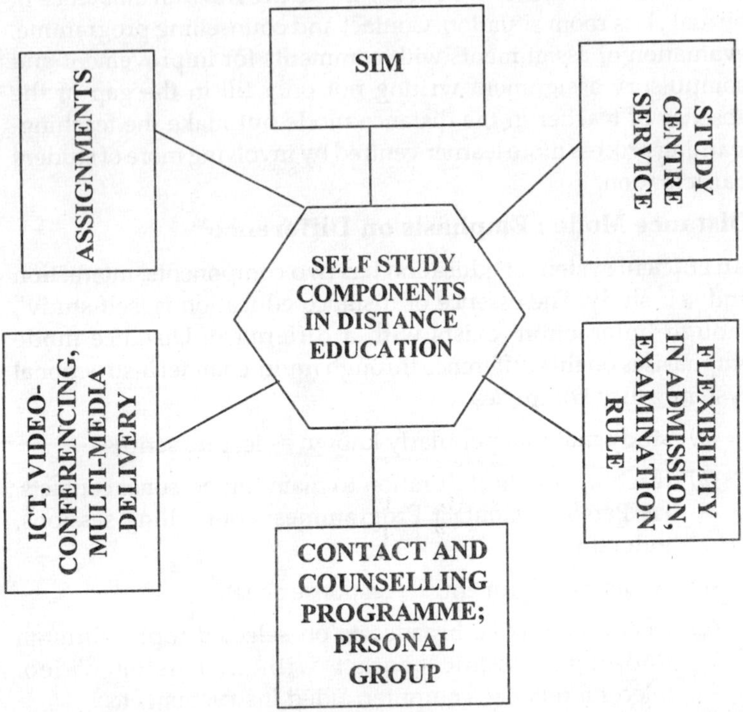

courses is required. The course recognised by DEC is recognised by all the universities and degree/diploma/certificate holders are eligible to central government jobs. However, there are universities running distance mode without the permission from DEC which may not be recognised by other universities. But there has been a general tendency of looking down upon the degree holders obtained from distance mode by conventional institutes in spite of MHRD instruction and DEC guidelines.

The challenges experienced under distance mode can be summarised as follows[21]:

1. acceptability of the degrees obtained from distance at work place and by universities;
2. practicability of imparting some of the subjects through distance mode;

3. method of conducting distance education courses; and
4. profit making attitude of degree giving institutions.

Besides, there is the challenge of quality assurance[22], for distance education has to promote skill, knowledge, competitiveness and competency in the job market which conventional education is lacking in the face of globalisation.

ARUNACHAL AT PERSPECTIVE

The challenges of Higher Education are same as they are for the whole country. However, there are also some problems specific to Arunachal Pradesh. The challenges in Arunachal Pradesh can be summarised in term of accessibility, affordability, acceptability and applicability[23]. Arunachal Pradesh is a mountainous state with the density of 13 persons per sq. km. The density per sq. km. ranges between 4 in Dibang Valley district and 42 in Lower Subansiri, Papum Pare and Tirap districts (See Table-1). The density also does not indicate uniform distribution of population in a district. There are many remote areas with widely separated and sparsely populated settlements which is evident on the basis of a comparison of circle wise density of population of census data. There are many remote areas with widely separated and sparsely populated settlements. Geographically, the state is divided into lower, middle and higher zones. There are no colleges or any technical institute at the higher zone of the state. The colleges are located in lower and middle zones especially in urban centres. Moreover, all the 10 colleges, 2 Technical Institutes, 1 Homeopathic College and 1 Agricultural College are located in 8 districts out of 16 districts of the state. Obviously, 50% of the districts are not covered by colleges. It is to be mentioned that out of 15 institutes of higher education, including one University and another Deemed University, 12 are located in urban centres. As per 2001 census 20.41% of population are urban population. Moreover, all the 17 urban centres (2001 census), do not have any institute of higher education. Roughly about 6.00% of urban and rural population have access to higher education in terms of close proximity. The rural areas spread over hills and mountains with transport bottle-necks do not have access to higher education. It is very much clear when about 80% of the population is engaged in primary sector activities. In other words, people live in backward areas and thus do not have access to higher education. The rural-urban gap in literacy rate is indicative of difference in access to education in general (Table-2). As per the statistics available in the Department of Higher and Technical Education, about 3 percent of the eligible age group of 17-24 years has access to higher education, though the literacy rate (2001 census) in the state is 54.74.

The socio-cultural factor in Arunachal Pradesh also affects the accessibility to higher education. Child and early marriage, responsibility towards family, health factor, etc. deprive many of the accessibility to higher education.

Coupled with this problem of accessibility there is the issue of affordability. Most of the rural areas are not significantly monetised; people still depend on traditional subsistence livelihood. Those who have a little income have to share among a number of children, their health care, traditional rituals and so on. As a result they fail to finance the higher education of children even though higher education is subsidised by granting stipends and free hostel facility.

The Higher Education in Arunachal Pradesh suffers from quality because of many reasons. This is very much clear from higher rate of S.T work participation in Primary Sector (87.16) and lower rate of participation in Secondary (2.98) and Tertiary Sectors (9.86). There are many unemployed youths in the state and most of them hesitate to compete outside even though they are entitled to ST quota. The quality of Higher Education is not encouraging because of shortage of infrastructure, non-conventional course, etc[24]. The medium of instruction being English also does not provide ambience to the rural people for understanding and learning in a right perspective. As a result, the knowledge which they learn does not have applicability even in their jobs in which they are employed on reservation quota. There is a charge labelled against Arunachalee employees working in offices that they do not work. This is because the competency required for their work is found to be lacking due to low level of quality achievement through education. Because of this lack of quality and skill they avoid work which has developed into a loss of work culture in the state. Here also the higher education suffers in applicability front.

There is a decline in the share of budget allocation under education sector in general and in the share of higher education in total budget allocation under education in particular (Table-3). The

Table 3

Budget Grant of Education Department (Rs. in Crore)

Financial Year	*Higher and Technical Education*				*School Education*	*Education Department Grant Total*
	DHE	*R.G. University*	*R.G. polytechnic*	*Total*		
2001-02	9.66 (39.57)	3.75 (13.81)	11.00 (45.06)	24.41 (12.10)	177.51	201.92
2002-03	9.21 (38.04)	4.00 (16.52)	11.00 (45.44)	24.21 (13.70)	152.63	176.84
2003-04	14.08(59.71)	4.00 (16.96)	5.50 (23.32)	23.58 (11.43)	182.80	206.38
2004-05	10.72(35.37)	8.59 (28.34)	11.00 (36.29)	30.31 (22.60)	103.77	134.08
2005-06	12.64(28.13)	8.59 (19.12)	23.70 (52.75)	44.93 (18.59)	196.81	241.74

Source : Begi, J., *op.cit.*

Note : *(i)* The total grant include both plan and non-plan grants.

(ii) Figures in the parentheses show % to total of each category.

allocation is not sufficient to provide necessary infrastructure and teachers[25] at least to maintain standard of education, not to speak of expansion.

Status of Distance Education

The distance education programme has been launched in the state with the pioneering effort of IGNOU and Rajiv Gandhi University. The IGNOU with its Regional Office at Naharlagun, established in 2000, and 9 study centres in the state provides education in both conventional and non-conventional courses. There are also 15 centres of National Open Schools accessing education at school level but preparing youths for higher education thereby. Rajiv Gandhi University has just launched distance education programme from 2004-05 starting with five subjects and 64 enrolments at undergraduate level. It has four study centres in colleges at Bomdila, Deomali, Tezu and Changlang.

During 2005-06 two more subjects namely Hindi and Sociology have been introduced. The Centre is preparing to launch Certificate Course in Fisheries Technology and to introduce Tribal Studies as a subject at undergraduate level from the session 2007-08.

During the session 2006-2007, 250 students have been enrolled to first year degree course. Of these 250 learners, there are 230 Arunachalee and 15 non-Arunachalee students. These non-Arunachalees belong to Manipur, Kerela, Assam, Bihar, U.P and Meghalaya but work in Papum Pare, Changlang, and Tirap districts of the state. Of Arunachalee students 133 are male and 102 female, while among the non-Arunachalees there are 9 male and 6 female learners. Further, out of the total enrolment, 208 are from formal mode of education, mainly from CBSE, and the remaining are from Open School (36) and from Diploma and Nursing courses. In fact Distance Education draws students from both formal and non formal streams. The eligibility criteria under formal stream is +2 and above. The non-formal sources include Open School and other equivalent standards. Under Open school, +2 and above is the eligible criterion for admission to BA 1st year degree course. However, under equivalent category candidates are required to have at least 2 years diploma in any subject or nursing, after 10th standard in order to be eligible for admission.

Except Dibang Valley district, candidates belonging to 15 districts of the state have got admitted themselves during the session 2006-07. The total candidates from Papum Pare are 84 out of which 73 belong to the district itself. This is followed by 34 from Lower Subansiri, 33 from West Siang and 21 from Tirap. The Arunachalee learners belong to Nyishi, Adi, Apatani, Khampti, Hills Miri, Khamba, Tagin, Galo, Monpa, Wangcho, Meyor, Miju Mishmi, Tangsa, Miji, Nocte, Tutsa, Sulung and Sherdukpen communities of the state. Because of the study centres at Tezu, Deomali, Bomdila and Changlang, it has become possible to cover many districts and tribes inhabiting there. The centre provides self instructional materials, conducts contact and counselling programme and evaluates assignments with necessary comments as mechanism of interaction with the student in the absence of class room interaction.

PLANNING A DISTANCE MODEL

In view of non-accessibility to remote area, the resource constraints faced by the State Government, socio-economic backwardness of the masses and the need of higher education for human resource development in the process of economic growth, a model of planning and management of distance education is presented.

1. In every district without any college there shall be a Study Centre under the charge of Centre Coordinator. As in District and Sub-Divisional Head Quarters there are Higher Secondary Schools, the resource persons in concerned subjects can be drawn from the Senior Teachers during the contact and counselling programme. Laboratory in Schools can also be promoted and utilised for providing education in the Science subjects. This will not only make best use of available resources but will have backward linkages in strengthening Higher Secondary Education. The teachers who will be involved as resource persons will not only update their knowledge but will be academically active. Their involvement will strengthen the Higher Secondary Education with update knowledge in the subjects. In the subjects in which resource persons will not be available from centres, peripatetic faculties may be appointed to take care of such shortcomings in different study centres.

2. The Centre can be used as *library-cum-reading room* for the public.

3. The centre can also organise *career counselling programme* and *coaching* for entrance examinations either online or in collaboration with other service providers on the subject. The Study Centre can also organise programmes and introduce courses in collaboration with various departments like medical, industry, fisheries, etc., for creating awareness on health, human rights, consumer's rights, etc. The Centre also can help in introducing courses to promote the existing indigenous knowledge in the area. The Government and the University shall be stakeholders from the Administration side. The Government shall look after infrastructure facilities, employment of human resource with an initial investment as the courses in Distance Education are largely self financing. The Centres will generate own revenue. The University will control the Academic performance through the Centre for Distance Education and conduct performance audit on the basis of which the State Government shall execute incentives, promotion, etc.

Collaborative networking, externalities by way of undertaking related activities and benefits of decentralised study centres are shown in charts 3, 4 and 5 respectively.

The target shall be those who are in service, those who are physically challenged, those who are confined in the home, those who want value addition in their profession and those who are not in a position to get formal education. The UGC spelt out the following categories of learners who would benefit from distance mode[26]:

1. students who had to discontinue their formal education owing to pecuniary and other circumstances;
2. students in geographically remote areas;
3. persons who want to learn and earn simultaneously;
4. students who had to discontinue their education because of lack of aptitude and motivation but who may later on become motivated;
5. students who cannot find a seat or do not wish to join regular college or university department although they

have the necessary qualifications to pursue higher education;

6. individuals who look upon education as a life-long activity and may either like to pursue their knowledge in an existing discipline or to acquire knowledge in new areas; and
7. in-service persons.

Significance in Arunachal Pradesh

Challenges before higher education in the state is manifold. In one of the recommendations.[27] Begi argues for distance mode of education to meet up the challenges of higher education in the state. Distance mode of education for the state has significance for other counts as follows :

Efficienting formal mode : In the face of infrastructural deficiency and shortage of teaching staff, distance mode will reduce the pressure on formal educational institutes. Moreover, the teachers involved in distance education will update their knowledge in the subject which will benefit the students. Course materials on different subjects prepared by experts drawn from colleges will also be available. The existing infrastructure shall not be overused given the learners an alternative and a good mode of education. Optimum use of resources is always efficient and hence the formal education shall be efficient when the colleges will cease to be overcrowded.

Reduced burden on state exchequer : As students are entitled to stipend and free accommodation, distance mode will relieve financial burden of the state exchequer to a great extent. Arunachal Pradesh is sparsely populated and the government on public demand and as a part of social and political commitment[28] is found opening up colleges with inadequate infrastructure and managing with existing teaching staff in the state. Moreover, the enrolments in colleges will be very less making the education very expensive in spite of inadequate infrastructure and shortage of teaching staff.

Value addition : Presently, a job seeker with a simple degree does not have an edge over others in the job market who have some value addition through distance education. Simultaneous admission to degree, diploma and certificate courses are permitted under distance mode[29]. A Commerce graduate with a certificate, say in Tally Programme gets an edge over a simple Commerce graduate. Through distance education the in-service persons can

Chart-3 : Outsourcing and Sharing

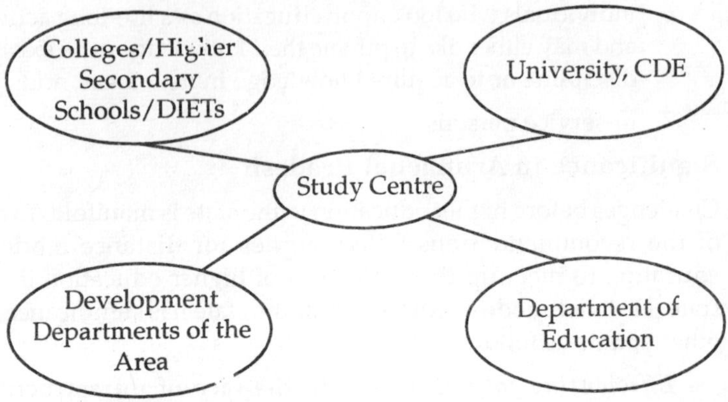

add value to their professional requirements, which in turn will help in promoting work culture.

Skill Upgradation : In-service persons experience transfer/promotion to branches dealing with new subjects. Efficient dealing with the subject may require the skill which the person may not have acquired during his/her previous posting. A short course in the related matter will help in skill upgradation and familiarity with the new job requirement. Some times, there may be technological innovation into the working system like the introduction of computer in place of manual typing. In such cases, skill upgradation through distance education will train the workforce to take up the new challenges which may come with the introduction of new innovation.

Meeting of market demand for human resource : The government of Arunachal Pradesh is all set to benefit from globalisation and liberalisation and therefore is inviting MNC investment and trying to promote border trade and cultural tourism. But unfortunately the quality of human resource required is not as per demand. As mass population does not have resource for quality education in private institutes, distance education can be only a viable alternative in this regard.

Motivator of study habit at home : Generally, Arunachalee homes do not provide a study atmosphere and children do not have a study habit. When adults will pursue education and study at home, for, at a matured age they may hate failure and distance mode promotes self study, the children may be motivated to study.

Promotion of work culture : Because of the reservation, many Arunachalees enter into service with minimum qualification. The knowledge they acquire may not be in the tune of requirement of the profession given the problems of education in the state. As a result, they avoid normal routine work leading to a decline in work culture. Promotion to post requires higher qualification. This works as a motivator for many to go for higher studies. Many may pursue it to acquire the working knowledge required for the job. When opportunity is provided for higher education without remaining absent from the job, then many get motivated to pursue studies. This enhances knowledge and develops skill of the in-service persons. They develop familiarity with the job requirement through enhanced knowledge which they acquire through distance mode. Familiarity through acquiring knowledge encourages involvement which in turn may promote work culture.

Controlling youth delinquency : As mere degree does not fetch a job, many degree holders are found unemployed. Moreover, they do not have access to further studies due to one reason or the other. In the changing situation, the traditional mode of life does not ensure bare recessities like health care, a decent dressing, etc. They remain frustrated and a vulnerable section of population for religious conversion, delinquent activities, joining ultra groups or easy target for the politicians to manipulate. When there is a way out for a better life and means available to achieve it, then normal youths will not venture for ultra activities. Distance mode of education promises such an alternative because of its non-formal nature, diverse courses, and flexible operation and by transporting knowledge to the aspiring people.

Infusing a sense of self-esteem : In Arunachal Pradesh, education is a highly subsidised commodity. The learners do not understand the importance of quality education as they do not pay for earning it. They do not give much importance to learning and therefore there is high incidence of dropouts and stagnation. In distance education, the education is partly or wholly self-financed and learners understand the worth of getting it. They do not take it lightly as they pay for it. It develops a sense of self-esteem when a person gets education by paying for it. Naturally, a distance learner tries to get the best for his money and this ensures quality along with his self esteem.

Minimising political interference : In principle distance education is not state sponsored programme and thus de-links political interference. The decision about management or organisation of courses is not a mater of state intervention like that of permitting for or opening of a college or introducing a course. Distance education is free from political manoeuvring to greater extent and thus does not suffer from quality fronts like state control education system.

Chart-4 : Auxiliary Role of Study Centre

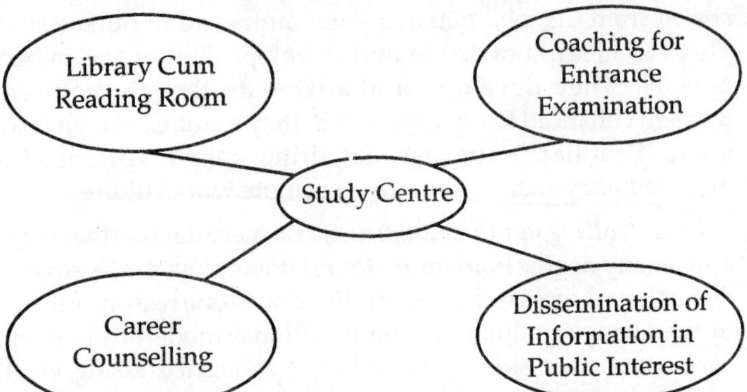

Flexibility in utilising service of faculties : Under traditional mode, when a course becomes redundant, it does not become easy to reduce the expenditure on it given the maintenance of infrastructure and salary of regular employees. To switch over to other courses existing teachers need professional training or proficient teachers need to be appointed. Either, training or appointing new teachers by keeping the old ones and not utilising their services productively has a financial burden. But the case of distance education is different because the courses are mostly self-financed. The Centres of Distance Education can make provision of professional training to teachers involved in different courses if there is a switch over to new or related courses. Under regular mode, which is more formal, the qualification of teacher matters most in order to be in a particular department even if the course is very much related to another department. Even if the teachers are not to be permitted academic involvement in new courses, there shall be enough management works where their services can be productively utilised unlike in colleges where expansion of management has a very limited scope.

A Few Recommendations

Keeping in view the challenges of distance education a few recommendations are made.

1. There is a tendency of looking down upon the degrees obtained by the distance mode by the agents and institutes of conventional education. While the degree of a University through conventional mode is recognised its degree under distance mode is questioned. The problem does not lie in the degree of the university but in the conventional mind-set of the people. Therefore, there should not be any mention of distance mode in the mark sheets and certificates as is the practice followed in Delhi University.
2. As distance education is non-formal, flexible, diverse and reversal in approach by transporting education to the learners' home keeping in view the changing market demand, the administrators and academics of conventional mode who are to be involved in distance mode need to be properly oriented, because the later requires a totally different understanding, vision, mind-set and work culture.
3. Management of distance education should be de-linked from conventional system of management or linked, if required, through a clear-cut policy measure especially in such Universities which provide both regular and distance modes of education.
4. The government should play the role of a facilitator.
5. When the Centre for Distance Education does not have resource persons or can not introduce a course having demand in the market, then it should enter into MoU with institutes providing quality education in the subject.
6. The University running distance education should open its own study centres without giving franchise to any organisation.

Chart-5 : Advantages of Decentralised Study Centres

Direct	Study Centre	Indirect
Easy access to learners		Strengthening Secondary Education
Cost effectiveness		Employment generation
Optimum use of State resources		Creating awareness
Fulfilment of social and developmental commitments of the State by providing opportunities of accessing to higher education		

REFERENCES

1. Kulandai Swamy, V.C., 2002, *Education for Knowledge Era—Open and Flexible Learning*, Edited by Suresh Garg and Santosh Panda, Kogan Page, New Delhi, pp. 1-2.
2. See Ram Reddy, G., 1988, : "Distance Education : What, Why and How?" in Koul. B. N., Singh, B., and Ansari, M.M. (eds), *Studies in Distance Education*, Association of Indian Universities and IGNOU, New Delhi, pp. 15–18.; Also see Takwale, Ram 1988: " Dimensions and Extensions of Distance and Open Educational Systems" in Koul. B. N., Singh, B., and Ansari, M.M. (eds), *Studies in Distance Education*, Association of Indian Universities and IGNOU, New Delhi. pp. 26-30.
3. See various issues of Human Development Reports.
4. "The crucial role of higher education, in the process of development and modernization was well recognized from the beginning of Indian Planning... This recognition is abundantly evident in the observation of its first Prime Minister, Jawaharlal Nehru, that, if all is well with the Universities, it will be well with the nation" (GOI,1996 : Planning Commission, p. 1).

   Kothari Commission has also said : "In a world based on Science and Technology, it is education that determines the level of prosperity, welfare and security of the people" (GOI, 1964-66 : Education Commission, p.1). Also see *World Development Report*, 1991, pp. 31, 55-56.
5. See Haugley, M., 2000, "A global society needs flexible learning", in Jakupec, V. and Garrick, J. (eds), *Flexible Learning, Human Resource and Organizational Development : Putting theory to work*, Routledge, London, pp. 11–29.

6. Sharma, B.B., 1993, "Dynamics in Distance Education : some Innovative Approaches". in *Academic XII, Directors' Meet*, Special Number (April 22-24, 1993), Academic Staff College, HP University, Shimla, vol. V, No. 1, April 1995, p. 41; Also see Takwale, R.,1988: *op.cit.*, pp. 29–30.
7. Prasad, V.S. and Venkaiah, V., 2005, *India's First Open University – Experience of two decades*, GRADE, Dr. B. R. Ambedkar Open University, Hyderabad, see Ch. II for 'access and equity', Ch. III for 'flexibility', Ch. IV for 'innovation' and Ch. V for 'quality' in distance mode.
8. Kulandai Swamy, V.C., 1993, 'Open University', in Chatnis, Suma and Altbach, Phillip G. (eds.), *Higher Education Reform in India*, Sage, New Delhi, p. 366.
9. Quoted in Goel, Aruna and Goel, S.L., 2001, *Distance Education in the 21st Century*, Deep and Deep, New Delhi, p. 32; Also see Ram Reddy, G., 1988 , *op.cit.*, pp. 15-18.
10. Quoted in Goel, Aruna and Goel, S.L., *op.cit.*, pp. 39-40.
11. Kulandai Swamy, V.C., 2002, *Education for Knowledge Era—Open and Flexible Learning*, Edited by Suresh Garg and Santosh Panda, Kogan Page, New Delhi. The programme specific cost per student proved that OUs were less expensive, about 1/3 of the cost than the corresponding programmes in CUs, p. 142.
12. Power, K.B., 1997, "Globalisation of Distance Learning System—Implications for Developing Countries", in University News, January 27, 1997, AIU, New Delhi.
13. Kulandai Swamy, V.C., 2002, *op.cit*, p. 10.
14. Takwale, R., 1988, *op.cit.*, p. 30.
15. Keegan, Desmond, 1983, "On Defining Distance Education" in Stewart, David, *et al.*, (eds) *Distance Education-International Perspective*, Croom Helm, London.
16. Goel, A. and Goel, S.L. 2001, *op.cit*. p. 31. Also See the STRIDE Hand book on *Development and Revision of Self-Learning Materials*, STRIDE, IGNOU, New Delhi, Handbook No. 5, 1989.
17. STRIDE Handbook No-5, *ibid*. Also see *Guidelines for Design, Development and Delivery of Programmes/Courses Through Distance Mode*, Distance Education Council, New Delhi, 1999.
18. Chatterjee, T.K., 2006, "Best practices in University Administration in the contemporary perspective", presented at the National Seminar on *Challenges of Higher Education in the Present Perspective and the Role of instance Mode*, November 3–4, 2006, Tripura University, Agartala.

19. According to Michael Moore, the distance mode of education departs from the conventional mode because of the use of the multi-media communication approach in the former. Moore, M.G., 1973: "Towards a theory of Independent learning and Teaching," *Journal of Higher Education*, Vol. 44, p. 664.
20. Kulandai Swamy, V.C., 2002, *op. cit.*, p. 10-11; Goel, A. and Goel, S.L. 2001, *op.cit.*, p. 41-42.
21. Sarkar, Sanjay Gopal, 2006, "Abstract', presented at the National Seminar on *Challenges of Higher Education in the Present Perspective and the Role of istance Mode*, November 3–4, 2006, Tripura University, Agartala. The *Abstract* is published in the Souvenir on the occasion by Tripura University officers' Association, pp. 11-12.
22. For quality assurance in distance education see different research papers in Gupta, S. P. (ed.), 2005: *Quality Assurance in Distance Education*, UP Rajarshi Tandon Open University, Allahabad.
23. Based on the "Observations" made by Prof. E. Balagurusami, Chairman, Governing Body, Consortium of Educational Communication, New Delhi, at the Policy Seminar on *Development of Content and Capacity Building Programmes on Northeast EDUSAT Network*, 22nd November, 2006, Rajiv Gandhi University, Itanagar.
24. Begi, Joram, 2006, "The Growth and Evolution of Education in Arunachal Pradesh: A Study in Historical Perspective", *Ph.D. Thesis* of Rajiv Gandhi University, Itanagar. Chapter –VIII has elaborately discussed the problem of higher education in the state.
25. There are shortage of teachers, curtailing of library grants, etc. Begi, J., *ibid*.
26. University Grants Commission, *Annual Report*, 1981-82.
27. Begi, Joram, *op.cit*. see Chapter-IX.
28. See Begi, *ibid* for the influence of politicians on education in the state and subsequent impact on quality.
29. IGNOU, 2003: *Manual on Student Registration and Evaluation Systems*, IGNOU, New Delhi, pp. 30, 32.

18

Understanding the Learners

—*T. Madhusudan*

If the Industrial Age was built on people's backs and the information Age on people's left hemispheres, the conceptual Age is being built on the people's right hemispheres.

Introduction

Students have different learning styles—characteristic strengths and preferences in the ways they take in and process information. Some students tend to focus on facts, data, and algorithms; others are more comfortable with theories and mathematical models. Some respond strongly to visual forms of information, like pictures, diagrams, and schematics; others get more from verbal forms—written and spoken explanations. Some prefer to learn actively and interactively; others function more introspectively and individually.

Learning style modes provide good framework for designing instruction with the desired breadth. The goal is to make sure that the learning needs of students in each category are met at least part of the time. This is referred to as "teaching around the cycle." Students may be :

- ***Extraverts*** — try things out, focus on the outer world of people
- ***Introverts*** — think things through, focus on the inner world of ideas

- ***Sensors*** — practical, detail-oriented, focus on facts and procedures
- ***Intuitors*** — imaginative, concept-oriented, focus on meanings and possibilities
- ***Thinkers*** — skeptical, tend to make decisions based on logic and rules
- ***Feelers*** — appreciative, tend to make decisions based on personal and humanistic considerations
- ***Judgers*** — set and follow agendas, seek closure even with incomplete data
- ***Werceivers*** — adapt to changing circumstances, resist closure to obtain more data.

Learning Styles

Let us try understanding the learners by analysing their learning styles based on different genesis.

Classifying the students as having a preference for

(1) *Concrete Experience* or *Abstract Conceptualization* (how they take information in)

(2) *Active Experimentation* or *Reflective Observation* (how they internalize information)

The four types of learners in this classification scheme are :

***Type 1 : "Why?"* (Concrete, Reflective)**

A characteristic question of this learning type is *why?* These types of learners respond well to explanations of how course material relates to their experience, their interests, and their future careers.

To be effective with *Type 1 students, the instructor should function as a motivator.*

***Type 2 : "What?"* (Abstract, Reflective)**

A characteristic question of this learning type is *what?* These types of learners respond to information presented in an organized, logical fashion and benefit if they have time for reflection.

To be effective, the instructor should function as an expert.

Type 3 : "How?" (Abstract, Active)

A characteristic question of this learning type is *how?* These types of learners respond to having opportunities to work actively on well-defined tasks and to learn by trial-and-error in an environment that allows them to fail safely.

To be effective, the instructor should function as a coach, providing guided practice and feedback.

Type 4 : "What if?" (Concrete, Active)

A characteristic question of this learning type is *What if?* These types of learners like applying course material in new situations to solve real problems.

To be effective, the instructor should stay out of the way, maximizing opportunities for the students to discover things for themselves.

Traditional engineering instruction focuses almost exclusively on formal presentation of material (lecturing), a style comfortable for only Type 2 learners. To reach all types of learners, a professor should

- Explain the relevance of each new topic (Type 1),
- Present the basic information and methods associated with the topic (Type 2),
- Provide opportunities for practice in the methods (Type 3),
- Encourage exploration of applications (Type 4).

Classifying students on the basis of psychological mode

Sensing Learners (concrete, practical, oriented toward facts and procedures)

Intuitive Learners (conceptual, innovative, oriented toward theories and meanings)

Visual Learners (prefer visual representations of presented material—pictures, diagrams, flow charts)

Verbal Learners (prefer written and spoken explanations)

Inductive Learners (prefer presentations that proceed from the specific to the general)

Deductive Learners (prefer presentations that go from the general to the specific)

Active Learners (learn by trying things out, working with others)

Reflective Learners (learn by thinking things through, working alone)

Sequential Learners (linear, orderly, learn in small incremental steps)

Global Learners (holistic, systems thinkers, learn in large leaps).

Brain Dominance

Before settling down how to teach all the types we shall try understanding the human brain dominance, based on the Task specialized functioning of the physical human brain.

Brain is divided into two hemispheres. Each side of the brain has its own unique and special abilities. The right side of the brain is intuitive, while the left side of the brain is logical.

Even though both hemispheres of the brain have independent functions, an individual benefits from the integration of the processing of information performed by each side. The hemisphere best suited to perform the particular activity will process information; this allows an individual greater understanding and learning potential of the situation that initiated the brain processing information.

Research has shown most people have a dominant side of the brain. Individuals who are predominately left sided tend to be more verbal, analytical, and problem solvers; while individuals who are predominately right sided tend to be artsy, good with math, and are more visual in nature. Dominance goes into affect when thinking becomes increasingly more complex. Although each hemisphere has its own set of functions in information processing and thinking, research data supports the notion these functions are not exclusive to one hemisphere.

Hemispheric Dominance

Right Hemispheric Functions :	*Left Hemispheric Functions :*
1	2
• Connected to left side of the body	• Connected to right side of body

1	2
• Integrates many inputs at once	• Deals with inputs one at a time
• Processes information more diffusely and simultaneously	• Processes information in a linear and sequential manner
• Deals with space	• Deals with time
• Responsible for gestures, facial movements, and body language	• Responsible for verbal expression and language
• Responsible for relational and mathematical operations	• Responsible for invariable and arithmetic operations
• Specializes in recognizing places, faces, objects, and music	• Specializes in recognizing words and numbers
• Does intuitive and holistic thinking	• Does logical and analytical thinking
• The seat of passion and dreams	• The seat of reason
• Crucial side for artists, craftsman, and musicians	• Crucial side for wordsmiths and engineers

Females Test Better On :	*Males Test Better On :*
• Perceptual speed	• Spatial tasks
• Verbal fluency	• Target direct motor skills
• Determining the placement of objects	• Spotting shapes embedded in complex diagrams
• Identifying specific attributes of objects	• Mathematical reasoning
• Precision manual tasks	
• Arithmetic calculations (simple math)	

Myths and Learning

There are several myths associated with hemispheric dominance. Myths related to :

- Handedness—No correlation between hemispheric dominance and being right handed vs. left handed.
- Intelligence—No evidence to support right-sided hemispheric dominance is superior to left side hemispheric dominance and *vice versa*. There is no correlation to intelligence.
- Genetics—No evidence that dominance is hereditary.
- Gender—Females tend to be more left hemispheric dominant and males tend to be more right hemispheric dominant.

Task-specialized Functioning of the Physical Human Brain

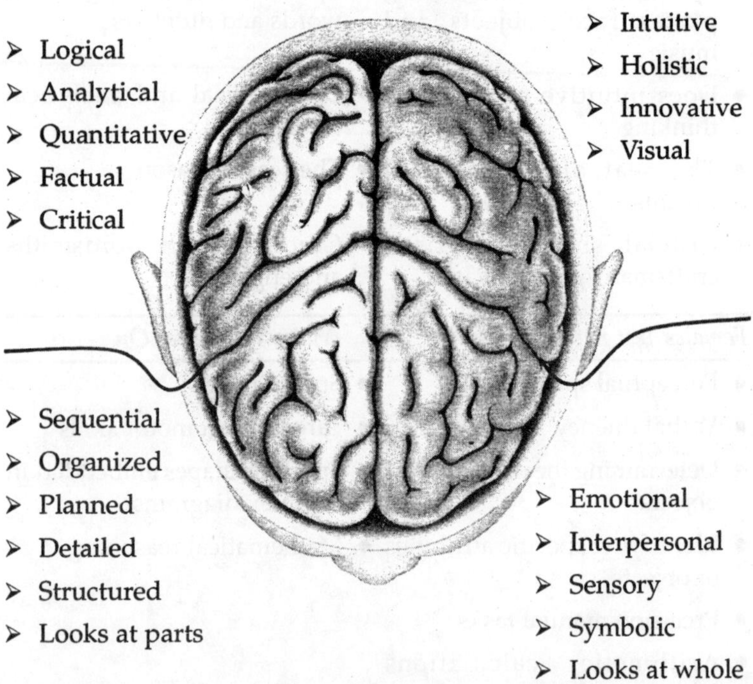

The study says "If the Industrial Age was built on people's backs and the information Age on people's left hemispheres, the conceptual Age is being built on the people's right hemispheres!!!

Technologies are proving they can outperform the left brain. They can execute sequential computational work better, faster and more accurately than even those with highest IQs. Stock brokers, lawyers, financial agents all are feeling the heat of automation. It is not fantastical to imagine a day when certain types of left brain jobs need not be outsourced to India because they can be automated. Paradoxically, the left brain can create machines and software that can do the left brain's jobs.

Moving from information age to conceptual age explains that the present world operates on a much more emotional, creative level where designers have more scope.

Earlier days most engineering instruction consequently focuses on left-brain Analysis and Methods and Procedures associated with that analysis, neglecting important skills associated with Right brain *i.e* teamwork, communications, creative problem solving, systems thinking, synthesis, and design. This was causing imbalance. Based on the research the new versions of curriculum have increased the components to maintain the balance.

TEACHING TO ALL TYPES

Here are some strategies to ensure that the courses present information those appeals to a range of learning styles. These suggestions are based on the Psychological mode.

- *Teach theoretical material by first presenting phenomena and problems that relate to the theory* (sensing, inductive, global).

For example, don't jump directly into free-body diagrams and force balances on the first day of a static's course. First describe problems associated with the design of buildings and bridges and artificial limbs, and perhaps give the students some of those problems and see how far they can go before they get all the tools for solving them.

- *Balance conceptual information* (intuitive) *with concrete information* (sensing). Intuitors favor conceptual information—theories, mathematical models, and material that emphasizes fundamental understanding. Sensors prefer concrete information such as descriptions of physical phenomena, results from real and simulated experiments, demonstrations, and problem-solving algorithms.

For example, when covering concepts of vapor-liquid equilibria, explain Raoult's and Henry's Law calculations and nonideal solution behaviour, but also explain how these concepts relate to barometric pressure and the manufacture of carbonated beverages.

- *Make extensive use of sketches, plots, schematics, vector diagrams, computer graphics, and physical demonstrations* (visual) *in addition to oral and written explanations and derivations* (verbal) *in lectures and readings.*

For example, show flow charts of the reaction and transport processes that occur in particle accelerators, test tubes, and biological cells before presenting the relevant theories, and sketch or demonstrate the experiments used to validate the theories.

- *To illustrate an abstract concept or problem-solving algorithm, use at least one numerical example* (sensing) *to supplement the usual algebraic example* (intuitive).

For example, when presenting Euler's method for numerical integration, instead of simply giving the formulas for successive steps, use the algorithm to integrate a simple function like $y = x^2$ and work out the first few steps on the chalkboard with a hand calculator.

- *Use physical analogies and demonstrations to illustrate the magnitudes of calculated quantities* (sensing, global).

For example, tell your students to think of 100 microns is about the thickness of a sheet of paper and to think of a mole as a very large dozen molecules. Have them pick up a 100 ml. bottle of water and a 100 ml. bottle of mercury before talking about density.

- *Occasionally give some experimental observations before presenting the general principle, and have the students (preferably working in groups) see how far they can get toward inferring the latter* (inductive).

For example, rather than giving the students Ohm's or Kirchoff's Law up front and asking them to solve for an unknown, give them experimental voltage/current/resistance data for several circuits and let them try to figure out the laws for themselves.

- *Provide class time for students to think about the material being presented* (reflective) *and for active student participation* (active). Occasionally pause during a lecture to allow time for thinking and formulating questions. Assign "one-minute papers" near the end of a lecture period, having students write on index cards the lecture's most important point and the single most pressing unanswered question. Assign brief group problem-solving exercises in class that require students to work in groups of three or four.
- *Encourage or mandate cooperation on homework* (every style category). Hundreds of research studies show that students who participate in cooperative learning experiences tend to earn better grades, display more enthusiasm for their chosen field, and improve their chances for graduation in that field relative to their counterparts in more traditional competitive class settings.
- *Demonstrate the logical flow of individual course topics* (sequential), *but also point out connections between the current material and other relevant material in the same course, in other courses in the same discipline, in other disciplines, and in everyday experience* (global).

For example, before discussing cell metabolism chemistry in detail, describe energy release by glucose oxidation and relate it to energy release by nuclear fission, electron orbit decay, waterfalls, and combustion in fireplaces, power plant boilers, and automobiles. Discuss where the energy comes from and where it goes in each of these processes and how cell metabolism differs. Then consider the photosynthetic origins of the energy stored in C-H bonds and the conditions under which the earth's supply of usable energy might run out.

Conclusion

Understanding the learning styles is useful for providing balancing instruction. Which model educators choose is almost immaterial, since the instructional approaches that teach around the cycle for each of the models are essentially identical. This is also useful for the educators who are designing a course or curriculum, writing a textbook, developing instructional software, forming cooperative learning teams, or helping students develop interpersonal, leadership, and communication skills.

The intelligence is our singular, collective ability to act and react in an ever changing world.

REFERENCES

1. R.M. Felder, "Reaching the Second Tier : Learning and Teaching Styles in College Science Education," *J. Coll. Sci. Teaching*, 23(5), 286–290 (1993).
2. B. McCarthy, *The 4MAT System : Teaching to Learning Styles with Right/Left Mode Techniques*, Barrington, IL, EXCEL, Inc., 1987.
3. J.N. Harb, S.O. Durrant, and R.E. Terry. "Use of the Kolb Learning Cycle and the 4MAT System in Engineering Education," *J. Engr. Education*, 82(2), 70–77 (1993).
4. N. Hermann, *The Creative Brain*, Lake Lure, NC, Brain Books, 1990.
5. M. Lumsdaine and E. Lumsdaine. "Thinking Preferences of Engineering Students : Implications for Curriculum Restructuring." *J. Engr. Education*, 84(2), 193–204 (1995).

Section—V
Other Frontiers

19

System Approach to Quality Training

—*Debabrata Maji*

A clear definition of any system requires defining of the inputs, the outputs, the description of the mechanism and procedures that are to be used in the process and most important, the identification of the specific objectives.

Abstract

A system is nothing but the logical network for accomplishing objectives. It is defined as "a set of components, which, with some specified objectives, uses certain process to transform input into outputs". A clear description of any system requires defining of the inputs, the outputs, the description of the mechanism and procedures that are to be used in the process and the most important, the identification of the specific expected objectives. The system approach to training makes a training programme successful as it relates training to the terminal behaviour, carefully specifies training objectives in terms of performances, modifies training on the basis of results, designs training to fit the people concerned, shifts attention away from the contents and methods of training courses, focuses on the objectives and achievements of training process and provides framework for describing and utilizing a training activity. The paper logically presents system components, elementary system of training, a training system (open) and a training system with closed loops.

Introduction

Quality is an important measure of quality or productivity; this is also true in any educational system. It is contemplated that the future market forces would not be controlled by the raw of supply and demand but by technological innovations such as biotechnology, genetic engineering, science of the formalist and search for new materials.

Scientists in developing nation were working at standard like ISO 9000; those in advanced countries were seeking recognition for IOS 14000 which demands higher standards of quality, environmental impact and more rigorous environmental audit system. Not surprisingly, the source of quality in Industry originates from the quality imparted in the educational system.

Need of Technical Education

It had been a century old appraisal that the knowledge imparted as part of technical education and training should be directly adaptable in practice. In other words, the gap existing between technical education and practice should be bridged. In order to attain this requirement, the following major needs are identified with regards to technical education and training.

1. There should be closed interaction between the end use and knowledge and skill imparted.

2. Appropriate provision should be made to impart agility in the technical education and training.

The first point is self explanatory and the second need explores the need to reorient and reorganize frequently. The technical education and training programme so that maximum productivity in term of applying knowledge and skill in practice is ensured. These two needs are considered to be customers' needs and the features of attaining quality in technical education and training by quality management.

System Approach

A system is a logical network for accomplishing objectives. It is defined as "a set of components, which, with some specified objectives, uses certain process to transform input into outputs". Thus a clear description of any system requires defining of the inputs, the outputs, the description of the mechanism and procedures that are to be used in the process and the most important the identification of the specific expected objectives. Thus an engineering system, say a generating plant has :

(a) Principle input	—	Coal
(b) Output	—	Electric power
(c) Process	—	Burning the coal to raise steam and using the steam to turn the turbine, which rotates the generator armature.
(d) Objectives	—	To generate electric power with the greatest possible efficiency and most economically.

System Components

The components of a system contribute to the transformation of given inputs into outputs, which may or may not be optimal or best with respect to some appropriate measure of effectiveness. Also every system is a part of a larger system and includes many sub-systems.

Fig. 1. Open System.

The system in Fig.1 is an "Open System" since there is no means of controlling the output.

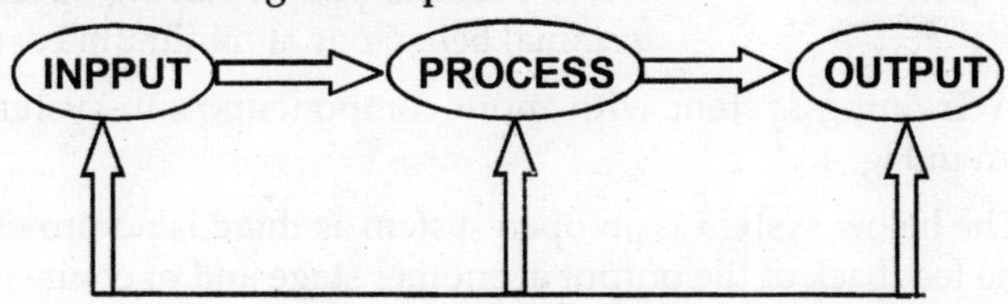

Fig. 2. Closed System.

In Fig. 2 another system, called 'closed System' is shown. In this the sample of the output is feedback which enables the control of the quality of the output by making necessary changes either in the input or in the process. As this system is closed and dynamic it is also called a 'Cybernetic system'. In an open system, the output depends only on the inputs and process. In closed system, the output is made to depend not only on the inputs and processes, but also on sample of the output used as a feedback. Also, the more frequently and accurately the output is sampled and feed back the more likely the system is to reach its specified objectives.

System of Training

Training is imparted for learning. Learning is defined as a relatively permanent change or modification in the behaviour of learner. Based on the system approach a very simple and elementary system of training is shown in Fig. 3.

Fig. 3. Elementary System of Training.

In a training system the—

(*a*) Principal Input — is trainees with initial behaviour *i.e.* education, experience, aptitude etc. but more importantly an inability to perform as required on the job whatever it is.

(*b*) Output — are trainees with terminal behaviour *i.e.* ability to perform as required on the job.

(*c*) Processes — are training courses, on the job experiences etc.

(*d*) Objectives — are to produce people having specified terminal behaviour at minimum cost.

A Training system with more components/sub-system is shown in Fig. 4.

The below system is an open system as there is no provision for the feedback of the output at another stage and of course, this is sadly true for most of the training programmes. Trainees come in, they are trained, and they go on to the job and everyone hopes that some good has been done. The objectives are not specified in performance terms and there are no means of contrasting performance with the objectives and then taking appropriate action.

The most important element of the training system is defining the objectives in performance terms. All training objectives should contain :

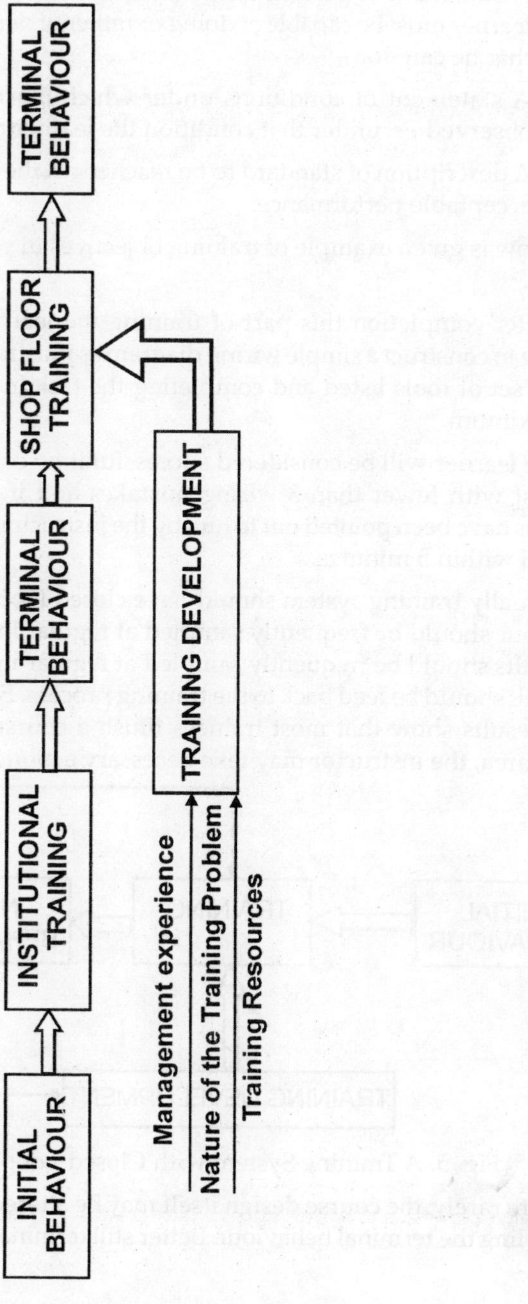

Fig. 4. A Training System (Open).

(*a*) A Statement of performance (behavior) required *i.e.* what learner must be capable of doing or rather of demonstrating that he can do.

(*b*) A statement of conditions under which mastery will be observed *i.e.* under that condition the learner must do it.

(*c*) A description of standard to be reached *i.e.* the standard of acceptable performance.

Below is given example of training objectives in performance terms :

"After completion this part of training the learner must be able to construct a simple wiring diagram as illustrated." Using the set of tools listed and completing the task in 30 minutes maximum.

The learner will be considered successful if he completes the post test with fewer than 3 wiring mistakes and if, after these mistakes have been pointed out to him by the instructor, he corrects them all within 5 minutes.

Actually training system should have closed loops. Terminal behaviour should be frequently sampled at regular intervals and the results should be frequently sampled at regular intervals and the result should be feed back to the training process. For example, if test results show that most trainees finish a course week in a certain area, the instructor may take necessary action to rectify it.

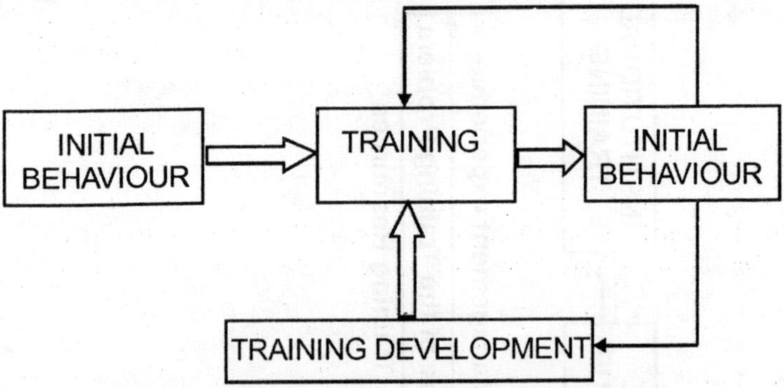

Fig. 5. A Training System with Closed Loops.

More rarely, the course design itself may be altered as a result of sampling the terminal behaviour. Better still terminal behaviour

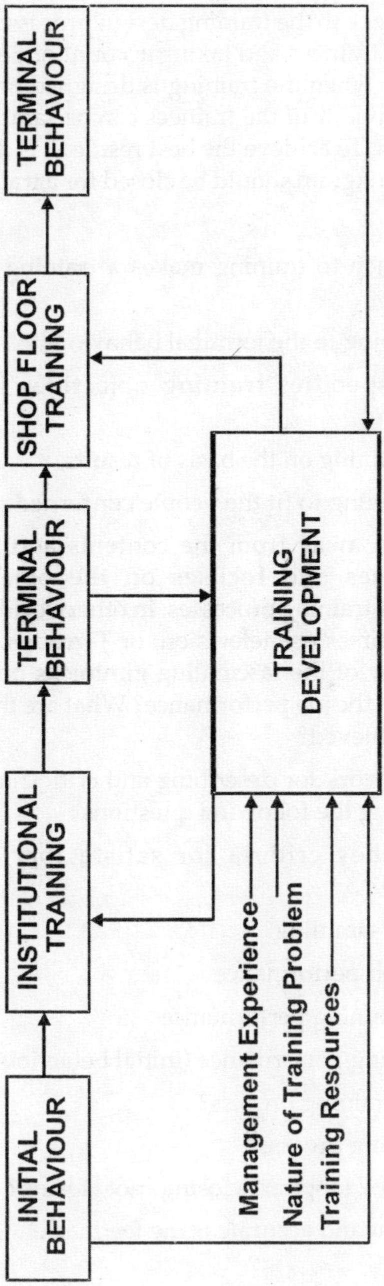

Fig. 6 : A Training System with Closed Loops.

after institutional training and shop floor training can be frequently sampled and feedback to the training design process. This implies actual follow up of trainees and taking account of defects in their terminal behaviour when the training is designed or redesigned; also the initial behaviour of the trainees can be sampled, and fed into training design. To achieve the best results it is desirable that all the loops in the diagram should be closed for a training system.

Conclusion

The system approach to training makes a training programme successful as it :

1. *(a)* relates training to the terminal behaviour,
   (b) carefully specifies training objectives in terms of performances,
   (c) modifies training on the basis of results,
   (d) Designs training to fit the people concerned.
2. Shifts attention away from the contents and methods of training courses and focuses on the objectives and achievements of training processes. In otherworld never mind whether the courses use television, or T-groups, or teaching machines or any of the fascinating gimmicks on offer. How do they relate to the job performance? What are the objectives and are they achieved?
3. Provides framework for describing and criticizing a training activity by asking the following questions :
   (a) What are they criteria for satisfactory on-the-job performance?
   (b) How are we sampling?
      (i) On the job performance
      (ii) End of training performance
      (iii) Pre-training performance (initial behaviour)
   (c) What is the training process?
   (d) How is training process?
   (e) What feedback loops are closing/not closing?
   (f) How frequent and accurate is the feedback?

In answering these questions a very revealing evaluation of any training system can be made.

REFERENCES

1. Mangal, S. K. (1990), "*General Psychology*", Sterling Publishers Private Ltd.
2. Young, J. G., "*What is creativity?*" The Journal of Creative Behaviour, Vol. 19, pp. 77–87.
3. Perkins, D. N. (1986), "*Knowledge as Design*", Hillsdale.
4. Allen, "*Media in Higher Education and Research*", Holt Publication, New York.
5. Hughes, E. H. and Hughes, A. G., "*Learning and Teaching*", 3rd edition, Longmans.
6. Davies Ivory K., "*The Management of Learning*", McGraw Hill Book Co. (UK) Ltd.
7. Briggs L.J. and Gagne R. M. "*Principles of Instructional Design*", Holt, Rinehart and Winston Publication, New York.

20

Role of NCC in Arunachal Pradesh

— *Akhilesh Kr. Gupta*

The role of NCC is broadly overall development of personality of an individual through inculcating the courage and confidence with an aim towards "Nation Building".

Abstract

The aims and objectives of the NCC have been highlighted with an emphasis on its role in the overall developmental process of the states and the country. Certain aspects have also been discussed which only NCC can handle effectively. The role of NCC in developing the overall personality of a person has been given more emphasis simply because a trained and educated person can be an asset to the society.

1. Introduction

Dr. A. P. J. Abdul Kalam, our President, has said,

> "Dream, Dream, Dream
> Dream transform into thoughts
> And thoughts result in action"

Every one of us has a dream to be on the top of the world. Our forefathers, the torch-bearers of our country and our leaders also had a dream to see our India becoming the world leader in all spheres of life. There is an old Chinese proverb,

> For your country—
> If you plan for a year——sow paddy

If you plan for a decade——plant trees
If you plan for future——Nurture youth.

It is said that, *"Today's youth is tomorrow's promising citizen"*. Youth is nation's strength. How will this youth force get the required inspiration to emerge as a worthwhile force to face the challenges of the changing and fast moving facets of the society? Who and where can the youth get the capsule that has the qualitative and quantitative nourishment so that the youth faces the challenges of the world with needed strength and courage and confidence so that his/her country is proud of him/her? Perhaps NCC is the only organization which can contribute to overall grooming and development of life skills of the youth. I have said this because the main task of NCC is to build a strong force that aims at *"Nation Building"*.

Sir Aurobindo pointed out, *"The future belongs to the young. It is the youth which has to shoulder greater responsibility towards the Herculean task of Nation Building. They have a big role to play. Today the youth has been distracted and divested towards wrong path. They are wasting their energies for the wrong reasons. The need of the hour is to emphasise on the character building of the youth"*.

2. What is NCC?

The National Cadet Corps is abbreviated as NCC. It is the world's largest uniformed government youth organization. Although NCC is very popular in the urban and sub-urban areas of our country, it is little known in the rural and the remote parts of the country where there are no schools. The students of schools and colleges are given training by the NCC Officers trained by specialized instructors from the army. Besides the military training, the students are also taught the ideals of good citizen, nationalism, secularism, national integration, etc.

3. Brief History of NCC

The roots of NCC in India date back to 1917 when the University Corps (UC) was founded to train potential soldiers for emergency assistance, to curb anti-government subversive activities and to channelize youth energy through military training. The UC was renamed as University Training Corps (UTC) in 1920 and as University Officers' Training Corps (UOTC) in 1942. The Women Auxiliary Corps was also set-up during the same year. 1943 saw the formation of the Indian Air Training Corps and the Sea Scouts Corps. The Indian Government constituted the NCC Committee in the year 1946 in view of the failure of UOTC and also to give military training to the youth. The NCC Committee submitted its report in 1947. At last the NCC was formally inaugurated on the 15th July, 1948 through the Act of Parliament.

In the beginning, the Colonel was the Director of the Directorate of NCC at Delhi. In 1954 a Brigadier became the Director of NCC. A Maj. General was to head the NCC from 1961. The post of the Director-General was created in the year 1962. Since 1982 a Lt. General started heading the NCC.

The National Cadet Corps was given an Inter-Service image in 1950 when the Air Wing was added, followed by the Naval Wing in 1952. Earlier, in 1949, the Girls' Division had been brought in to give equal opportunity to school and college going girls of the nation.

The NCC training was made compulsory during Pandit Jawaharlal Nehru's period in 1963 but, due to the resentment of the youth and financial constraints, it was decided to revert back to NCC being voluntary in 1968.

The Corps which started in a small way with a cadet strength of 1.67 lakh has now grown to 13 lakhs. The network of 774 NCC Units is spread over the country through 4880 colleges and 7783 schools. In 1952, the NCC curriculum was extended to include community development as part of the NCC syllabus. During 1962, 1965 and 1971 Wars NCC served as the second line of defence and took charge of civil defence in many bordering districts of country.

4. Aims of NCC

(i) To develop character, comradeship, discipline, leadership, secular outlook, spirit of adventure and the ideals of selfless service amongst the youth of the country.

(ii) To create a human resource of organized, trained and motivated youth, to provide leadership in all walks of life and to make always available for the service of the nation.

(iii) To provide a suitable environment to motivate the youth to take up a career in the Armed Forces.

5. Motto of NCC

The motto of NCC is———"**UNITY AND DISCIPLINE**"

6. Cardinals of NCC Discipline

—Obey with a smile

—Be Punctual

—Work hard and without fuss

—Make no excuses and tell no lies

7. NCC Flag

It has three colours——red, deep blue and light blue signifying the Army, Naval and the Air Wing respectively. It has NCC written in English at the center surrounded by a circle of 16 buds depicting the 16 Directorates. Below the circle is inscribed the motto of NCC in Hindi.

8. NCC Oath

I promise that I shall follow the rules of NCC and serve the country with truthfulness and devotion and obey the orders of my Commanding Officer to attend every parade and camp sincerely.

9. Who can join NCC?

As per the NCC Act, all the educational institutions can opt for NCC. Only the *bona fide* students can join the NCC.

10. What is NCC Training?

The activities of NCC can be broadly divided into the following distinct categories :

— Institutional Training
— Community Development Programmes cum Social Service Activities
— Youth Exchange Programmes
— Adventure Training and Sports

There are two advisory committees to advise and pass policies about implementing various schemes of the government. The Central Advisory Committee (CAC) is the highest policy making body at the National level. State Advisory Committee (SAC) is chaired by the Chief Ministers of respective states.

11. Benefits to the Students

There are a number of vacancies at various levels reserved in the Defence Forces for the NCC "C" certificate holders. Besides, 2–10 bonus marks are awarded to the NCC cadets for the recruitment in the Paramilitary Forces and the Department of Telecommunications. Certain state governments also give preference to the NCC cadets for various state services. Many industries also give preference to the NCC cadets for recruitment. Some universities give certain bonus marks for admission to higher classes. There are various types of cash awards for excellence in sports and games. For academic excellence also some scholarships are given by the NCC Directorate as well as the Sahara Group of Companies.

NCC trains the cadets to be bold, energetic and enthusiastic. It trains them to seek opportunities, accept responsibilities, select a challenging and worthy goal and keep their attention concerned on the single objective. NCC training teaches them to be resolute and not to stop, come what may, till the goal is achieved. They learn to face obstacles, enroute to success, with courage and perseverance. They learn to become optimistic, cheerful and enthusiastic as enthusiastic people can turn even very routine, mundane and boring jobs into a thrilling enjoyable and enthralling adventure.

12. Role of NCC in Arunachal Pradesh

NCC has been playing a pivotal role in shaping our youth for taking up various responsibilities. The institutional training imparted to them helps in getting a good career in the Armed Forces. NCC also teaches how to lead a community life. The cadets are asked to attend various locally and centrally organized camps where they are trained as a tough citizen who can adapt himself/herself in adverse conditions. They are also taught lessons on discipline, courage, national integration and various other aspects relating to military training. They are also made aware of the various types of social services they can do for the society and needy people of their own locality. They are taught about sanitation and self defence. Adult literacy programmes, Campaign against drug abuse, AIDS awareness, First aid, etc. are very important topics/social evils about which an NCC cadet is made well aware of.

It is quite clear that a trained NCC cadet is an asset to the society. Everybody should try to utilize the services of the NCC cadets for the betterment of the society. It is the duty of the senior members of the society to ensure that our youth takes the right path in his/her life. Proper monitoring of the youth and proper guidance is the responsibility of the guardians, teachers, elders and most importantly it should be the top priority in the minds of the policy makers to see to it that the useful energy of our youth is channelized in the right direction and for the betterment of the society in particular and the country at large.

The real meaning of the word cadet can be assessed from the following description which I read some where :

C is for **Camaraderie**

A is for **Assured**

D is for **Disciplined**

E is for **Enthusiastic**

T is for **Talented**

The importance of NCC can not be narrated in a paper or article of this size. It can be felt by anybody who is desirous of making India better, stronger and wealthier. Its potential can be compared with that of the nuclear energy which can cause disaster if misused in the form of an atom bomb and can also be a boon if used constructively in providing us with the nuclear power for running the mighty industries.

Rightful use of NCC will, therefore, depend how we plan our policies for future? There are ample opportunities and ways in which we can utilize the NCC cadets for the betterment of the society and just for no extra cost.

Arunachal Pradesh is still a new state of our country. Like other North-eastern states it was also neglected so far until recently when the Govt. of India realized the importance and potential of these states. The whole of the North-East India is very rich culturally. Arunachal Pradesh has an edge over the other North-East states in the sense that it has the privilege of having the world's richest bio-diversity. There are no big industries in this state. On capital front it will take many long years to develop. The education in the state is picking up. The geographical diversity of Arunachal Pradesh is also a big bottleneck in the way of its development.

In order to have fast development the kind of Human Resource a state has is of prime importance. People need to have a sincere will to develop. They should have a true sense of belongingness for the state. They should be properly trained and educated in order to serve their state better.

The whole of North-East India is under the devilish grip of Drug-abuse and AIDS. Arunachal Pradesh is no exception. There are so many different kinds of superstitions existing in the society. The social evils of the society need to be removed for an overall development of a state. At the same time we should not forget to keep in our mind that out customs and traditions are our treasure and we must preserve them in their originality before they vanish out of the earth. Still there can be a parallel way to keep developing and at the same time preserving the tribal thread of the state intact. In my opinion NCC can play a very important role in shaping the state for a better tomorrow. In the following paragraphs I have tried to highlight some of the ways in which NCC may be utilized to inculcate the qualities of a good citizen in the youth of this state which can, in the long run, benefit the state to achieve what it wants to.

(i) Role of NCC in Adult Literacy

There are various schools in Arunachal Pradesh where NCC units are functioning. The cadets of NCC can be used to educate the illiterate adults of the state in a phased manner. Most of the adult illiterates are already earning their livelihood either by farming or by selling small items in a shop. Some people are involved in the indiscriminate deforestation as it gives them fast earning without doing anything. It becomes, thereofore, the responsibility of the state government to implement popular schemes for the adult illiterates so that they can learn as they earn. This will not only stop indiscriminate deforestation but also develop a literate and educated lot who will contribute to the development of the state. The NCC cadets can be used to educate the adult illiterates so that they can develop a sense of belongingness for their parents and the downtrodden people of the state. The education to the females particularly will bear better fruits.

(ii) Role of NCC in AIDS Awareness

Arunachal Pradesh has gone into the grip of the dreaded disease in its early stages of development. This is, in no way, a good sign. Our youth is the victim of this social evil. It clearly means that our future is going to be in the wrong hands if we do not awake today. NCC Cadets are given lessons on AIDS awareness. Our youth is quite unaware of the safe sex due to lack of proper education. If they are given good rewards after their education in the form of jobs perhaps it may reduce the probability of spreading AIDS. Periodic seminars, Workshops and regular lectures on AIDS awareness will also help curbing this menace to a great extent. It requires a strong will on the part of our youth at the same time to abstain from the bad habits. NCC teaches how to develop will power. The State Government may involve the NCC Officers and other educated lot of the state to spread the awareness about the AIDS through various schemes. The search for the AIDS victims and their rehabilitation should be the top priority of the state government as it will help controlling the dreaded disease from further spreading.

(iii) Role of NCC in Combating Terrorism

Terrorism has become a very fast means of big earning for the youth. That is why they are easily attracted towards indulging in the terrorist activities. They do not care for others. Such people are mentally retarded people as they have lost the sense of belongingness for their society. They do not have any self confidence. If the self confidence is inculcated among the youth then probably they will abstain from joining such heinous acts. The students may be taught to fight terrorism together. This can happen when they are also given some military training together with the ideals of good citizen. The state government should provide ample job opportunities for the youth so that they take up a job before starting to join the terrorist activities. The NCC cadets can resolve together to fight against terrorism. The state government should also try to persuade the terrorists and try to rehabilitate them appropriately.

(iv) Role of NCC in Developing Patriotism and Secularism

India has always remained a land, where the followers of different religions have existed in harmony with one another. India has had the unique capacity of accepting and embracing the people of every religion into its folds and that is why India has emerged through every crisis and has existed through the history to the present age. The subject of National Integration is debated in every school, college and has become an important national issue.

National Integration is a difficult thing to achieve in a country which is multiethnic, multi-cultural and multi-lingual. India also has a sizeable population which is illiterate. The growing influence of communalism, casteism, linguistic chauvinism and other such divisive tendencies are threatening the very integrity of the nation.

Almost similar situation exists in almost all the states of our country and Arunachal Pradesh is no exception. All that is required at this hour is the emotional integration. The children at their tender age while they are in NCC can be groomed in an environment of patriotism and belongingness. The NCC training is basically aimed at achieving this very goal. In this respect, it becomes, therefore, very important that the NCC should be incorporated in all the schools and colleges as a part of their curriculum so that every student is given the same type of teaching with respect to patriotism and secularism.

(v) Role of NCC in Disaster Management

Every NCC Cadet is expected to attend the centrally and locally organized camps wherein he/she is given rigorous training aimed at making them strong physically and mentally. They attend the parades and drills. They are expected to follow the daily routine strictly. Thus they are able to learn how to lead a disciplined life. Besides, they also learn how to live together in complete harmony with one another. They are also engaged in various types of team works. They learn the sportsmanship and leadership. In fact, each student is given ample opportunity to develop his/her leadership qualities.

At the time of flood or earthquake or an accident the immediate help to the public comes from the local inhabitants. If the locality has trained NCC cadets, the job of rescue becomes very easy. On many occasions of local and national need NCC has already shown its strength and ability to work efficiently. In this respect I feel that every student should get a chance to enroll himself/herself in NCC during school or college education so that, in turn, he/she may be of use in case of an emergency.

(vi) Role of NCC in controlling Drug-Abuse

Today, the youth has been infected with the menace of drug-abuse. They think that the drug addiction is a very easy way to get rid of the mental tension they suffer from. It is solely because of the lack of awareness among them towards the ill effects of drug-abuse.

The North-East India is the most affected by drug-abuse. The tribal youth particularly is fascinated by the western culture and they feel proud in resorting to the drug-abuse. The illiteracy in this part of India is one of the most important cause of spreading of such deadly social evils. Poverty and unemployment are some of the other related reasons for the increasing rate of drug-abuse in this part. It is a matter of great concern for all of us as it is going to affect the future generations adversely and, in turn the whole of India's development may get jeopardized.

It is, therefore, very important that our youth must be aware of this social evil that is engulfing them. The training of NCC in their childhood can be very effective in making them aware of their duties and responsibilities towards their state and country. Various types of educative programmes can also be organized by NCC in the nearby areas to educate the local public against the ill effects of the various social evils. The state government may also take measures to check the illegal drug-trafficking in their states and at the same time it is the duty of the state government to create better job opportunities so that the youth get easy and fast employment.

(vii) Role of NCC in Creating Consumer Awareness

Illiteracy and lack of awareness among the public with respect to their rights and duties towards the society are very important aspects which require immediate attention of the state government and the non-governmental organizations. The consumer exploitation has become a very common practice today. The traders always aim at the maximum profit. That is why, they try to cheat the consumers by weighing or measuring less and also by selling the adulterated or inferior quality products that too at a higher price. This is very important, therefore, that the public is made aware of various aspects related with the consumer protection. NCC cadets can be engaged in making the public aware of the rights and duties of the consumer. If the youth is aware of their rights and duties then perhaps the traders will also start abstaining from ill practices.

(viii) Role of NCC in Creating Awareness about the Human Rights

Human Rights are being violated freely and openly and in every corner on the earth. Many innocent persons and the children are becoming the victim of this and are being exploited. It is shameful to speak of the technological and social development when our own brothers and sisters are living in their own country as slaves. We do not have any right to exploit anyone. Human is a social animal—this has become a misnomer now a days. It becomes the prime duty of every citizen, who claims to be a human, to protect the human rights of every body in the society. We must start making the public aware of their rights and duties so that they are not exploited any more. This job can be given to the NCC Officers and the NCC cadets so that they can work in a time-bound frame-work to give the relevant information to the public and report the cases of violation to the respective authority so that punitive measures may be initiated against the culprits and thus a sense of confidence can be built in their minds. The institutional training is given to the NCC cadets with this very aim of educating them and also to educate the local public. However, a strong support from the state government is imperative to safeguard the interests of everybody.

***(ix)* Role of NCC in Civil Defence**

The NCC cadets are given basic military training in which they learn the skills to fight war. They also learn how to protect themselves in case of any type of emergency. They are given training about the first aid, Fire-fighting skills, and the art of good and healthy living. Thus, an NCC cadet has in him/her every quality a good citizen and a patriot is ought to have. In the case of state emergency and at the time of any type of law and order problem such as holding elections at various levels, etc., the NCC Officers and the NCC cadets can be used effectively.

13. Conclusion

The discussion in the previous paragraphs has made it clearly understandable that NCC is an uniformed government youth organization which is the largest of its kind in the whole world so far. I have tried to highlight some of the potentials which NCC has in it and which can be harnessed by everybody for the betterment of the society in particular and the country in general. Every state has a huge resource of manpower at its disposal which can be utilized in a more effective manner. Only thing what is needed is to give a thought to plan how best the NCC can be engaged in the development of the state. The role of NCC is quite explicitly outlined in its aim given in the earlier paragraphs. Let us take an oath today that we shall try our best to help NCC so that it can help the state on its turn.

21

Role of NSS in Higher Education

—V.N. Sharma

Through NSS, students/youths receive additional knowledge in order to develop their personality through physical labour, service, character and renouncement. The realization that my knowledge, my labour, my energy are not for me alone but it is important for you and the entire society, the feeling of 'Not Me But You' is developed.

India has the largest education system in the world. In the pre-independence period between 1947 and 1950, India had 25 universities, 200 colleges, 1500 teachers and one lakh students. About one percent persons were taking higher education. Today we have 247 universities + 98 deemed to be universities, more than sixteen thousand colleges, ninety seven lakhs students and 4.5 lakhs teachers in India. In the changing scenario these students must be able to support themselves. In spite of the tremendous increase in the number of students undergoing higher education all the eligible youth are not yet able to get education. In the age group of 17 to 24 years, only seven percent youngsters are pursuing higher education.

The maxim " Higher Education for a limited few" has been replaced by Dr. Punjabrao Deshmukh movement "Mass Education for all homes". According to Pandit Jawaharlal Nehru, " The university should work to impart lofty thoughts to a person and thereby help in building the nation. The universities are symbols of humanitarian/tolerant, logical, progressive and courageous thought and search for the truth. Universities should strive to uphold the higher goals of the human race." The Nation considers education as a medium to impart the legacy of cultural, social and political values to the coming generation. One of the learned educationists and writers has stated three roles of the higher education namely learning and teaching, research and extension. Extension is now a compulsory obligation of the Higher Education.

Being an organization which gives higher education, the university is marked upon as an important agency in this regard. As a part of its social communication activity it has been given the responsibility of extension education and it is expected that education, research and extension activities would be carried out under one roof.

Extension education which is a third objective by UGC according to its new policy of 1976, has been accepted by all universities as a social obligation and responsibility towards the neglected segment of the society.

Objective of Extension

Extension is an educational process, communicating useful information to people, helping them to learn how to use it to build a better life for themselves, their families and their communities.

Mahatma Gandhiji visualized the extension of knowledge of the universities to the community. To make his vision true, numerous commissions and experts recommended some kind of service to be rendered by the students to the community and some kinds of institutional mechanism to facilitate optimum utilization of education for the welfare of the community.

Extension education tries to develop the social behaviour of the people, their different groups and the intra inter-relationship of these social groups. In general, the concept of Extension education is used in educating people.

History of NSS

In the pre-independence period it was a dream of Mahatma Gandhi that students should utilize the leisure time available to them during education for service to the nation on 23th August, 1959 under the chairmanship of Dr. C. D. Deshmukh National Service Committee was constituted. The Committee suggested that the college students will have to render compulsorily their services to the nation for one year. In May, 1969 in joint meeting of the ministry of education and UGC, it was accepted that national service could be an effective medium for national integration. Accordingly in the 4th five year plan NSS was accepted as a pilot scheme and was started in a few chosen institutes and universities. On 24th Sept., 1969, the central minister for education Dr. V. K. Rao inaugurated the NSS which was started in 37 universities in India with 40,000 volunteers by coincidence the scheme was started on the birth centenary of Mahatma Gandhi. Now 24 lakh volunteers are enrolled.

Importance of NSS

Through NSS students/youths receive additional knowledge in order to develop their personality through physical labour, service, character and renouncement to give them an experience of practical life, this programme has distinct role in college and social field. The realization that my knowledge, my labour, my energy are not for me alone but it is important for you and the entire society, the feeling of *'Not Me But You'* is developed and instead of craving for money, power and selfish motives the young generation is to give lessons of renouncement and service by this programme and hence it is important. This makes their personality more carrying, creative and progressive, hence I consider this activity entirely valuable.

NSS Regular Activities

Under Regular Activities programme, students undertakes various programmes in the adopted villages, college/school campuses and urban slums during week ends or after college/school hours. By these programmes NSS volunteers would be truly useful in students' empowerment.

NSS Special Camping Programme

In special camps, volunteers have to go in village and have to work continuously for 10 days in adopted villages or urban slums during vacations with some specific projects by involving local communities.

Index

C

D

H